THE POLITICS OF CIVIL SOCIETY

Big society, small government?

Fred Powell

P P

First published in 2007
Second edition published in Great Britain in 2013 by

The Policy Press
University of Bristol
Fourth Floor
Beacon House
Queen's Road
Bristol BS8 1QU
UK
Tel +44 (0)117 331 4054
Fax +44 (0)117 331 4093
e-mail tpp-info@bristol.ac.uk
www.policypress.co.uk

North American office:
The Policy Press
c/o The University of Chicago Press
1427 East 60th Street
Chicago, IL 60637, USA
t: +1 773 702 7700
f: +1 773-702-9756
e:sales@press.uchicago.edu
www.press.uchicago.edu

British Library Cataloguing in Publication Data
A catalogue record for this book is available from the British Library.

Library of Congress Cataloging-in-Publication Data
A catalog record for this book has been requested.

ISBN 978 1 44730 714 3 paperback
ISBN 978 1 44730 715 0 hardcover

Cover design by The Policy Press
Front cover: image kindly supplied by www.alamy.com

In my humble study I am the most virtuous …
I strum my plain old zither, read Buddhist sutra,
No music to grate my ears
No office to tire my mind and soul.

My Humble Study by Liu Yuxi (772–847)

Contents

Acknowledgements

In preparing this book, I am much indebted to four research colleagues, Donal Guerin, Martin Geoghegan, Margaret Scanlon and Katherina Swirak, with whom I had the good fortune to work on three major research projects on civil society in Ireland that resulted in three books: *Civil Society and Social Policy* (Powell and Guerin, 1997), *The Politics of Community Development* (Powell and Geoghegan, 2004), *Youth Policy, Civil Society and the Modern Irish State* (Powell et al, 2012). Their intellectual collaboration has helped to shape my understanding of civil society. I would also like to thank Andrea de Dominicis and Silvia Lombardi of the Centro Italiano di Solidarietà di Roma for including me in a European Union study that encompassed the third sector in the Czech Republic, Denmark, Germany, Ireland, Italy, Slovenia, Spain and Sweden. In addition, I am grateful to Anna Kwak and Marek Rymsza of the University of Warsaw for facilitating my visit to Poland during the 1990s and the Council of Europe for funding a ten-country study on the socioeconomic status of youth during 2007–08, which enabled me to link the experience of civil society to childhood. I would also like to thank Demos for generously furnishing me with its relevant reports during a visit to London. Particular thanks are due to the late Jo Campling for her advice and support in producing this book. Finally, I am much indebted to Rebecca Jeffers, Sinead Hanley, Orla McDonald and Maura O'Brien for their patience and diligence in the production of the manuscript, my School Manager, Fionnuala O'Connor, for keeping me eternally organised and, finally, my family for their support, understanding and love, and particularly my late father, Dr Anthony Powell, for his inspirational belief in humanity.

Introduction

To-day the Arab Spring dominates the Arab airwaves.
Egypt in particular, where the awakening flowered with
the removal of Hosni Mubarak, occupies the Arab psyche
as a bellwether, a litmus test of how this new political phase
is progressing.

> Nasrine Malik, in the *Guardian* (27 December 2011)

Saturday 3 December 2011 saw a hugely successful pre-
budget 'Parade of Defiance' against the IMF-imposed cuts
throughout the streets of Cork. This was a creative protest
organised by Occupy Cork to show the city's opposition to
austerity measures and to raise our voices together against
the undemocratic forcing of these cuts on the people of this
country. Between 1,000 and 1,200 people marched behind
banners with messages such as 'Not my Debt' and 'This is
not a Recession, this is a Robbery'.

> *Occupy Cork* (Issue 3, 2011)

The Little People came suddenly. I don't know who they
are. I don't know what it means. I was a prisoner of the
story [IQ84]. I had no choice. They came, and I described
it. That is my work.

> Haruki Murakami, in *New York Review of Books*
> (8 December 2011)

Three recent events captured the essence of our times. First, the Arab
Spring, which, like a tidal wave of liberty, displaced large numbers of
tyrants in the Maghreb–Mashreq region and introduced a new politics
of hope. Second, the Occupy movement, which began in Wall Street,
New York City on 17 September 2011 and spread across the world.
The message of the Occupy movement is a simple one. It opposes the
austerity measures imposed on ordinary people around the world, the
99% who, it argues, have been expropriated by the wealthiest 1% of
the population. Third, the much-anticipated Haruki Murakami novel
published in 2011 entitled *IQ84*, while clearly inspired by George
Orwell's *1984* allegory about Stalinist tyranny (Orwell, 1989), takes
the reader into a counterworld of unreality, where surveillance is all-
pervasive and the 'Little People' hide from a weirdly unsettling Lewis

Carroll wonderland of horrors and the horrifying exercise of power over the mesmerised. Both the Occupy movement and Murakami's *IQ84* illuminate aspects of the world that we currently inhabit: the dominance of unaccountable and largely invisible systems of power, but also the willingness of citizens to globally struggle against these dark forces. The 'Little People' have become the 'unsignified signifiers' probing behind the mirror of power (Baxter, 2011, p 25). The counterpoint with Orwell's 'Big Brother' is striking. Power has become invisible. 'Big Society' is an invented concept, intended to give social meaning to an empty political space.

While events such as the 2012 Olympics remind us that there still exists a visceral loyalty to the nation, the authority of the state, both as an abstract idea and as a tangible set of institutions (for example, public services, parliaments, courts), is increasingly contested. Clearly, in the case of tyrannical states, such as Eastern Europe during 1989 and the Maghreb–Mashreq region in 2011, uprisings against the state are directly attributable to the existence of repressive regimes. However, the protest movements in the West during 2011, such as the Occupy movement, *los indignados*, the German Wutbürgers and English riots, occurred in democratic regimes. The totality of these events suggests that the tectonic plates are shifting and the communicative power of citizens is redefining state–civil society relations. Civil society has emerged in this changing context as a force beyond the institutions of the state, family and community that is harnessing new communication technologies (for example, Facebook, Twitter, blogs, Wikileaks, texting and so on) to reframe social and political relations in a globalised world. The pace and scale of these changes is reflected in discursive voices that increasingly take shape outside traditional politics in the forms of digital activism, citizen journalism and new social movements.

These struggles represent a cacophonous struggle for political change that (a) knows no borders, (b) is committed to civility in the form of non-violence, toleration and respect for difference – in terms of ethnicity, gender, religious affiliation, sexual orientation and so on – and (c) is driven by experimentation, innovation and learning that reflects Umberto Eco's concept of 'wild thinking'. In an age of fragmentation, atomisation and deepening scepticism, civil society has morphed into a new lifeworld – a citizen-led theatre of global debate and digital action, whose many emerging socio-political narratives take experimental form (Blaagaard, 2012). In this new communicative reality civil society defines our collective self in the postmodern world – isolated, sometimes angry and concerned about the future.

The second edition of *The Politics of Civil Society* is intended to update but also expand on the arguments of the first edition in 2007. Much of this book is rewritten, reflecting the rapid and reflexively changing nature of the topic. Throughout the book we will compare and contrast the forces of light (as the 18th-century Enlightenment humanists liked to portray themselves) against the forces of darkness, most visible in the co-option of civil society in Nazi Germany during the 20th century, but also evident in the democratic deficits of the 21st century that are being challenged in the Middle East, Europe and other parts of the world. Ayçoberry (1999, p 210), in reference to Nazi Germany, observes: 'civil society turned into a kind of kicked-in anthill'. It is a fitting metaphor regarding the fragility of civil society. The book sets out to understand and historically contextualise the renaissance of civil society over the past three decades, notably during the emblematic years of 1989 and 2011. It has been expressed in a dramatic explosion of democratic energy against Stalinist tyranny in Eastern Europe in 1989, led by playwright Vaclav Havel (1936–2011), an exponent of the theatre of the absurd. The 2011 Arab Spring was clearly influenced by Havel's 'Velvet Revolution'. Havel captured the link between the unreal world of the political imaginary and the world of the *realpolitik* that civil society straddles. His vision is also echoed during 2011 by the Occupy movement in cities around the world. *Occupy Cork* captures the essential message of this protest movement:

> A hugely important aspect of the protest was the involvement of Cork Community Art Link, who brought a real creative and artistic colour to the demonstration. This combines the importance of our presence on the South Mall in the heart of the city with an appreciation of the need to move in more creative directions, opening up the Occupy movement to all. This is about making the movement accessible and welcoming to all, and bringing that together with the principles of equality and democracy that are central to what we do. In a time where there is such an overwhelming amount and range of advertising constantly being forced down our throats, we need to work in ways that really engage with people, and the wide and open nature of the Occupy movement is bringing something really new to the table.
>
> Creative protests such as the Parade are testament to a DIY ethic producing our own culture, one that can be defiant through creativity, but this shouldn't be seen as the

be-all and end-all of how we're to organise ourselves for this fight. We should not feel bound to the past to feel we owe today's struggle to those who've come before us – we should try to see ourselves within the tradition of human beings standing up for potent ideas of justice, equality and dignity. How we interpret that challenge of building a new society should be across the whole spectrum of human capacity – the creative and cultural shouldn't be seen as opposed to the political, to the practical task of organising and mobilising in cooperation with one another, against those whose interests are currently served by our rights being stamped on. (*Occupy Cork*, Issue 3, 2011, p 11)

Similarly, the Libyan poet and Arab Spring activist Khaled Mattaira writes a poem 'Now that We have Tasted Hope', asking 'why would we live again in the tombs we'd made out of our souls?'. The Arab Spring represented a fundamental change in consciousness. While the Arab Spring constitutes a struggle against despotism in the Maghreb–Mashreq region, in Western civilisation, civil society addresses economic oligarchy in the form of neoliberalism that is, arguably, eroding democracy from within by locating power in distant and largely unaccountable elites. The protest of the Occupy Cork movement evokes a titanic battle between democracy and capitalism in the post-2008 crash conditions. Professor Wolfgang Streeck (2011, p 13) has observed: 'where democracy as we know it is effectively suspended, as it already is in countries like Greece, Ireland and Portugal, street riots and popular insurrection may be the last remaining mode of political expression for those devoid of market power'. He concludes:

More than ever, economic power seems today to have become political power, while citizens appear to be almost entirely stripped of their democratic defences and their capacity to impress upon the political economy interests and demands that are incommensurable with those of capital owners. In fact, looking back at the democratic-capitalist crisis sequence since the 1970s, there seems a real possibility of a new, if temporary, settlement of social conflict in advanced capitalism, this time entirely in favour of the propertied classes now firmly entrenched in their politically unassailable stronghold, the international financial industry. (Streeck, 2011, p 13)

Streeck's stark warning reminds us that modern democracy is a relatively recent development. Born in the *agora* (a site of political assembly or marketplace) of ancient Greece, democracy had lain dormant for 2,500 years, until it was awakened during the 18th-century Enlightenment in Europe and America. The point Streeck is seeking to make is that democracy, as a mass movement of citizen power, does not easily coexist with market capitalism – with the former (99%) seeking the redistribution of wealth and the latter (1%) seeking to defend its accumulation of capital. It is an age-old struggle between democracy (majority) and oligarchy (elite) that is traceable back to ancient Greece. However, it shapes society. That is why it is so fundamental to the quality of life and the human experience.

Civil society – as a communicative space – finds itself located between these competing forces, which in turn seek to bend it to their particular interest. Proponents of civil society, which was reborn in its contemporary form in the battles against oligarchies of power in Eastern Europe (Stalinism) and Southern Europe (Fascism), and latterly, despotism in the Arab world, find themselves once again challenged to defend democracy, following the 2008 financial crash and the ensuing austerity policies. That is what makes civil society political, and provides the intellectual purpose of this book. At a point in history when power, as Haruki Murakami suggests, has become a dark and invisible force in the world – subordinating the citizen to the rule of mysterious and unaccountable interests – civil society may be the last refuge of democracy.

The Politics of Civil Society is composed of eight chapters based upon the premise that, in order to understand the present, we need to look into the past. Chapter One focuses on 'the Big Society: Small Government' project as an exercise of mapping the changing and variable geography of the contemporary political imaginary through doublethink. Chapter Two seeks to (i) locate civil society in its historical context in antiquity, (ii) describe the significance of its extraordinary reimagining during the Enlightenment, when a 'revolution of the mind' led to revolution(s) of fact, and (iii) explore the fertile relationship between civil society and the contemporary political imaginary that is called 'the renaissance of civil society'. Chapters Three and Four explore the interaction between civil society, democracy and civic virtue during the modern era that ultimately led to a fusion between the state and civil society – the welfare state. Chapter Five demonstrates the fragility of this democratic achievement in the violent reaction to modernity that underpinned the tyranny of Nazi Germany. Chapter Six addresses the connected issues of human rights, moral protests and civic revolts in the form of: the velvet revolutions, the Arab Spring and the Occupy movement in the West. In Chapter Seven the author explores the relationship between culture wars and civil society in the United States, as a pitched battle between realism and unrealism for political hegemony. The final chapter moves the argument on to the disputed territory of globalisation and poses the question 'Is global civil society a myth or reality?'. This brings us back to the central problematic of the book – making sense of reality/unreality in a world of opaque power that is too often secreted behind 'the mirror of power', out of sight of the citizens.

The Politics of Civil Society seeks to look behind 'the mirror of power' to discover the reality of civil society, or 'Big Society' as it is sometimes called. It finds not one but three forms of civil society: radical, liberal and conservative. In a complex interplay between state and civil society, the author argues, citizens contend for power through civil society in the pursuit of civic virtue. This is both an age-long pursuit dating from antiquity and a contemporary democratic struggle between competing visions of modernity that determine the *real* in politics, as experienced by the citizens. *The Politics of Civil Society* shifts the scholarly debate about civil society onto the new ground, offering an accessible and compelling analysis of one of the central issues of our times.

ONE

Doublethink: the 'Big Society, Small Government' debate

To know and not to know, to be conscious of complete truthfulness while telling carefully constructed lies, to hold simultaneously two opinions which cancelled out, knowing them to be contradictory and believing in both of them, to use logic against logic, to repudiate morality while laying claim to it, to believe that democracy was impossible and that the Party was the guardian of democracy, to forget, whatever it was necessary to forget, then to draw it back into memory again at the moment when it was needed, and then promptly to forget it again, and above all, to apply the same process to the process itself – that was the ultimate subtlety; consciously to induce unconsciousness, and then, once again, to become unconscious of the act of hypnosis you had just performed. Even to understand the word 'doublethink' involved the use of doublethink.

George Orwell, *1984* (1989, pp 37–8)

In general, Liao Xun [theorist of Chinese 'Big Society, Small Government' project] was in favour of a state construction that was reduced as much as possible, and quoted Thomas Jefferson as saying: 'The best state is the state that governs as little as possible' (guanli zui shao da zhengfu, jiu shi zui hao de zhengfu). Liao Xun also maintained that he was attracted by the theory that the individual should be considered the basic cell of society. This means that the state should serve the individual and should not interfere in everything. In fact, Liao Xun envisioned that in the future the state would serve three main functions: as a 'soccer referee' (zuqui caipan), as a 'traffic cop' (jiaotong jingcha), and as a 'fire fighter' (xiaofang duiyuan). In serving the first function, the state would issue a set of ground rules, and it would only interfere when citizens intentionally 'bumped' into each other or committed 'offside'. In the second function, the state would 'clear the streets and bridges' and establish an orderly flow of transport and communication. Finally, in the third function as a 'fire fighter', the state would intervene if fire or disaster occurred or if relief was necessary.

K.E. Brodsgaard, *Hainan* (2009, p 88)

Zygmunt Bauman likens the contemporary idea of civil society to the ancient Greek concept of *agora* as a site for political assembly, or town square, an interface between the public and private spheres of social life that created the idea of a political community or republic based upon active citizenship (Bauman, 1998, pp 86–7). He argues that in modern society the *agora* has come under sustained attack. While its enemy during the 20th century was totalitarianism, as we enter the 21st century, some argue that it has become neoliberalism as a global capitalist hegemony (Davis, M., 2006; de Sousa Santos, 2006; Klein, 2006). Neoliberalism has been defined by David Harvey (2005, p 2) as 'in the first instance a theory of political economic practices that proposes that human well-being can best be advanced by liberating individual entrepreneurial freedoms and skills within an institutional framework characterised by strong private property rights, free markets and free trade', adding, 'the role of the state is to create and preserve an institutional framework appropriate to such practices'. The challenges for civil society as the embodiment of the civic republican tradition of participative democracy are both institutional and socio-political. A debate about the roles and responsibilities of the public sphere in the form of the 20th-century welfare state is at the centre of this discussion. The renaissance of civil society based upon civic republicanism has challenged not only despotic states but also democratic societies to rethink citizen participation, particularly in relation to welfare. The debate focuses on the relationship between civil society, citizen participation and the state. In doing so, it seeks to change the social and political grammar of our politics.

In this chapter we will argue that the socio-political meaning of civil society as a 'Big Society' has become a central element in the debate about welfare reform, civic republicanism and political community. The chapter advances four narratives of civil society and examines their socio-political and institutional implications for renegotiating state–society relations. Narrative 1 examines Big Society with Chinese characteristics. Narrative 2 analyses British Conservatives' advocacy of a welfare reform agenda that equates civil society with 18th-century Burkean 'Little Platoons' in the modern form of voluntary associations, as an alternative to state welfare provision. Narrative 3 explores how social democracy has offered a Third Way through a neo-institutionalist model of social partnership and generative politics between an 'enabling' state, a resurgent market and civil society in the production of 'modernised' social services, based upon active citizenship. Narrative 4 discusses post-Marxist theorists of radical democracy and social activists who advocate 'democratising democracy' as a means to involving citizens in the delivery of social services in a new social contract between the state and civil society that envisages the co-production of welfare.

Narrative 1: Big Society with Chinese characteristics

Brodsgaard (2009, p 113) observes that 'during the 1980s and most of the 1990s the critique of big government was the dominant theme of public policy and debate. Conservative ideas in the form of neoliberalism re-emerged throughout most of the developed world and following the Thatcher and Reagan regimes Western political economy thinking shifted towards the right advocating "small government, big society"'. Remarkably, Brodsgaard in his study of the Chinese island provinces of Hainan also notes similar developments under an entirely different ideological regime, officially communist. The political theorist and reformer Liao Xun published a tract addressing Marx and Engels' purported view of 'small government' and also argued the case for economic liberalisation. Liao Xun's tract suggested that Marx and Engels (through their theory of 'the withering away of the state') favoured small government, unlike the big government of the Russian Soviet model. Liao Xun presented the case for downsizing bureaucracy and government as a key element in socialist reform (Brodsgaard, 2009, p 86). In Liao Xun's view, the role of the state needed to be shrunk to the core functions: 'traffic cop', 'soccer referee' and 'fire fighter'. The rest was up to civil society. However, his project in Hainan failed (partly because of a property bubble that collapsed the local economy in 1996) (Brodsgaard, 2009, p 9). There is also a deeper problem in replacing politics with economic rationalism. It fails to connect with the public because it lacks a political imaginary (Robin, 2011, p 162).

Despite Liao Xun's failure in Hainan due to local economic and political factors, his ideas were adopted at national level. Boychuk (2007, p 201) notes that the 'Big Society, Small Government project' was mainstreamed by the Chinese government in 2004:

> Under the slogan 'Big Society, Small Government', the 2004 National Congress for the Communist Party of China (CPC) endorsed efforts to construct a 'system of social protection,

including social security, social assistance, and charitable undertakings', in which 'civilian organisations have become bridges and belts linking the Party and government with the mass, an indispensable force to promote economic development and social progress, and play an important role in the harmonious development of a socialist civilization'. In addition to granting explicit official recognition for the first time to non-profit organisations (NPOs) in China, the CPC also committed itself to expanding the non-profit sector under the rubric of party leadership, government responsibility, and citizen participation. Put another way, citizens shall support the growth of the NPOs and these social organizations will assist the Chinese government, all under the broad direction of the CPC.

Both Brodsgaard (2009) and Boychuk (2007) locate their analysis within the neo-institutionalist framework that addresses state–society relations. Boychuk (2007, p 202) asserts that while the dominant debate in the West is framed by neo-Tocquevillian ideas predicated upon the liberal-pluralist perspective that views civil society as being independent of both the state and the market, for neo-institutionalists civil society exists in degrees. Neo-Tocquevillianism promotes a highly idealised version of civil society as community, in contrast to neo-institutionalists. The neo-institutionalist perspective links civil society directly to systems of governance. The 'Big Society, Small Government' project is closely linked to market liberalisation, regardless of official state ideology, in the neo-institutionalist approach. Neo-Tocquevillianism is the ideal: neo-institutionalism the reality.

In the case of China, under the reformist leadership of Deng Xiaoping, economic liberalisation emerged in what was called 'socialism with Chinese characteristics'. The policy change has created major economic growth but also produced severe inequalities and compromised social harmony. China has the second-largest number of billionaires (115) after the US (412). By the end of 2011, the number of millionaires was expected to have doubled in three years to 590,000, with the richest 10% of the population controlling 45% of the country's wealth. Changes in the official poverty level from €0.34 per day to €0.43 are estimated to triple the number living in extreme poverty to 100,000 million people – the UN puts the figure at 245,000 million people (*Irish Times*, 25 May 2011). In an editorial comment the *Irish Times* (25 May 2011) was led to conclude that 'Socialism with Chinese characteristics' in reality was 'Socialism with Capitalist characteristics', balefully adding: 'Karl Marx's contradictions live on.' The 'Big Society, Small Government' project in China is reflected in the key narratives and counter-narratives that are shaping state–society relations in the West.

China is a very old society seeking to re-establish its influence in the world. Its economic success gives it political authority. 'Socialism with Chinese characteristics' has moved China in the direction of prodigious economic growth. In two decades it is likely to overtake the United States as the strongest economy in the world. Its political and social models are therefore important in global terms. China is undergoing an intensive internal political debate about reform. Liao Xun's concept of the 'Big Society, Small State' is therefore very important. His vision of the state as 'soccer referee', 'traffic police' and 'fire fighter' offers a vision of the future that we need to take seriously. It is a very different to the European welfare state. Liao Xun's 'Big Society: Small Government' project failed in Hainan, ostensibly because of an economic collapse. The Chinese premier, Wen Jiabao, warned the National People's Congress (parliament) at its 2012 meeting that without structural reform China faced a return to Mao's Cultural Revolution (*Financial Times*, 15 March 2012). The purging of Bo Xilai in 2012 suggests that not everybody in the CPC agrees. Politics continues its hold over the public imagination. Mr Wen's advocacy of reform resonates with British Conservatives, who are part of a wider Western restoration of conservative ideas and values, based upon a post-socialist order.

Narrative 2: conservatism, Big Society and 'little platoons'

The conservatism of the 21st century has been tempered by a reassessment. There is a growing recognition among Conservatives that their unqualified espousal of free market individualism has left them open to the charge of promoting selfishness and endorsing callous indifference to the plight of the poor (Blond, 2010). Poverty is a global problem of catastrophic proportions (Davis, M., 2006). Moreover, the social fracture that has become the legacy of neoliberal economics (exacerbated by the 2008 financial crisis) has caused a spiralling sense of public angst in Europe, requiring a new political and social narrative. Evoking the spirit of Bismarck, Shaftsbury and Disraeli, the distinguished conservative philosopher, Roger Scruton, has observed that 'no one doubts the value of economic freedom or the spirit of enterprise; but the exclusive emphasis on these things looks like so much self-serving rhetoric on the part of those whose only interest is profit and whose concern for the community goes no further than the search for customers' (*Observer*, 9 February 1997). A decade later, British Conservatives were embracing civil society as a compassionate alternative to the state in social policy. In a Green Paper (Conservative Party, 2008, p 4) called *A Stronger Society: Voluntary Action in the 21st Century*, the Conservatives assert: '[t]he time has come for us to think of the voluntary as the first sector; not just in recognition of the historical origin of the public services and the institutions we rely on today – but as the first place we should look for answers that neither the state nor the market can provide'. The Conservatives view the redefinition of voluntary organisations from third to first sector as reflecting a new social and political grammar. They argue: '[t]he post-bureaucratic age demands that we change government so that it is more open to being driven by a vibrant civil society' (Conservative Party, 2008, p 6). The Conservatives believe that 'volunteers are the beating heart in Britain's civil society' (Conservative Party, 2008, p 20). For Conservatives, civil society is the antidote to the 'broken society', because it builds social capital, which they view as the basis for a new political and social grammar (Blond, 2010; Norman, 2010). They call it 'compassionate conservatism', a term first associated with George W. Bush's crusade to introduce faith-based charity in the United States as an alternative to the state. During 2004, the US federal government transferred €2 billion to faith-based charities (Goldberg, 2006, p 108). The anti-statist movement in America, known as the Tea Party, continues the campaign for a smaller state, with considerable popular support. The Republican contender for the 2012 US presidential election, Mitt Romney, echoed this conservative view on a visit to Poland: 'a march towards economic liberty and smaller government has meant a march towards higher living standards, a strong military that defends liberty at home and abroad, and an important and growing role on the international stage' (*Guardian*, 1 August 2012). British Conservatives have located their 'Big Society' project in the 'little platoons' of civil society. Evoking the 18th-century conservative thinker Edmund Burke (1729–97), latter-day conservatives have sought to equate Burkian 'little platoons' with 'Big Society'. Apart from the obvious asymmetry, there is an uncomfortable Orwellian ring to the concept of 'Big Society' – redolent of 'Big Brother' – in the 'little platoons'.

Philip Blond's (2010) book *Red Tory* seeks to move British Conservative politics away from neoliberalism and towards the 'Big Society' ideal that combines economic equity with social conservatism in a new conservative narrative. Blondist conservatism is based on the disaggregation of civil society from the state in a social project that would ultimately replace the welfare state with charity, including faith-based charity. But there the problems begin. Bruce Anderson (2011), writing in the *Financial Times*, asserts: 'no one knows what "Big Society" means. The word "big" is vaguely threatening.' He concludes: 'the Big Society is not about coercion. It is about freedom, creativity and responsibility.' In reality it is about civil society replacing the state as the 'first sector', rather than the 'third sector'. It is manifestly a big political project but, like Murakami's 'little people', the 'little platoons' are, by their nature, invisible. That makes the concept 'Big Society' vaguely unsettling.

Clearly, in this brand of conservatism, the voluntary sector is fundamental in defining civil society that is agreeable to the tenets of 'compassionate conservative' philosophy. Blondist conservatism argues that civil society has the potential to forge a new social and economic settlement by decentralising power, wealth and social and economic organisation (Blond, 2008). This is a persuasive argument. But realities of charitable giving are not propitious, as the Conservatives frankly acknowledge:

- Charitable giving by individuals is struggling to keep up with the GDP growth and is falling as a proportion of the voluntary sector's income.
- The level of giving in 2006/07 was down by 3% on the previous year – the proportion who gave also fell from 57% to 54%.
- Giving levels in the US are more than twice those in the UK – 1.7% of GDP compared to 0.7%.
- In Britain 7% of the population accounts for around 49% of all giving.
- There is a very generous minority, which is not one and the same as the wealthy minority – three-fifths of high value donors have annual incomes of less than £26,000 and giving as a proportion of income is roughly equal across all income groups. (Conservative Party, 2008, p 10)

The fact that 'the most generous contributors to charity, as a proportion of their income are not the richest groups but those below average income', according to the Conservative Party (2008, p 15), suggests that the tradition of mutual aid among the working class constitutes the most vibrant element in today's charity. It also suggests that the traditional ethical construction of charity, as the rich helping the poor, may be little more than a myth. Mutual aid is part of the utopian socialist tradition. In an era of demutualisation its policy potential would seem to be problematic. Furthermore, mutual aid is a form of horizontal redistribution of wealth from rich to poor – a reality that has been accepted in the UK since the People's Budget of 1909. It emerged in the same year as the publication of the Royal Commission on the Poor Law (1909). In a minority report, Fabian socialists convincingly demonstrated the failure of both charity and the Poor Law to eradicate poverty. One hundred years later, Conservatives plan to reverse that policy logic by embracing the 'Big Society' project based upon harnessing 'the civil middle in British public life' and 'changing the architecture of institutions' (Blond, 2010, p 63). From the Conservative perspective, the 'Big Society' is the antidote to the 'post-democratic politics' inspired by the 'Fabian Takeover' (Norman, 2010, pp 79–81).

The scale and metrics of charity underlines the political limits of 'compassionate conservatism'. There are over 190,000 voluntary organisations in England and Wales. Across the United Kingdom there are 400,000 community groups, reminding us of the embeddedness of civil society in democratic practice. Each year, 6,000 new charities are registered, underlining the health and vibrancy of the third sector – the term used to describe the combined voluntary and community sectors. The total income of registered charities is now in excess of £27 billion, and they employ a workforce of 600,000. But the Charities Act 2006 promises to provide the biggest change in charities' legal status since the 1601 Poor Law Act (*Guardian*, 20 February 2006). Polly Toynbee (2006), however, has pointed out that expenditure on charity, when compared to public expenditure from taxation in the region of £400 billion per annum, is infinitesimal. Furthermore, 40% of voluntary sector funding comes from the state, and accounts for 1% of GDP. These figures put the voluntary sector into perspective. The fiscal gap between public expenditure and charity is on a scale that underlines the flawed logic of the proposition put forward by the British Conservatives. Toynbee concludes: 'there is such a thing as society; it's just not the same thing as the state'. The *Independent* (20 July 2010) questioned whether the 'Big Society' project was merely 'a cover for spending cuts'. The scale of the public expenditure cuts being imposed by the Conservative–Liberal Coalition in the UK suggests that the *Independent* may be correct in suggesting that the 'Big Society' project is merely political fiction. Zoe Williams (2011) concludes: 'for all the big society talk, "philanthrocapitalism" looks a lot more like capitalism than it does philanthropy'.

Arguably, the fallacy in the Conservative narrative of welfare reform based upon the 'Big Society' project is the fictional notion that it is possible to roll back the state without running the risk of returning society to the Dickensian conditions of the Poor Law and reliance on charity for the 'deserving' poor. Blond's (2010, p 206) citation of the 1890s Primrose League directly connects the 'Big Society' project to its Victorian antecedents. M. Davis (2006) has compellingly demonstrated the abject quality of social life in states without state welfare, where slum conditions resemble those of 19th-century England described by Engels in 1844 (Engels, 1999). Civil society in the neoliberal form of charity arguably provides little in the way of a solution to structural poverty and weakens the bonds that hold democracy together, because of its association with the welfare reform agenda that is driven by the political objective of ending social justice as the basis of political community. This suggests that the 'Big Society' project may turn out to be a political fiction rather than a new political narrative. Albeit, Norman (2010, p 204), in presenting 'the contractual case', argues that the 'Big Society' is ultimately about a new subjectivity, which he calls ICE – 'institutions, competition and entrepreneurship'. The archaic image of Burke's 'little platoons' has done little to persuade the public that 'Big Society' is a positive political subject. There are too many unanswered questions. The imagery is wrong in a democracy. Social democrats have also been influenced by this 'Big Society' thinking.

Narrative 3: The Third Way and Big Society

Tony Judt (2010, p 143) observes: 'Social democracy, in one form or another, is the prose of contemporary European Politics'. His book *Postwar* (Judt, 2005) was in many respects a tribute to what he called 'the social democratic moment', which spanned the period between the late 1940s to the 1970s and was widely regarded as the Golden Age of the welfare state. For Judt (2005, p 559), social democracy was the master narrative of the 20th century. Judt (2012, p 368) in his valedictory book, *Thinking the Twentieth Century*, concludes: 'But even a well educated citizenry is not sufficient protection against an abusive political economy. There has to be a third actor there, beyond the citizen and the economy, which is the government.' He characterises social democracy as 'the banality of good'. Social democrats have latterly sought to incorporate civil society into a project of renewal, which has involved adapting to neoliberalism in a post-socialist order. As the socialist imaginary that underpinned the Enlightenment republican ideal of human progress has dimmed, social democrats have sought to reinvent themselves. It has not proved to be an easy task. Chantal Mouffe (2005, p 9) observes that social democracy 'has proved incapable of addressing the new demands of recent decades, and its central achievement, the welfare state, has held up badly under attack from the right, because it has not been able to mobilize those who should have interests in defending its achievements'. The 'Third Way' has emerged as the defining philosophy of a relaunched social democratic project. Paradoxically, the Third Way has proved to be the most influential in the Anglophone world, where classical social democracy has been weakest. The Third Way has been social democracy's alternative to the compassionate conservatism of the 'Big Society'. Jordan (2010, p 191) observes: 'the Third Way can be represented as the last in a long line of attempts to regulate capitalism in line with some version of morality'. He concludes that the Third Way had the instrumental function of providing a response 'to the subversion of welfare states by globalisation in the 1980's' (Jordan, 2010, p 191).

Anthony Giddens, in *Beyond Left and Right* (1994), seeks to tackle the challenging problems of social democracy in late modernity by addressing the changed solidarities that are reshaping the relationship between the individual and collectivity, through the concept of 'social reflexivity'. In terms of forging a new political and social grammar, Giddens' work is impressive. He advocates 'democratising democracy' through 'generative politics'. Evoking the ancient Greek republican *agora*, Giddens (1994, p 15) argues that 'generative politics is a defence of the politics of the public domain ... it works through providing material conditions, and organisational frameworks, for the life–political decisions taken by individuals and groups in the wider social order'. Building active trust, participation in the decision-making process and community development are all part of this Third Way strategy, in which links between state, business and community are integral to the process of building a partnership society.

Giddens has produced the definitive text on the 'Third Way' project, entitled *The Third Way: The Renewal of Social Democracy* (Giddens, 1998). In this book, Giddens advocates his project as not just a possibility, but a necessity, in a globalised world dominated by neoliberalism. While 'Third Way' politics is particularly associated with Tony Blair's New Labour government in Britain and Bill Clinton's 1990s Democratic administration in the US, Giddens presents it as a universal model. However, as Pierson (2001, p 127) points out, 'the quest for something that is not-quite capitalism and not-quite socialism is more than a hundred years old' – the welfare state. Traditional social democracy is the historic third way between capitalism and socialism. Its architects – Léon Blum, John Maynard Keynes, Clement Atlee, Luigi Einaudi and William Beveridge – had a shared vision of a big society based upon public-spirited railways, superb state schools that promoted equality of opportunity and an excellent, nationalised health service free on the basis of need (Buruma, 2012, p 31).

The novel element in the 'Third Way' is its professed futurism based upon an enabling state. But critics question its policy substance. Selbourne describes this 'Third Way' thesis as 'phoney blue-skies thinking' (*Guardian*, 4 January 2008). The French sociologist Alain Touraine (2001, p 90) characterises the impact of Giddens' 'Third Way' in social policy terms: 'essentially, it means replacing welfare policy with enterprise policy which presupposes both flexibility at the level of the social organisation and the empowerment of actors'. Giddens, with New Age resonance, defines the distinction between classical social democratic concepts of welfare and the 'Third Way' narrative as a shift from an economic paradigm to a 'psychic one': 'not only is welfare generated by many contexts and influences other than the welfare state, but welfare institutions must be concerned with fostering psychological as well as economic benefits' (Giddens, 1998, p 117). This is the core of the enabling state that emphasises opportunity as well as well-being, avoiding the charge of creating a dependency culture by fundamentally restricting state–society relations. Jordan (2010, p 43) argues that the 'Third Way' is essentially a moral project that seeks to 'reconcile individual freedom with collective solidarity and security'. His argument is essentially about an attempt to construct a new social and political grammar in post-structuralist society, based upon a renegotiated moral consensus – a Big Society?

Behind the futuristic narrative there are clear strategic principles intended to change state–society relations. At a structural level, Giddens (1998, p 118) argues: 'we should recognise that the reconstruction of welfare provision has to be integrated with programmes for the active development of civil society'. Giddens sets out his goal for 'the renewal of civil society' as follows:

- Government and civil society in partnership
- Community renewal through harnessing local initiative
- Involvement of the third sector
- Protection of the local public sphere
- Community-based crime prevention
- The democratic family. (Giddens, 1998, p 79)

He asserts: 'an open public sphere is as important at local as at national level, and this is one way that democratization connects with community development' (Giddens, 1998, p 85). These are the basic rules of Giddens' political and social grammar designed to forge a

Third Way in politics, based upon neo-institutionalist principles that are redefining the relationship between the state and civil society by incorporating civil society into the apparatus of governance. Norman (2010, p 29) has characterised this strategy as 'faking civil society'.

The import of Giddens' model envisages a reinvention of local governance with social partnerships offering the basic ingredients of political community – a late modern *agora*. It is presented as a narrative of 'democratic renewal'. The positive contribution offered by local partnership is that it theoretically reframes the relationship between the users of social services and the providers in a democratic and empowering manner called 'co-production' (Skidmore and Craig, 2005, pp 30–3). Shortly after it was elected to office, in 1997, the New Labour government announced a 'national compact' between the voluntary and community sector and the state for England (Home Office, 1998). It suggested a new post-ideological political dynamic, in which the government was trying to forge a developmental model of social democracy, in partnership with civil society. The think-tank Demos has called this 'co-production', a system where citizens have a 'real voice not meaningless choice' (Parker and Heapy, 2006, p 10). With the UK 'service economy' accounting for 74% of GDP, service design has become a critical policy issue. The experience of social partnership in Ireland suggests a model of civil society as an instrument of governance (Powell and Geoghegan, 2004). This is far from the goal of 'democratising democracy'.

The Third Way version of social democracy seeks to respond to a metachange in capitalism from 'Fordist' manufacturing to a post-Fordist 'knowledge economy', based upon service industries and information technology. It assumes that the second way (socialism) is dead. Traditional class politics is replaced by a 'business friendly' social democracy that seeks to embrace the market as the driver of economic growth. The Third Way is, therefore, an acceptance of the first way (capitalism). While there have been signs that this pro-business model of social democracy may be under electoral strain in the form of (1) the election of Respect candidate George Galloway in the Bradford West by-election in 2012 on a radical anti-capitalist and anti-imperialist platform and (2) the impressive performance of the Left candidates in the 2012 French presidential election and the Greek general elections, there are some signs of policy change towards economic growth in a world where the market-led model of development remains dominant, despite the 2008 financial crash. Is this policy shift an illusion? Jean Luc Emlenton, the Front de Gauche (Left Front) candidate in the French presidential election, thinks so and rejects 'the illusion that there could be a good capitalism'. He asserts: 'look, we have to smash this prejudice that the rich are useful just because they are rich'. Emlenton has called for a 'civic insurrection' in France against the forces of capital (*Irish Times*, 20 April 2012).

From Mélenchon's perspective, 'capitalist propaganda always managed to make people think that the markets were in humanity's interests. For too long people have been made to feel that they were some kind of drain or problem for expecting free education, free health care or being able to stop working when they are old and spent.' Emlenton proclaims that his Front de Gauche has emerged 'at a time of renaissance and reorganisation of the progressive camp on the ruins of social democracy and state communism' (Mélenchon, quoted in the *Guardian*, 7 April 2012). This critique reads very much like an obituary notice for social democracy and a dismissal of François Hollande, the Social Democratic winner of the French presidential election in 2012 and champion of a policy shift toward economic growth within the EU. But there are exceptions that indicate that 'Big Society' and 'welfare state' can coexist in a progressive partnership, based on the social democratic model.

The exceptions to the rule reside in the Nordic states, which are based upon 'the Nordic economic paradox', where highly developed welfare states, partial decommodification of labour and high taxation regimes coexist with successful economies close to the top of the global league tables (Wilson, 2011, pp 9–10). Underpinning this Nordic success have been high levels of state investment in the labour force, which have attracted Foreign Direct Investment (FDI). A 'smart society' has underpinned a 'smart economy' based upon 'flexicurity', which protects labour from the vagaries of the market. This is the developmental model of social democracy at its best. Contrary to Mélenchon's critique, the Nordic model proves that social democracy can work.

The key to this Nordic success has been the positive relationship between civil society and the welfare state. Swedish social democracy has been based upon the 'popular mass movement model', which embraces the traditional labour movement and the new social movements (NSMs) of the 1960s – women's, environmental and peace movements – as well as consumer cooperatives, sporting and educative bodies (Wilson, 2011, p 6). In Sweden these popular mass movements (*folkrörelser*) define the meaning of civil society in its common usage, rather than the third sector based on charity, in the Anglo-Saxon world. In both Sweden and Denmark civil society has been traditionally relegated to a marginal role. Wilson (2011, p 6) notes that charity (*välgörenhet*) 'acquired a negative connotation during the 20th century, with welfare coming to be understood as a matter of civil and social rights'. The Nordic model demonstrates the compatibility of a democratic 'Big Society' with the 'welfare state', based upon citizenship rights and supported by a 'popular mass movement' model of civil society. There are, however, signs of change in which the values of social democracy and the welfare state have started to erode in Nordic societies.

In Sweden, Wiig et al (2003, p 154) have reported:

> During the 1960s, '70s and '80s, the roles within the Swedish welfare system stayed the same and were quite stable. Few people at the time would have questioned the fact that the welfare producers belonged to the Public Sector. There were of course critical voices questioning how different authorities worked. Usually the critics accused the State and Council of too little action. During the 1990s we see tendencies of change, and the Public Sector's ability to solve welfare problems is questioned. Along with this in Sweden, (the so called) Idealistic Sector's welfare potentials are starting to attract more attention. The reputation of charity has been restored. Idealistic organisations are employed by the State and municipalities for welfare services. At the same time these organisations are expected to stay independent, even from their employer.

In Denmark, Viggo Jonasen (2003, p 42) also observed a growing level of interest in the third sector, which he dates from the 1970s:

> The 1970's brought an oil crisis, growing unemployment (and therefore growing public unemployment expenses), poverty-polarisation, state-criticism and monetarist policies to many countries – even to some degree in Denmark. In the 1980's a new conservative headed government launched the idea of mobilising more people to do voluntary social work might be used as a means of reducing the growth in the public sector. The same period brought a rise in criticism of the public sector: 'Public bad, private good'. A doubt about the capacity of the welfare state to solve (all) social problems at that time had also been creeping into the hitherto staunch welfare state adherents in the labour party. This political climate also gave rise to a growing academic focus on the third sector. The idea: cut public expenses by having volunteers working for free, however,

soon disappeared from most of the discussion in Denmark. In fields of budget cuts politicians normally claim 'necessity' and 'higher efficiency' – not asking volunteers to take over.

It is clear that the social solidarity that made the Nordic countries a social democratic haven during the 20th century is beginning to unravel, and with it the much-vaunted Scandinavian welfare state. Is this the end of the welfare state, and what are the consequences for society?

A report by Jason de Parle in the *New York Times* (8 April 2012), entitled 'Welfare Limits Left Poor Adrift in Recession', observed: 'perhaps no law in the past generation has drawn more praise than the drive "to end welfare as we know it", which joined the late '90s economic boom to send caseloads plunging, the employment rate rising and officials of both parties hailing the virtues of tough love'. De Parle goes on to highlight the social consequences of ending welfare:

> The poor people who were dropped from cash assistance here, mostly single mothers, talk with surprising openness about the desperate, and sometimes illegal, ways they make ends meet. They have sold food stamps, sold blood, skipped meals, shoplifted, doubled up with friends, scavenged trash bins for bottles and cans and returned to relationships with violent partners – all with children in tow.

These victims of poverty make up one in four of US low-income single mothers, amounting to roughly four million women and children living in poverty in the richest country in the world (*New York Times*, 8 April 2012). This is the consequence of abandoning the 1930s New Deal that formed the basis of America's welfare state and 'the Great Society' programme of the 1960s. Yet it was a social democrat, President Clinton, who ended 'the welfare state as we know it'. President Obama also spoke favourably about the policy of 'ending welfare as we know it' during his 2008 election campaign. He has been notably silent on the issue during his presidency, which has been characterised by high unemployment and sluggish economic growth (*New York Times*, 8 April 2012).

The Third Way project has, arguably, failed as a 'Big Society' narrative for three reasons. First, the welfare state project was a successful third way between capitalism and socialism that has captured the public imagination as a 'Big Society' moral project and has been sustained over many decades by democratic consensus. The Third Way version of the 'Big Society, Smaller Government' project did not offer a convincing alternative to this tried and tested welfare state collectivist project. The objective of making citizens and communities more responsible for their own welfare, while superficially evocative of civic republicanism, became a welfare reform narrative of smaller government with serious social consequences for the poor. Second, British conservatives managed to turn the Third Way narrative around into a 'Big State' narrative that basically served to deepen governance at the expense of solidarity. Jordan (2010, p 19) asserts: 'because the Third Way model saw government as enforcing a contract with self-responsible individual citizens, the Conservatives could describe New Labour in the UK as creating an authoritarian "surveillance society" symbolised by identity cards, CCTV cameras and unnecessary regulations'. Third, Conservatives managed to transform the New Labour Third Way narrative into a moral discourse of social failure, which they called 'the Broken Society'. It enabled Conservatives to question the moral basis of the welfare state. Blond (2010, p 76) asserts: 'the great tragedy of the modern welfare state has been the corrosion of the long standing social values held by the working-class, and thereby the effective erosion of the mutualism these values enshrined'. As a narrative, the 'Third Way' manifestly had its limitations in terms of a neo-institutionalist agenda based upon social responsibility that has had a limited democratic purchase. Judt (2010, p 144) asserts: 'Social democracy needs a more convincing narrative, based upon a new political and social grammar, that replaces its exhausted language.' This new language has begun to be forged on the social Left in a project that seeks to 'democratise democracy'.

Narrative 4: strong democracy, 'Big Society' and social Left

Shortly before his untimely death in 2011, Tony Judt sent an e-mail to his fellow New York intellectual Ian Buruma about the need to find a 'radical epistemology with which to counter the coherence of Right wing universalism'. Judt concluded, 'the failure and collapse of the Soviet Union undermined not just communism, but a whole progressive narrative of advance and collectivisation ... when that story lost its anchor, much else went adrift' (Buruma, 2012, p 31). Ironically, the movements and mobilisations of 2011 suggest that radical civil society is very much alive. The demands of the Greek protestors for 'equality, justice and dignity', or the Egyptian demands for 'bread, freedom, dignity and humanity', echo the language of the 1789 French Revolution (Anheier et al, 2012, p 19).

The evidence so far suggests that the Big Society, Smaller Government project is predominantly a neo-institutionalist narrative that facilitates the renegotiation of state–civil society relations, in which the state seeks to downsize and transfer responsibility to the citizens. Alternatively, it has the potential to counter-intuitively deepen democracy through mobilising citizens. This has become the narrative of the social Left. Radical democratic theorists suggest that the project of democracy remains contested and incomplete. Anne Marie Smith (1998, p 7) observes:

> As mere ideas, 'liberty' and 'equality' do not change anything. Democratic discourse cannot exert this interruption effect upon relations of subordination until the democratic imaginary becomes embodied in norms and institutions. The extension of democratic principles into new spheres of the social did not take place until actual democratic struggles won some concrete strategic ground through political struggle. Political struggle does nevertheless depend in part on the ability to imagine alternative worlds.

The social Left evokes the poor people's movement of the 20th century, whose campaign in the US led to the 1964 Civil Rights Act and the 'Great Society', which enlarged government in the interests of the poor (Piven and Cloward, 1979). The idea that there is a 'social Left' composed of an active citizenry organised at grassroots democracy level and committed to deepening democracy is radical. Its *indignados* (outraged) philosophy is embodied in the anti-capitalist and the Occupy movements that espouse the principle 'democracy is something you do not something you have' (Ainger, 2012). Whether the social Left is a communicative space (such as a town square or *agora*) or a 'movement of movements' is open to question. It is probably both a space and a movement at the same time, given its centrifugal nature. In Spain, the *indignados* (who inspired the Occupy movement) grasped early on that the economic crisis was also 'a political crisis, and their struggle is for fundamental renewal of democratic politics. While the markets can destroy livelihoods in milliseconds, the slow halting meetings in the plazas and the small local assemblies that spread from neighbourhood to neighbourhood, embody participatory democracy' (Ainger, 2012). The Occupy movement, which is a response to economic and social injustice and the popular belief that 'the 99%' are being exploited by society's wealthiest '1%' extends across six continents, over 60 countries and has inspired up to 2,600 demonstrations (*Guardian*, December

2011).Alan Touraine has defined the meaning of the term 'social Left',
noting the ideological dominance of the political left and right, based
upon top-down power pyramids that operate in a centripetal way. He
argues that 'the social left in contrast takes as its starting point the idea
that all social movements begin with active defence of a social reality
and rights' (Touraine, 2001, p 87). Furthermore, he asserts 'it is a matter
of defending the cultural rights of all (and especially of minorities)
against forced assimilation, irrespective of whether it is forced upon
a market-dominated mass culture or by a communitarian power'
(Touraine, 2001, p 87). The view espoused by Touraine detects a rupture
with the past and the emergence of a new democratic imaginary in
the future, building on human rights achievements. Hardt and Negri
(2004, p 106) have argued that the Marxist subject – the working
class – has been transformed into an 'open and expansive' concept that
they call 'the multitude', linking all people who work in a project of
emancipation. Diversity is a core principle of the social Left, envisaging
planetary citizenship as an alternative to the globalisation or post-
globalisation vision of the future. The Occupy movement has become
the theatre of radical democratic discourse opposed to neoliberalism.
It offers a radically different model of democracy that challenges the
role of elites at a time of economic crisis and growing perceptions of
democratic deficits.

The eviction of the Occupy movement in New York, London
and Dublin (among other places) has the resonance of an Orwellian
'thought crime' being suppressed. This clearly was not the decision
of health and safety officers but of the 'thought police'. The slogan
of the Occupy movement, that they were representing the 99% of
citizens expropriated by the 1% oligarchy, had a powerful resonance
in the public imagination, inviting citizens to reclaim social justice as
the project of democracy. A shift towards the political left in elections
in France, Greece and Germany suggests that public opinion is being
influenced by this anti-capitalist critique.

Ulrich Beck (1997) regards the political rupture identified by
Touraine as a development that is leading to the reinvention of politics.
Beck (1997, p 104) advocates 'subpolitics', meaning 'social arrangements
from below' in a 'subpoliticised society' that 'could become (among
other possibilities), the civil society that takes its concerns into its
own hands in all areas and fields of action of society'. He concludes
that whilst mass political parties may have taken on the appearance
of 'dinosaurs from a fading industrial age', they still retain power. The
central challenge, according to Beck, is to reinvent politics by 'moving
organised interests back into society and elevating unorganised interests,

which nonetheless endanger or protect the public interest, to be central tasks and axes of the political system'. The French philosopher Alain Badiou (2012) advocates 'real politics' in opposition to what he calls 'parliamentary cretinism'. He defines 'real politics' 'as a necessity to invent a politics that is not identical with power. Real politics is to engage to resolve problems within a collective with enthusiasm'. This is the essence of the *agora*. Badiou (2010) elaborates his ideas in *The Communist Hypothesis*, which essentially presents a Maoist perspective.

Beck's Third Way, as has been argued above, bears no relationship with Giddens' Third Way, which seeks to adapt social democracy to neoliberalism. For theorists of radical democracy, socialism was a necessary historical moment in the evolution of democracy because it demanded an end to the conditions of social and economic oppression (Smith, 1998, p 9). But socialism failed to achieve a coherent and sustainable narrative for human liberation. Nonetheless, its politics of redistributive justice represents a vital element in the evolution of democracy. But the imperative of recognition based upon identity politics has introduced an alternative site for the narrative of human liberation. Social policy is challenged to embrace the imperatives both of redistribution and of recognition in an evolving civil society–welfare state consensus that expands government, while making it more accountable to citizens in a 'Big Society, Strong Democracy project'. Is it possible to create a discourse coalition around this transformative democratic narrative of 'Big Society'? We may be witnessing its birth in social movements like the *indignados* and the Occupy movement. This is reflected in the rise in European anti-austerity parties, such as Syriza (Left Coalition) in Greece – a conglomeration of ex-Maoist, Trotskyists and Greens – at the expense of traditional parties including New Democracy and Pasok. However, the success of the Far Right in 2012 French presidential election reminds us that a political rupture may produce diverse results, which have also appeared in Greece in the form of Golden Dawn.

If civil society is to become a project of transformation with all the suggested potential in a diverse world, it will need to harness its future to deepening democracy as a global project and reject its use by the state as a vehicle for the deepening of governance. The project of deepening democracy is often called 'strong democracy'. Benjamin Barber (1984, p xxii) in his justly celebrated book, *Strong Democracy*, declared: 'strong democracy tried to revitalise citizenship without neglecting the problems of efficient government by defining democracy as a form of government in which the people govern themselves in at least some public matters at least some of the time'. He configured the pursuit of the so-called 'Big Society' with the position of strong democracy – 'Big Society, Strong Democracy'.

Prugh et al, (2000, p 10) have asserted that strong democracy offers immediate advantages over the 'thin democracy' of the representative variety, emphasising (i) the sociality of the conception of a social 'us' inherent in notions of community; (ii) the dispersal and redistribution of power away from special interests; and (iii) engaging citizens in the challenges and problems of governance. They add: 'we need politics of engagement, not a politics of consignment' (Prugh et al, 2000, p 220). De Sousa Santos (2006, p xliii) asserts: 'democracy is a new historic grammar'. He adds: 'this grammar implied the introduction of experimentalism in the very sphere of the state transforming the state into an absolutely new social movement' (De Souza Santos, 2006, p xlv). This democratic experimentation envisages reconfiguring state–society relations in favour of civil society but not at the expense of an active state. The welfare state becomes more accountable but is not downsized. Central–local relations are also likely to be reconfigured in a constitutional process driven by citizens within the state.

The idea of radical democratisation in the form of a 'Big Society, Strong Democracy' project has become fundamental to a new social and political grammar that is at the heart of the reinvention of politics. In a postmodern world the pursuit of a strong and reflexive democracy has become the compass for a social change process that seeks to radicalise late modernity. The emergence of new social movements concerned with social and economic injustice, women's rights, environmental protection, ethnic minority rights, gay rights, peace and neutrality etc. embodies the spirit of reflexive democracy. Grassroots social movements have given the socially excluded a collective voice through which they can interrogate both capitalism and nation regarding their democratic and social intent. This, arguably, presents late modern society with transformative possibilities. Within this context the subpolitics of active citizenship has given impetus to the pursuit of strong and radical democratic realignment with civil society at its heart – a 'project of projects' in which participatory democracy complements representative democracy.

The World Social Forum embodies the principles of radical democracy. Latin America has become the main theatre for radical democratic projects, having abandoned neoliberalism since the new millennium began. The New Bolivarianism that has swept the Latin American continent has provided the ideological driving force. Porto Alegre, a Brazilian city, is its iconic symbol (Kirby, 2003). It represents a convergence between socialism and democracy. Traditional socialist values of social justice, equality, solidarity are linked to participative democracy and human emancipation in the new Bolivarian political project.

Radical democratic theorists view the struggle for democratisation as open ended (Laclau and Mouffe, 1985; Mouffe, 2000). As Smith (1998) puts it:

> In the nineteenth and twentieth centuries, subjects with a long history of struggle such as workers, peasants, slaves and the colonized, took on new identities – as trade union members, citizens, anti-colonial nationalists, anti-imperialist internationalists and so on – as they demanded rights in innovative ways. New subjects also emerged – women, racial/ethnic rights-based claims in language borrowed from previous struggles.

According to this analysis, 'the multitude', as Hardt and Negri (2004) put it, is the new revolutionary subject that has replaced the working class of classical Marxism in driving the locomotive of history.

But there are sceptics who regard the idea of 'Big Society, Strong Democracy' as utopian. Giddens (1998, p 133), in a critique of the radical democratic perspective, observes: 'the aim of a multiculturalist politics is entirely laudable – to counter the exploitation of the oppressed'; but he adds: 'this cannot be done without the support of the broad national community, or without a sense of social justice that must stretch beyond the claims or grievances of any specific group'. He is raising the related issues of cultural essentialism (sectionalism) and the challenge of forging an intersectional approach to radical democratic politics – one that takes class, race, gender, sexuality and ecology into account. Clearly, unless radical civil society can address the challenge of intersectionality and form a democratic matrix, its internal contradictions are likely to undermine potential political coherence. Gray (2007, p 38) asserts that multiculturalism is 'an illusion of the Enlightenment'. But Chantal Mouffe (2005, p 60) argues that 'the question of political identity is crucial and that the attempt to construct citizens' identities is one of the most important in democratic politics … such a project requires the common political identity among democratic subjects'. However, unifying Hardt and Negri's (2004) 'multitude' as a common political subject analogous to Marx and Engels' working class is fraught with centrifugal elements that are likely to undermine its coherence. These are clearly not easy issues to resolve. Fraser and Honneth (2003) have pointed out how challenging this task is, encompassing both epistemological and political dimensions because it involves reconciling recognition (diversity) and redistribution (equality). Gray (2007, p 41) concludes that the underlying rationale of radical democracy is 'an epistemological impossibility'.

Radical democratic theorists are more hopeful. Chantal Mouffe (2005, p 4) suggests that 'once we accept the necessity of the political and the impossibility of a world without antagonism, what needs to be envisaged is how it is possible under those conditions to create and maintain a pluralistic democratic order'. She argues the case for a new social and political grammar based upon the principle of 'agonistic pluralism', that provides 'a framework for the articulation of the different democratic struggles' (Mouffe, 2005, p 7). Mouffe (2005, p 8) concludes that radical democracy is based upon a paradox: 'such a democracy will therefore always be democracy "to come", as conflict and antagonism are at the same time its condition of possibility and the condition of impossibility of its full realisation'. De Souza Santos (2007, p lxiii) similarly concludes 'from this substantive point of view, there is no true democracy, there is only democratization, a process without end'. The social Left is an attempt to forge a political alternative based upon the aspiration to design a map of action towards building a new world, in which 'old world' hegemonies and tyrannies are overcome. Whether it is a space or a movement or both, it offers a profound institutional and philosophical critique of late modern society that is shaping our consciousness of the political and social in the 21st century. Its promised 'new world' may be the outline contours of a post-globalised era. Only time will tell whether this radical social subjectivity proves to have any meaningful political purchase as a new narrative or simply is another political fiction. President Barrack Obama's decision to endorse gay marriage during the 2012 US presidential campaign adroitly interposed a connection with the Civil Rights movement of the 1960s, highlighting the power of political fiction to shape social reality and promote a transformative agenda in an increasingly multicultural society (*Observer*, 19 May 2012).

Conclusion

In this chapter we have set out four narratives exploring the relationship between civil society and the state. All four are problematic. First we addressed the 'Big Society, Smaller Government' concept in China. It involved a paradoxical inversion of the Marxist theory of 'the withering away of the State'. Socialism with Chinese characteristics means a party state dedicated to economic rationalism and social polarisation. It conflicts with the official goal of social harmony in China. Secondly, we examined the British Conservative Party and its endorsement of a modernisation project, based upon neoliberalism and the civic conservatism of the 'Big Society, Smaller Government' project. For those who are excluded from the consumer society, civic or 'compassionate conservatives' advocate civil society in the form of a rediscovery of charity as the solution to poverty. There are real problems of scale and metrics, apart from the politics. Charity accounts for little more than a small fraction of public expenditure. Giving appears to be primarily in the form of horizontal redistribution from people on relatively low incomes to people on very low incomes. This has more the characteristics of mutual aid (a form of utopian socialism) than of charity in its historically constructed form of the benevolence of the rich towards the poor. Third, we discussed the Third Way – social democrats in the Anglophone world, seeking to adapt to the neoliberal project, have sought to advocate social partnership between the state, civil society and the market. This neo-institutionalist agenda denies the reality that the state in the late modern era has resituated itself towards the market. Critics view partnership as a mechanism that seeks to incorporate civil society into a project of deepening governance at the expense of democracy. Fourth, we turned to the idea of deeper democracy as 'Big Society'. Radical democrats seek to harness the civic republican tradition of democracy in the pursuit of a project aimed at 'democratising democracy' through active citizenship, which we have called a 'Big Society, Strong Democracy' project. But there are major challenges in terms of transcending cultural essentialism (sectionalism), forging intersectionality and overcoming antagonistic relations with the state and parliamentary democracy, which radical democrats contend is based upon an outmoded form of governance. All of these approaches share a common theme in endorsing the concept of active citizenship as the basis of political community. This represents a shift away from the social citizenship of the welfare state, where entitlement defined the citizen's relationship with the state. We are left with the question: is the future going to be a choice between an activist state or an activist society or both in a new synergy that will rewrite the exhausted social and political grammar of late modern politics? What is certain is that a new discursive framework is required. If there is to be a 'Big Society', it requires a project of reimagining politics that moves beyond political fiction into a narrative form, building upon and reshaping the political language of the twentieth century that rested upon the reality of social democratic prose. The financial crash of 2008 exposed the failure of neoliberalism as a project that is compatible with democracy. As we survey the ruins of our democratic architecture the task of forging a new narrative that is based upon a sustainable political future becomes more pressing. If we are to avoid a descent into the populist authoritarianism that characterised Europe during the 1930s, we need to find a new civic narrative that gives expression to social justice and political equality.

TWO

The renaissance of civil society

> Yes, but our sense of having lost the tradition of the
> Enlightenment is tied to the complete reversal of our vision
> of the world that has been imposed by the neoliberal vision
> that dominates today. I think (and here, in Germany, I can
> make this comparison), I think that the current neoliberal
> revolution is a conservative revolution – in the sense that
> one spoke of a conservative revolution in Germany in the
> thirties – and a conservative revolution is a very strange
> thing: It's a revolution that restores the past and yet presents
> itself as progressive, a revolution that transforms regression
> into progress – to the extent that those who oppose
> regression seem themselves to be regressing. Those who
> oppose terror come to seem like terrorists. It's something
> that we have both experienced: We voluntarily classify
> ourselves as archaic – in French, we are called *ringards* (old-
> timers), *arriérés* (outdated).
>
> Pierre Bourdieu, in *The Nation* (3 July 2000)

Bourdieu's observation describes the complexity of the time we live
in and the challenges involved in unravelling its political meaning.
Civil society has enjoyed a renaissance in our 'postmodern' world as
the symbol of a new phase in democratic development. It conveys the
image of a free and vibrant public sphere, where tyranny has finally
been laid to rest. But as modernity recedes into historical memory, real
concerns have been raised about a loss of hope in the possibility of social
progress. The metanarrative of modernity based upon human progress
and social justice has been eclipsed by a global narrative of development
driven by the acceptance of neoliberalism as the only model, despite
the 2008 financial crash. In this scheme of things, civil society appears
as little more than a toothless distraction to its critics on the political
left or, worse still, a Trojan horse that will unleash market dominance
over democracy in a full-blown conservative restoration. And yet, all
over our 'globalised' world civil society is re-emerging as a beacon
of hope for the future. What is its potential for human progress? This
chapter will argue that the renaissance of civil society is a significant

historical and political event. It will not simply present civil society, as its neoliberal partisans do, as the end of modernism, secularism and socialism. The 'end of history thesis' is much in favour on the Right (Fukuyama, 1992). But the idea of civil society is more complex than that, if for no other reason than it affirms that there is such a thing as society – a concept contested by conservatives. Cohen and Arato (1994, p ix) define civil society 'as a sphere of social interaction between the economy and the state, composed above all of the intimate sphere (especially the family), the sphere of associations (especially voluntary associations), social movements and forms of public communication'. Put simply, civil society is our collective self. It is us: our civic narrative. It will be argued in this chapter that, historically, civil society has been associated with the civic struggle to build a more virtuous political order, based upon democracy and freedom.

Civil society, democracy and politics

While civil society provided the democratic means to overthrow communism in Eastern Europe, its renaissance also coincided with the 'modernisation' of the welfare state in the West in the teeth of democratic opposition. Elites on both the political Left and Right began to argue the case for decentralising the welfare state and harnessing the potential of civil society. The implications have been profound. We need to discover what the renaissance of civil society means. Does it mean a new and more democratic future based on citizen participation? Or does it envisage the liberalisation of society in which the state is displaced by the resurgent market? Does this downsizing mean the end of the welfare state? Did it ever exist? Was it a metaphor for a virtuous society based on a welfare compromise? Is virtue being redefined in terms of individual agency in a world where welfare has become once again a matter of personal responsibility? Or can the *zeitgeist* of the welfare state be reinvented by a social Left on the basis of utopian socialist principles? Is Colas' (1997, p 323) contention that 'the State is the opium of civil society' correct?

In order to make sense of the relationship between civil society and civic virtue, we need to explain the origins and meaning of civil society. The respected authority John Keane (1998, p 6) offers a political vision of civil society: 'Civil society, as I used the term and still do, is an ideal typical category that both describes and envisages a complex and dynamic ensemble of legally protected non-governmental institutions that tend to be non-violent, self-organising, self-reflexive, and permanently in tension with each other and with the state institutions that "frame", constrict and enable their activities'. In this political vision, 'civil' appears as the antonym of violent or 'coercive' and is equated with civility in a participative democratic society that is tolerant and respectful of difference. Civil society is defined by the basic democratic freedom to associate. Citizens are entitled to create an association for any political, social or cultural purpose. But they are not allowed to form associations that promote disorder, terrorism or immoral objectives (for example, paedophilia). Sometimes associations are formed for contradictory purposes, such as pro-life and pro-choice, or the promotion of hunting as opposed to the protection of birds. However strongly we feel personally about these issues (for example, hunting), we recognise the other's right to associate as a basic expression of democratic governance. But it has not always been so. The right of association is intimately connected to the political struggle for democracy. Early welfare organisations based on utopian socialist principles, such as friendly societies, cooperatives and mutual aid organisations, were the product of these civic struggles. They challenged a paternalistic and egoistic tradition of charity that treated the recipient of assistance as a supplicant, whose socio-legal status was punitively defined as pauperism. The fear of fanaticism has long been a contradiction at the core of civil society, leading to public demands for restraints on the right to association (Colas, 1997). One person's liberty may be another's tyranny. The birth of modern democracy in the revolutionary ferment of France in 1789 linked welfare to a statist vision of citizens' rights, epitomised by the Jacobin dictum 'no one shall be allowed to arouse in any citizen any kind of intermediate interest and separate him from the public ideal through the medium of corporate interests' (cited in Archambault, 1997, p 28). This created a statist tradition based on the pursuit of equality that was to exercise a powerful constraining influence for two centuries on the development of civil society. It finally collapsed in 1989, with the fall of the Berlin Wall. But there was an alternative tradition that initially flourished in the utopian socialist 1848 revolution in France, which resulted in an explosion of non-profit organisations. Alexis de Tocqueville's account of the United States in the 1830s similarly reveals a world purportedly rich in associational activity. The success of the social credit and cooperative movements in Canada attests to a culture vibrant in mutual support (Finkel et al, 1993). Similarly, in Europe a civil economy of credit unions has flourished, alongside cooperatives (Murray, 2012, p 146).

The origins of the welfare state have been driven by an essentially Jacobin view of the world. There is a direct relationship between the state and the citizen in which the former contracts to provide for the welfare of the latter. The Fabian view of the welfare state in Britain evolved into an unchallengeable orthodoxy that welfare must be provided by the state, despite the Webbs' advocacy of 'parallel bars' between the state and the voluntary sector. The explanation probably lies in the belief that only the state can guarantee the citizen's right to entitlements in what came to be known as the post-war welfare settlement that led to the socialisation of the state (see Chapter Four).

The boom in associative activity since the 1960s, reinforced during the 1980s by a paradigm shift in governance, has fundamentally changed the political landscape. Lester Salamon (1994) has spoken of 'a virtual associational revolution'. However, it would be naïve to believe that the state has simply reached a new democratic compromise with civil society. Nobody doubts that the state is shrinking. But is it becoming more democratic? From the point of view of capital, the welfare state had become a Faustian bargain that it could not afford (Offe, 1984). The opportunity to shed this social responsibility was welcomed in a full-blooded conservative restoration after 1989. The primacy of the market became the dominant characteristic of a new global world order, where welfare was redefined as 'dependency' and the very idea of society, with its collectivist connotations, was questioned (Murray, 1984).

Margaret Thatcher's famous remark that there is 'no such thing as society' was as much an attack on civil society as on the state welfare. It was to unleash a major debate. The idea of a welfare state has been challenged in the Veit-Wilson–Atherton debate in the journal of *Social Policy and Administration*. Veit-Wilson (2000) believes that the welfare state has become emptied of analytic meaning, due to its undiscriminating application. He calls for a distinction between 'welfare' and 'unwelfare' states, arguing that without it the term is simply reduced to 'mystifying' and 'redundant noise'. While Veit-Wilson was writing from the British perspective, Atherton (2002) provides an American response, declaring that he uses the term 'simply as a matter of convenience'. Paradoxically, Atherton seems to favour dropping the term altogether, reminding us that America never had a welfare state as it is understood in the European sense, that is, the European social model that is now imperilled by the politics of austerity in post-crash conditions.

The historic reality, as Esping-Andersen demonstrated in his monumental study, *The Three Worlds of Welfare Capitalism* (1990), is that the idea of a welfare state is profoundly Eurocentric one. Esping-Andersen, in a subsequent study, *The Social Foundations of Post-Industrial Society* (1999), anticipates the Veit-Wilson–Anderson debate, arguing that 'precise definition in this concept [welfare state]' is 'probably futile', given that it 'serves to capture the Zeitgeist of an era' (Esping-Andersen, 1999, p 7). This acknowledgement of the symbolic significance of the term 'welfare state' suggests that it is essentially a normative rather than a descriptive term for a society that promotes social citizenship.

As we begin a new century a global conservative restoration, called neoliberalism, threatens to sweep equality and welfare away. Social justice is contested as a normative concept. Neoliberalism, based on balanced budgets, privatisation, low taxation and tight money, coupled with hollowing of the state, has redefined civic virtue. A leading conservative intellectual, Leo Strauss (1899–1973), whose influence over the American political elite has been very significant, has argued that a virtuous society is constructed on virtuous morally centred individuals, suggesting that an interventionist state has created a dependant class of welfare recipients at home and locked developing countries into a dependency relationship based on aid (Drury, 1997, 2005). The politics of austerity in the wake of the 2008 financial crash has polarised society by enforcing cuts in welfare, while simultaneously bailing out the banks from the public purse.

While elites on both the Right and Left of the political spectrum have accepted austerity, civil society has not followed their lead, sensing that oligarchy may be threatening democracy (Hardt and Negri, 2000, 2004; Klein, 2000; Hertz, 2001). And at times rambunctious protests composed of *indignados*, Aganakismenoi and Occupy movements represent the political face of radical global civil society, challenging the neoliberal orthodoxy and its austerity agenda, designed to shrink the welfare state. These concerns at global level are asserting citizens' rights in a campaign that is reharnessing radical civil society in the struggle for the restoration of social justice, challenging a perceived democratic deficit at the core of our governance. American communitarian thinkers, notably Etzioni (1993), Fukuyama (1995) and Putnam (2000), have responded to this challenge from radical civil society by promoting the concept of social capital as the basis for civic virtue that utilises civil society to promote trust. Critics of the idea of social capital argue that it is a depoliticising strategy aimed at pacifying society's discontents on the domestic front and in a global world that has discursively reshaped international development according to the prescriptions of the World Bank. For example, John Harriss (2002) argues that this depoliticising strategy has disconnected development from its democratic potential and reduced the role of civil society to the private sphere of sports clubs, confraternities and church-based organisations. These developments reflect the Straussian concept of privatising virtue and shrinking the role of the welfare state, which is viewed as the nemesis of liberty.

Some argue that civil society has become the voice of welfare in an era when the state is under siege from its critics. It offers the prospect of the 'reflexive continuation of the welfare state' as part of a 'reflexive continuation of the democratic revolution' (Cohen and Arato, 1994, p 26). Or does it?

There are signs of a divergence of views between Europe and America and among political opinion in Europe. The welfare state remains popular in successive public opinion polls in Europe and continues to prosper in Scandinavia, albeit with more modest horizons (Ross, 2000, p 19). While the political Left may have accepted neoliberalism and welfare reform, there is little evidence that it has sold the idea to the public. In the space vacated by the political Left, what the French sociologist Alan Touraine calls a 'social Left' has emerged, deeply rooted in radical democracy that seeks to harness service users as actors in their own civic narrative. In the United States, the enduring legacy of Tocquevillian traditions of civil society – these days represented in the concept of social capital – continues to survive, albeit, if Robert Putnam's analysis in *Bowling Alone* (2000) is to be believed, in a state of crisis (see Chapter Seven).

Will Hutton, in his influential book, *The World We're In* (2002), has explored the divergence between American and European models of society. This divergence is as much cultural as economic. America is a deeply religious society, as Hutton demonstrates, imbued with a resurgent Christian fundamentalism that has formed a powerful symbiotic relationship with free market liberalism, epitomised by the rise of the Tea Party. Americans prescribed this as a model for world development. Ironically, at home, subsidies to US banks, the car industry, savings and loan companies and the steel industry suggest that this model may be more for export than for domestic consumption.

Europe, on the other hand, is a post-Christian society, where civic humanism offers the only alternative to the harsh reality of the marketplace. The tradition of collectivism in continental Europe stands in marked contrast to the full-blown individualism of the United States, which is mirrored in more muted form in other Anglo Saxon societies. China offers an entirely different developmental model, but shares the 'Big Society, Small Government' strategy (see Chapter One). Other parts of the world, including Africa, India, Latin America and the Islamic world, point in divergent directions. These cultural and economic divergences are reflected and refracted in debates about the political meaning of civil society that go to the heart of the body politic and the pursuit of a virtuous society. The global crisis following the 2008 financial crash has turned many political assumptions of the past into aspirations that are increasingly being denied to needy citizens in Europe and the United States. What unifies the European and American traditions of civil society is their common history in classical civilisation. Civil society was present in ancient Greek democratic society, personified by Pericles (495–429 BCE), the great Athenian leader. The search for a virtuous society is a trend running through the history of Western civilisation. Without understanding its past, it is not possible to understand and locate civil society within present-day debates. We must now turn to the task of considering the metanarrative of civil society and its role in shaping Western civilization's search for civic virtue.

The metanarrative of civil society

Peter Hall (1998, pp 24–6), in his book *Cities in Civilisation*, has described Athens as the 'fountainhead' of Western civilisation. Ancient Greece provides us with the etymological and conceptual building blocks for understanding the interconnected concepts of civil society, citizenship and civic virtue. The word 'policy' has its origins in ancient Greece. The Greeks called it *politeia*. Its meaning in practice was much more complex than *politiké* (politics). They simply regarded politics as the art of government. On the other hand, *politeia* meant the pursuit of civic virtue through good governance. The nature and objectives of good governance were debated by Plato and Aristotle, laying the foundations for modern democratic politics and providing a foundational narrative for civil society (Table 2.1).

For Aristotle, *demos* and *polis* were inseparable concepts that linked civic association to political association. The *agora* (a site of political assembly or marketplace) became the metaphor for Greek civil society as Greece evolved into city-states from about 700 BCE. Athens was the dominant and defining paradigm but was part of a larger civic development into city-states that included: Sparta, Corinth, Thebes, Aegina, Delos and Ionian cities such as Miletus (Hall, 1998, p 35). Sandel (2012, p 195) concludes in relation to the pivotal significance of these developments for European civilisation: 'only by living in a *polis* and participating in politics do we fully realise our nature as human beings'.

Civility emerges in classical culture as the basis of community, social stability and mutual dependence. Citizens internalised social and cultural codes of behaviour that enabled them to communicate non-violently with neighbours and strangers – agreeing to disagree – in conflict-free communicative zones (Anheier, 2010, p 476). Civility is the cornerstone of civil society because of its association with the civilising process

Table 2.1: The metanarrative of civil society

Civilisation	Civil society	Political formation	Welfare model	Civic virtue
Ancient Greek	*Politike koinonia*	City-state/*polis*	Political community or *philos*	Civility and citizen participation
Roman	*Societas civilis*	Roman Republic/ Empire	Commonwealth based upon idea of justice and community of interest	Justice, the rule of law, civic life, community and civility
Medieval	*Civitas Dei/ civitas terra* dualism	Christian civil society and monarchy	Monasticism and courtly etiquette of giving	Charity, religious belief and Christian civility
Renaissance	*Societas civilis*	City-state	Patronage and guild system	Philanthropy and fellowship/civility
Enlightenment	*Bürgerliche Gesellschaft*	Monarchical state and republican revolution	Public charity/poor law	Humanist civility
Modern	Welfare state/ civil society fusion	Democracy/ nation-state	Welfare state	Social citizenship and collective civility of welfare state
Postmodern	Renaissance of civil society	Neoliberalism/ 'Big Society'	Downsizing of welfare state, privatisation – with civil society as 'first sector'	Active citizenship, social capital and individualised civility based on toleration and respect of difference

(Elias, 1994). Anheier (2010, p 477) concludes that 'civility creates predictability, and builds social capital through successful encounters'; in summary, civility provides the communicative competencies and spaces upon which civil society is constructed.

Aristotle (384–322 BCE) in both his *Politics* and *Nicomachean Ethics* identifies the political community as supreme (Molnár, 2010). Maritti Munkonen (2010, pp 1230–4) observes that the ancient Greeks adopted the oriental concept of *oikos* (household) as the basis of classical welfare. However, in classical Greece the concept broadened to embrace the idea of communal union (*koinonia*). Members of the community were citizens (excluding slaves, foreigners and probably women) who formed the Greek city-state (*polis*). *Koinonia politike* means civil society and encapsulates the sense of social bonds or *philos* (friendship) between the citizenry that formed the basis of the Greek *polis*. These concepts laid the foundations of Greco–Roman philanthropy. In the latter, civil society became *societas civilis*. In Roman times the Latin word *civitas* meant citizenship and *municipium* (municipality) the descriptor of the city-state within the Roman republic and later *imperium*. For Romans, the rule of law, justice and civility constituted the virtuous civil society based upon a community of interests.

With the fall of Rome in 410 CE, Europe entered the medieval period. Reason was displaced by faith in the new order. The philosopher Augustine of Hippo had laid down the political principles of medieval society in his great work *Civitas Dei* (City of God), commenced in 413, three years after the sack of Rome. It was completed 13 years later. In this major philosophical work Augustine sets out the basis of a Christian civil society. At the core of his thinking is a duality based upon the idea of two cities, an earthly city (*Civitas Terra*) and a superior *Civitas Dei* (City of God). The use of the word *civitas* or city is influenced by the classical political formation of city-state and should be understood as a form of governance or *polis*. The relationship between church and state is defined by the superiority of ecclesiastical authority in Augustine's dualism. Divine law transcended secular power. Christian civil society, based upon the premise of human frailty, embodied in the doctrine of the Fall of Adam and Eve, that is, original sin. Human sin makes political autonomy and individual choice impossible, according to Augustine's worldview. It produced a hierarchal order in which war, property, slavery and the state provide the pillars of political society. While the Church asserted its supremacy over the secular sphere, it enjoined the faithful to accept the state's authority in their daily lives. The reality of civil society in practice was often very different to its theological conception. But there was an overarching sense of Christian Commonwealth that defined civil society as a political and social construct. Medieval protest movements sometimes challenged this hegemony in the form of messianic movements, religious heresies or campaigns about customary agrarian use rights that were being eroded (Cohn, 1961). They were, according to Cohn (1961, p 313), abnormal in their destructiveness and irrationality. The link between religion and fanaticism was undeniable in this uncivil society (Colas, 1997). Yet these medieval protest movements are important because they represent popular mobilisation against authority.

Charity defines the care of the poor in medieval society as a Christian duty. In its idealised form, charity is presented as an individualistic and altruistic act, as a private affair between two parties, the benefactor and the beneficiary. In Christian cosmology, redemption was possible through charity, however venal the life. Ontologically, charity balanced the venal and acquisitive in moral and social compact with God. Justice was divinely ordained through divine law. The philosopher Thomas Aquinas defined the Christian principles of charity, ordering them into seven 'spiritual aids' and seven 'good works'. The spiritual aids included: *consule* (consel), *carpe* (sustain), *doce* (teach), *solare* (console), *remitte* (rescue), *fer* (pardon) and *ora* (pray). Added to these seven spiritual aids were seven 'good works': *vestio* (clothe), *poto* (give water), *cibo* (feed), *redimo* (redeem from prison), *tego* (shelter) *colligo* (nurse), and *condo* (bury). The recipients of charity varied greatly, from the poor, the homeless, the hungry, the sick and the dead to the imprisoned. The exercise of charity defined civic virtue in a Christian civil society (Davies, 1997, p 778). It retained the ideal of civility, which had been largely co-opted in the formalism of courtly etiquette in an attempt to establish its cultural superiority. Colonial adventurers were later to employ this strategy to achieve cultural domination.

In the medieval world those seeking Christian perfection joined monastic communities. Monasteries were, however, not simply a refuge for ascetics and scholars from an otherwise 'barbarous' world. They were also an important social experiment that provided a form of civil society, often in the midst of chaos. The monastery formed a complex micro-society enmeshed in the wider society outside it. The great abbeys of France such as Cluny (910), Clairvaux (1115) and Fontevraud (1099), as well as elsewhere, including, Heiligenkreuz (Austria) and Iona (Scotland), typified the emergence of the monastery as a major European institution with hospitals, herbal dispensaries and lepersariums, as well as libraries and scriptoria.

The significance of the monastery in European civil society during the medieval period cannot be overstated. Its communal form in Western Europe made it a centre for civil society. While the monks formed a discrete micro-society, they also interacted with the outside world through preaching, learning and healing. In the late Middle Ages, monasticism went into decline. The onset of the Reformation led to the suppression of monasteries, notably in Protestant countries such as England. Their role in civil society as the centre of communal activity in a largely rural society also began to be challenged by the emergence of urban life and the renaissance or rebirth of the classical humanist tradition (Powell, 2010a).

The Renaissance marked a fundamental change in European civilisation in which the humanist tradition of classical civilisation was rediscovered in an increasingly urban-led society. The classical legacy had been protected in the Near East by philosophers such as Avicenna (980–1037), Averrvoes (1126–1198) and Maimonides (1135–1204), who rediscovered the works of Aristotle and Plato. The re-emergence of the European city-states, like Florence and Venice, enabled civil society in its classical sense to revive. Humanism was back, embodied by the work of Dante Alighieri (1265–1321) and Niccolo Machiavelli (1469–1527). The world ceased to be mesmerised by religion. The Renaissance formed an intellectual bridge to Enlightenment humanism in the form of the morally engaged individual.

The Enlightenment, as interpreted by the *philosophe*, viewed itself as a return to classical civilisation based upon the ascendancy of reason. Humanism was reborn and democracy rediscovered. Democracy looked back to the ancient Athens of Pericles (490–429 BCE) for its inspiration. The grandeur of Rome provided the model for a classical cultural and architectural revival, where law and civility became synonymous with the common good. In an Enlightenment world, where scepticism, empiricism and a belief in progress shaped the age, human beings believed that reason had freed them from traditional forms of authority, whether religious (the Church) or political (monarchical absolutism). The triumph of reason over tradition promoted a belief in the political and civil rights to liberty and equality that underpinned democracy and civic virtue as the core elements of the modern governance. This was the context of change from rural to urban in which the idea of civil society was reborn and flourished both among scholars and in the public mind. In Ernest Gellner's (1994) view this transition was little short of a historic miracle.

Democracy gradually became a reality in modern society through the emergence of a mass print-media culture and a popular coffee-house society. The intellectual ideas of the *philosophe* reshaped human consciousness, creating a society that was informed by reason and secular values. This was to prove a liberating experience for a bourgeoisie society that redefined itself in terms of modernity and democracy. However, for the poor the experience was different. A system of public charity emerged. It redefined the meaning of charity eschatologically, reconstituting it as a system of social regulation midway between the state and voluntary associations that focused on the control of poverty through segregation and confinement.

A new style of social control emerged during the Enlightenment, based on the systematic regulation of poverty (Powell, 2010b). The effective organisation and financing of this burgeoning apparatus of charity necessitated the growing involvement of the state in the social arena. This process took place through the transformation of the institution of charity into a means for enforcing a system of values based on the work ethic. Moral responsibility for poverty was displaced from the rich onto the poor. Poverty was turned into a social issue and charity was the instrument of its regulation. Nonetheless, the defining achievement of the Enlightenment brought to life a new and radical set of ideas that proclaimed a revolutionary era, called 'modernity'. Radicals sought to harness the Enlightenment possibilities for a new order through a 'revolution of the mind' that paved the way for their political realisation in the emerging democratic society (Israel, 2010). Out of this revolutionary ferment ultimately came the welfare state, in which civil society is fused with the state in pursuit of a new commonwealth, based upon the principle of social justice and equality. Also out of this historical rupture emerged emancipatory social movements that were to shape and reshape human consciousness down to the present day. Jonathan Israel, in his trilogy *Radical Enlightenment* (2001), *Enlightenment Contested* (2006) and *A Revolution of the Mind* (2010), argues that there were three competing visions of the Enlightenment: a Radical Enlightenment, a Moderate/Liberal Enlightenment and a Conservative Counter-Enlightenment. His core thesis is that the Radical Enlightenment, which he argues began with the Dutch philosopher Benedict de Spinoza (1632–77), is the *real* Enlightenment:

> Radical Enlightenment is a set of basic principles that can be summed up concisely as: democracy; racial and sexual equality; individual liberty of lifestyle; full freedom of thought, expression, and the press; eradication of religious authority from the legislative process and education; and full separation of church and state. It sees the purpose of the state as being a wholly secular one of promoting the worldly interests of the majority and preventing vested minority interests from capturing control of the legislative process. Its chief maxim is that all men have the same basic needs, rights, and status irrespective of what they believe or what religious, economic, or ethnic group they belong to, and that consequently all ought to be treated alike, on the basis of equity, whether black or white, male or female, religious or non-religious, and that all deserve to have their personal interests and aspirations equally respected by law and government. Its universalism lies in its claim that all men have the same right to pursue happiness in their own way, and think and say whatever they see fit, and no one, including those who convince others they are divinely chosen by their masters, rulers, or spiritual guides, is justified in denying or hindering others in the enjoyment of rights

that pertain to all men and women equally. (Israel, 2010,
pp vii–viii)

Israel (2010, pp 122–3) dismisses the Moderate Enlightenment as
irrelevant in terms of the changing tide of history, while blaming it
for triggering the Counter-Enlightenment:

> In short, Moderate Enlightenment was simply unable to do
> the job that major portions of society required it to do and
> hence it eventually lost the initiative. By the 1780's control
> of events had passed to the radical enlighteners and, equally
> evident, to the out-and-out opponents of all Enlightenment,
> the ideologues of the Counter-Enlightenment. It was thus
> the moderate mainstream's comprehensive failure, more than
> anything else, that triggered both the 'General Revolution'
> following the wake of the Radical Enlightenment's
> 'Revolution of the Mind' and the simultaneous upsurge
> throughout Europe of a powerful Counter-Enlightenment
> culture of faith, anti-intellectualism, and reactionary thought
> and politics based on unquestioning rejection of democracy,
> equality and personal liberty.

What Israel is arguing is that the 'Revolution of the Mind' created the
revolutionary reality of the 18th century in the American Revolution
(1776–83) 'the Dutch Revolution' (1780–87) and the French
Revolution (1789–99).

These three versions of the Enlightenment shaped the ideological
basis of civil society into radical, liberal and conservative perspectives
as we understand it today. The forces for radical change, liberal
modernisation and conservative reaction have continued to influence
debates about the nature and meaning of civil society. They are in
essence what civil society in all its complexity is about in the modern
world. Postmodernity has added a further layer of complexity to the
debate about the meaning of civil society.

Postmodernity: the end of the grand narrative

Postmodernity as an analytic construct has transformed the discourse
of social science from an analysis of social structures into a study of
social meanings and the way they are represented in cultures. 'Grand
narratives' of human progress, including humanism, Christianity and
Marxism, are rejected by postmodernists as foundationalist, essentialist

or totalising theory. Influenced by French structuralism, notably the ideas of Jacques Derrida (1930–2004), Michel Foucault (1924–84) and Jacques Lacan (1901–81), attention has focused on discourses or social constructs. In this reconstructed worldview Marxism and social democracy, according to the postmodernists, have become outmoded because of their perceived authoritarianism. The distinguished German sociologist, Ulrich Beck (1993, p 87), observes: 'we increasingly confront the phenomenon of capitalism without classes but with individualised social inequality and all the related social and political problems'. This analysis would appear to suggest the death of collectivism. 'All power to the workers' has been replaced by 'all power to the individual'. However, this may be an illusion. One of the basic problems with postmodern social theory is its 'deconstruction of the subject'. In the postmodernist intellectual project, individual agency is dissolved into social construction. Seligman (1992) suggests that with the decline in individual moral and social agency there is an accompanying decline in trust. Modern individualism dates from the Renaissance and is predicated upon moral self-knowledge. Seligman (1992) views waning trust as an episode in the career of the modern subject and concludes that in the postmodern social order personal and social responsibility have been delegitimised. If Seligman's analysis is correct, there is little room left for emancipatory action. Enlightenment humanism has lost its civilising influence and been replaced by a political void in which civil society has been rediscovered in the 'Big Society: Small State' narrative of postmodernity (see Chapter One).

As the old uncertainties propounded by modernism have disintegrated, new perspectives are emerging. Many of these new perspectives arise in the context of globalisation. But there is also a sense of timelessness in some of the debates about the common good that are rooted in antiquity. Concepts such as civic virtue, civil society and citizenship are all derived from classical civilisation. Yet, in postmodern civilisation classical values have re-emerged with a renewed sense of importance and vigour. This is partly due to the growing sense of fragmentation and social disintegration that the postmodern era has engendered. In this uncertain landscape civil society has experienced a renaissance. What is most striking about this renaissance in civil society has been the re-emergence of the Enlightenment categories of radical (new social movements, 'democratising democracy', human rights and people power), liberal (active citizenship, social capital, the voluntary and community sector and NGOs) and reactionary (faith-based charity, the Tea Party and, arguably, a full-blown conservative restoration). This is the context of the renaissance of civil society, which has rekindled the philosophical debates of the modern era, with their emphasis on the civilising process and human emancipation.

Philosophical debates: civil society in Europe and America

In the debate about civil society as noted above the key terms – civil/ civic, society, virtue, politics, community – all originate in the ancient world. For our purposes, however, the debate in the modern world is traceable to the Enlightenment. Key early influences were Thomas Hobbes (1588–1679), John Locke (1632–1704) and Benedict de Spinoza (1632–77). Hobbes and Locke constructed civil society 'as a contractually produced and politically guaranteed instrument of individuals who came together to attain some conscious purpose' (Ehrenberg, 1999, p 91). Spinoza rejects Hobbes' conservative contractarianism as too negative in terms of constraining human freedom, most prominently in the latter's book *Leviathan* (Hobbes, 1968)). He similarly rejects Locke's more liberal reformulation of Hobbes. Instead Spinoza presents liberty 'as a positive good or inalienable potential', in which political freedom can flourish and where reason and virtue are connected in a benevolent relationship between the citizen and the state (Israel, 2001, p 259). The logic of Spinoza's argument is fundamentally radical. Leo (2008, p 76) asserts: 'it is Spinoza and Spinozism which promotes the adoption of secular reason and government, universal toleration and shared equity among all men, personal liberty, freedom of expression and democratic republicanism'. Conservatives rejected 'Spinozist claims as anarchic and atheistic innovations that quickly breach the limit of what is necessary to maintain order and morality in a civil (and religious) society' (Leo, 2008, p 77). Despite censorship and police surveillance, 'by the mid-1670's Spinoza stood at the head of an underground radical philosophical movement rooted in the Netherlands but decidedly European in scope' (Israel, 2001, p 285).

After Spinoza's death in 1677 a 'forbidden movement' inspired by his ideas spread across Europe, despite the constraints of censorship, suppression and hostility (Israel, 2001, pp 295–7). Liberal thinkers of more moderate persuasion also began to explore the importance of civil society – notably in Scotland. The Scottish Enlightenment sought to resolve the relationship between faith and reason through Scottish Common Sense, which put it at odds with the Radical Enlightenment of Spinozism (Israel, 2010, pp 180–5). Adam Smith's (1723–90) *Theory of Moral Sentiments* (Smith, 1759) 'offered a powerful conjecture about the way in which some citizens acquire that sense of fitness and ethical beauty which makes it possible for them to aspire to a life of virtue' (Phillipson, 2010, p 157). Ehrenberg (1999, p 96) concludes: 'it was Adam Smith who first articulated a specifically bourgeois conception of civil society. His effort to integrate economic activity and market processes in a more general understanding of the anatomy of civilized life is a milestone in the development of modern thought.'The explicit use of the term is first evident in a treatise by the Scottish Enlightenment thinker, Adam Ferguson (1723–1816), who first published *An Essay on the History of Civil Society* in 1773 (Ferguson, 2001). In this work Ferguson explores the tensions and paradoxes inherent in the concept of civil society.

In France Voltaire (1694–1778), who was famed as a philosopher, playwright and poet, popularised Enlightenment thought but carefully avoided the atheism and egalitarianism of Spinoza.While criticising the intolerance of institutional Christianity, Voltaire 'remained as convinced as ever that the common people required a strong brake on their unruly passions and this could only come from traditional religion and especially the promises and threats of retribution of a God who rewards and punishes in the hereafter – hence his insistence that ordinary folk neither could nor should be enlightened' (Israel, 2010, pp 217–18). Voltaire was quintessentially the voice of the liberal Enlightenment. In his view authority in the symbolic form of God was necessary to keep the masses under control.

The debate about civil society in modern social and political thought started in the OldWorld, but quickly crossed the Atlantic to the New World of the American colonies. Essential to the widening of the debate was Thomas Paine, raconteur, polemicist and republican, who dominated progressive political thought in Britain, France, America and Ireland during the age of revolutionary struggle against absolutist tyranny in the last quarter of the eighteenth century. In his highly influential pamphlet, *Common Sense*, published in 1776 (Paine, 1969), Paine introduced the term 'civilised society' as a natural and potentially self-regulating form of association, counterposed to 'Government', which was in his view, at best, a necessary and artificial evil. However, Paine was vague about what precisely he meant by civil society. Paine's key impact was to popularise the idea of 'civil society versus the state' (Keane, 1995, p 117). In doing so, Paine radicalised civil society in the public imagination and turned it into a crusade against despotic governments (Powell, 2010c).

Paine's revolutionary agitation in America, France, Britain and Ireland drew a conservative response from Edmund Burke (1729–97). Born and educated in the radical ferment of the late eighteenth-century

Irish politics, Burke became the political voice of Britain's conservative Counter-Enlightenment. Burke's *Reflections on the French Revolution* (1790) derided (his one-time friend) Paine and publicly questioned the fundamental principles of the Enlightenment emancipatory project. Paine responded with the *Rights of Man* (1791–92) (Paine, 1969), in which he likened despotic government to a fungus growing out of a corrupt society: 'if we look back to the riots and tumults, which at various times happened in England, we shall find, that they did not proceed from want of government but that government was itself the generating cause; instead of consolidating society it divided it; it deprived it of its natural cohesion, and engineered discontents and disorders, which otherwise would not have existed' (Paine, 1969, pp 187–8). Paine's powerful revolutionary rhetoric challenged Burke's eloquent conservative prose. But conservatives were finding their voice in resisting the political power of Enlightenment rationalism. The German philosopher Johan Gottfried Herder (1744–1803) also proved highly influential in campaigning against natural rights, rationalism, the autonomy of the individual and the first beginnings of liberalism (Sternhell, 2010, p 79). In the argument between Paine and Burke we witness the two extremes of the debate about the political meaning of the Enlightenment.

The French aristocrat Alexis De Tocqueville, who visited the United States in the 1830s, was a great deal more cautious. Liberal by political persuasion, De Tocqueville is sometimes regarded as having de-politicised the term 'civil society', celebrating any form of associational activity for its own sake in his study *Democracy in America*, first published 1835. In fact, De Tocqueville laid considerable stress on participation in local democracy as the best method for ensuring that civic association reinforced and protected democratic politics against tyranny. However, the core of his conception of civil society devolved on the health of intermediate institutions, usually the family, the community and churches. As De Tocqueville put it:

> Amongst the laws which rule human societies, there is one which seems to be more precise and clear than all others. If men are to remain civilised, or to become so the art of associating together must grow and improve in the same ration in which equality of conditions is increased. (De Tocqueville, 1956, p 202)

De Tocqueville, according to his biographer Hugh Brogan (2006, p 348), was 'uncomfortable in the new era'. His prescription for civil society strikes a careful balance between 'the weaknesses and dangers of democracy, only to end with a splendid affirmation' (Brogan, 2006, p 349). Howard Zinn (1999, p 218) has cast doubt on the reliability of De Tocqueville's positive vision of American civil society, which he regarded as profoundly divided between rich and poor.

The German philosopher, Hegel, explored the concept of civil society in the definitive version of his monumental system of political and social philosophy, as it appeared in the 1821 edition of *Philosophy of Right*. For Hegel, civil society incorporates the spheres of economic relations and class formation as well as the judicial and administrative structure of the state. He does not include pre-state relations, such as the family and community, which essentially define the term 'civil society' in its most common usage today. Ayçoberry (1999) has demonstrated the fragility of family and community life in a totalitarian society, citing Nazi rule in Germany.

On the other hand, Karl Marx (1818–83), who along with a group of fellow German refugees in Paris during the 1830s and 1840s established the League of the Just (later the Communist League) as a bulwark against capitalism, is widely regarded as having rejected civil society. Marx regarded 'civil society as an illusion that needs to be unmasked' (cited in Hann and Dunn, 1996, p 4). Fraser and Wilde (2011, pp 44–5), in textual analysis of Marx's thinking on civil society, suggest a more complex evolution. Marx accepted in his *Critique of Hegel's Philosophy of Rights* (1843a) Hegel's characterisation of civil society (*bürgerliche Gesellschaft*) as bourgeoisie or market society. His negative view of civil society as egotistical and market driven is evident in his essays on *The Jewish Question* (1843b) and *The Economic and Philosophical Manuscripts* (1844). However, Fraser and Wilde (2011, p 45) detect a shift in Marx's thinking in relation to civil society in his reflections in the *Preface to a Contribution to the Critique of Political Economy* (1859), in which he recognises that understanding the anatomy of civil society is as important as mastering the nature of the state and the market, in terms of his emancipatory project. The essential weakness in this position is that Marx's vision of civil society belongs to the realms of a utopian future (Klein, 2010, p 431). Later Marxists, notably Antonio Gramsci, who struggled against Fascist tyranny in 20th-century Italy, reworked the Marxist position. In his *Prison Notebooks*, commenced in 1929 at the beginning of a 20-year prison sentence, Gramsci wrote:

> What we can do, for the moment, is to fix two major superstructural 'levels': that one can be called 'civil society', and that of 'political society' or the 'State'. There two levels

correspond on the one hand to the function of 'hegemony' which the dominant group exercises throughout society, and on the other hand to that of 'direct domination' or rule exercised through the State and the judicial Government. (Gramsci, 1971, p 12)

For Gramsci, social inequality and class domination were exercised by a variety of cultural institutions that enabled the dominant group to impose its sense of reality on the rest of society. It was only through addressing the labyrinthine cultural complexity that 'the oppressed' could liberate themselves and wrest control of civil society from the bourgeoisie, which had traditionally opposed popular participation. In Gramscian terms civil society was conceived as the site of alternative hegemonies. The 'organic intellectual' had the capacity to reimagine the world and change it (Gramsci, 1973). For Gramsci, the revolutionary task was not about Jacobin–Leninist seizure of power, with its inevitable violence and totalitarian outcome. It was more about a struggle to liberate human consciousness than about hegemonic domination. There is a direct link between Spinoza and Gramsci in their emphasis on a 'revolution of the mind' as a prelude to human freedom. Both sought to address existing hegemonies of power by changing human subjectivity. We will return to a more detailed discussion of Gramsci's ideas in Chapter Four.

Ironically, it was the failure of Marxism as an ethical system of governance that led to the renaissance of civil society in recent times, reflecting postmodern realities. The fall of communism in Eastern Europe cast doubt on the capacity of totalitarian states to coexist with civil society because of their lack of civility and insistence on the totalisation of power in the state. Ernest Gellner (1925–95), in his classic book, *Conditions of Liberty*, published in 1994, sought to explain the collapse of socialism. He concluded that civil society was possible only in a pluralistic society in which the free market was encouraged. Clearly, participants in the Occupy movement would not share his faith in the free market as a guarantor of democracy.

Other scholars have taken a different view. John Keane, who is director of the recently founded Sydney Democracy Initiative, in a series of important books has linked civil society to its classical roots in antiquity. His seminal book *The Life and Death of Democracy* (Keane, 2009) explores the spread of democracy across the world, its disputed meaning and the threats it faces. Keane (2009, p 709) sagely advises: 'people need to become democracies within themselves'. His work and substantial contribution to the civil society debate has been to articulate the seminal link between civil society and democracy at a point in history when both are imperilled by an increasing lack of civility in the public sphere and collapse of the republican values (liberty, equality, solidarity) that defined the birth of modern democracy.

Civil society at 'the end of history'

Postmodern society is defined by risk, polarisation, global markets, chronic change and fragmentation. As Stokes and Knight have observed, 'today we seem to be plunging into a chaotic, privatised future, recapturing medieval extremes of wealth and squalor' (*Independent*, 15 January 1997). Postmodernity is characterised by extremes of wealth and poverty. It is presented as the present in a dialectical relationship with the modernist past. For Marxism, the collective struggle to wrestle freedom from necessity was the purpose of history (Anderson, 1998, p 53). That form of subjectivity, according to the postmodernists, is dead. It died in 1989, after 200 years of an active revolutionary life. Its obituaries cast the modernist, whether artists such as Picasso or Braque, writers like Joyce and Kafka or political revolutionaries such as Robespierre, Marx and Lenin, as part of a world constituted by entirely different subjectivities – unstable, violent and profoundly self-deluded. The death of modernity was peaceful. Postmodern society has democratically consigned it to the abyss. Or so the narrative of postmodernity tells us. Its critics point to its 'death of the subject' as a moral and political actor as a profoundly conservative conclusion that barely conceals a form of intellectual nihilism at the core of the postmodern analysis of our world. The American writer Cornel West, in his challenging book *Democracy Matters* (2004, p 26), cogently makes the point that 'what is most terrifying – including the perennial threat of cowardly terrorists – is the insidious growth of *deadening nihilisms* across political lives'. Perry Anderson (1998, p 56) shares this pessimism:

> Among the traits of the new subjectivity, in fact, was the loss of any active sense of history, either as hope or memory. The changed sense of the past – as either ague-bed of repressive traditions, or reservoir of thwarted dreams; and heightened expectancy of the future – as potential cataclysm or transfiguration – which had characterised modernism, was gone. At best fading back into a perpetual present, retro-styles and images proliferated as surrogates of the temporal.

The alleged nihilism that underpins postmodernity leads its critics to view it as a 'new medievalism' or 'savage capitalism'. They may be greatly mistaken. It is far more likely that postmodernity, as its supporters claim, is evidence of the historical dynamism of capitalism, which, contrary to Marx's prediction, continues to renew itself. American liberals, most notably Thomas Friedman in *The World is Flat* (2005), link a globalised present grounded in neoliberalism to a flattened global market, including developing nations, in a new capitalist narrative of globalisation. Friedman's bold metaphor is for a resurgent neoliberal subjectivity confident that socialism is an illusion that can be consigned to the dustbin of history. Such may be the stuff of postmodern myths (Dean, 2009). Yet such views cannot be dismissed as simple-minded 'hyper-modernism' or futurism. Postmodernism represents a triumphant neoliberalism that has popularised itself in Western culture. Neoliberals have not hesitated to take ownership of the concept of civil society and bend it to their political will in the form of communitarianism, trust, social capital and the revitalisation of charity in the concept of 'Big Society'. However, following the 2008 financial crash questions are being asked about neoliberalism and its relationship to the common good. How can the privatisation of banking profits and the socialisation of losses be justified in terms of the public interest? Is the resulting level of inequality compatible with democracy?

Communitarians who have sought to examine the nature and quality of trust and its connection with cooperation and prosperity argue they have discovered a positive correlation between development and civil society (Putnam, 1993; Fukuyama, 1995). Fukuyama (1995) found that developed societies such as the US, Germany and Japan were high-trust societies, as compared with less developed societies such as Latin American Catholic countries and (incorrectly) China, which he concluded were low-trust societies. Similarly, in Italy, Putnam found higher levels of civic trust in the more developed northern region, 'Padania', than in the less developed south. Communitarians conclude that, despite its tendencies towards fragmentation and polarisation, postmodernity can engender social participation and more sophisticated forms of communication between people that promote empathy and trust. This is either the paradox of contemporary civilisation or a Panglossian reading of social reality.

On the face of it, it is a two-world theory of an economic world defined by the utilitarian values and a social world defined by communitarian values. However, Fukuyama (1995) and Putnam (1993, 2000) contend in their theses on trust and communitarian values in the public sphere that these are positively correlated with the creation of prosperity in the economic sphere. In reality, they claim to have discovered a civilizational configuration between altruism and self-interest that they call 'social capital'. It is not simply the product of individual altruistic effort, but is expressed through the networks that human cooperation creates. Interconnectedness is the hallmark of social capital. Capitalism and society are, it is argued, compatible, both are mutually supportive in a symbolic relationship that drives development and yields prosperity. The importance of the concept of social capital in reshaping our understanding of postmodern civil society cannot be overstated. The welfare state emerged through a fusion of the nation-state and civil society that defined the modernist age. Social capital seeks to create a new fusion between civil society and the market that is the defining feature of postmodern welfare. In order to achieve this fundamental transition postmodernists have claimed that modernity is dead. They have also proclaimed the need to reshape the world through a new metanarrative of development driven by free market capitalism in the form of the 'Big Society, Small Government' debate.

It is an end of civilisation thesis that has been around for half a century. It was originally propounded by Harvard professor Daniel Bell (1962) in his famous book *The End of Ideology*, which claimed that the modernist project was exhausted and the acceptance of 'managed capitalism' was the only available political choice. The 'grand narratives' or 'big ideas' of the modern age were bankrupt. History was, after all, unchangeable. The future would be conservative. We have reached ideological terminus of historical development, according to Bell. Similarly, Francis Fukuyama's book *The End of History* (Fukuyama, 1992) claimed just that – the great ideological debates of the previous two centuries were over and liberal democracy in the form of market capitalism was triumphant. Socialism and transformative views of history were dead. Both Bell and Fukuyama and their many imitators in the millenarian preoccupation with 'endisms' were somewhat premature in their pronouncements. It is certainly true that the Western tradition of Enlightenment rationalism and belief in progress are in crisis. Whether this proves to be a terminal crisis remains to be seen. Both Bell and Fukuyama may be wrong in assuming that the future will be liberal and Western in the shape of American values. The Japanese philosopher Takeshi Umehara has observed that 'the total failure of Marxism ... and the dramatic break-up of the Soviet Union are only the precursors of the collapse of Western liberalism, the main current of modernity. Far from being the alternative to Marxism and the reigning ideology at the end of history, liberalism will be the next domino to fall' (cited in Huntington, 2002, p 306). Slavoj Žižek, in his book *Living in the End Times* (Žižek, 2011), shares their apocalyptic vision, arguing that the Four Horsemen of the Apocalypse have arrived in the form of: worldwide ecological crisis;

imbalances within the economic system; the biogenetic revolution; and exploding social divisions and ruptures. There is a fundamental divergence between Fukuyama's hubristic belief in the victory of capitalism and liberal democracy over socialism and Žižek's theory of a terminal global crisis. Ferenc Miszlivetz (2012) comments that the hubris of the 1990s has given way to the nemesis of the post-2008 crisis, as a journey from *annus mirabilis* to *annus horribilis*. The post-1989 years represented a 'third wave' of democratisation, which has tended to be equated with westernisation, explaining the triumphalism of Fukuyama's position. However, Miszlivetz (2012, p 55) suggests that the reality is a great deal more complex, arguing that since the collapse of the bipolar conflict between Soviet communism and the 'free Western world' the focus has shifted to the quality of the democratic experience driven by two key forces:

* the increase of freedom and choice aspirations
* the aspirations for the improvement of life chances or simply for the good life.

The consumerist aspirations have kept alive the bipolarity between socialist frugality versus capitalist abundance, fuelling unrealistic development expectations. The result has been a global crisis evidenced by 'irreversible imbalance, chaos, uncertainty and unpredictability in market capitalism that may be permanent, leading towards a transformation into the unknown' (Miszlivetz, 2012, pp 55–6).

Postmodernity, consciousness and democracy: in search of a new political imaginary

The financial crash of 2008 underlines the fragility of the capitalist system in its current neoliberal form and the need for a new, more socially cohesive model of development. Keane (2009, p xvii) argues the case for 'monitory democracy', based upon the novel idea of citizens keeping their politicians under surveillance through the agency of civil society. The advent of citizen journalism has helped to democratise the media, assisted by new technologies such as Twitter, Facebook and so on (Blaagaard, 2012). In this bottom-up reconceptualisation of the political role of civil society in democracy, Keane raises important questions about human consciousness and agency. Has neoliberalism undermined civil society? If it has, do we live in a post-democratic era? These questions have been taken up by Jodi Dean in her book *Democracy and other Neoliberal Fantasies* (2009). She suggests that the political pessimism of many on the political Left is unwarranted. Dean argues that a conservative restoration is in reality a 'neoliberal fantasy', created by what she calls 'communicative capitalism' – a constellation of consumerism, the privileging of the self over group interests and the embrace of the language of victimisation. She concludes that a 'psychotic politics' has been enabled by the web and other networked communication media, pacifying political energies that have been reduced to the registration of preferences in opinion polls and the transmission of feelings in a virtual reality. This, she contends, has marginalised reasoned argument and real political debate. She argues the case for citizens retrieving democracy and political sovereignty. Civil society clearly provides the context and means of redressing this democratic crisis.

Dean (2009) invites us to rethink the nature of democracy as an imaginary act. Castoriadis, in his book *The Imaginary Institution of Society* (1987), has argued that radical politics needs to move beyond the socialist (Marxist) exclusive preoccupation with capital. He redefines modernity as a struggle between the radical democratic project of autonomy (that is, personal freedom to determine one's own future without structural manipulation) and the institutional project of mastery by a disciplinarian state. In an assessment of the import of Castoriadis' contribution to re-theorising modernity, Gerald Delanty (2005, p 276) concludes that 'the focus on creativity offers an alternative theorisation of modernity echoing the idea of *homo faber* (man the maker) in Aristotle and Marx: the idea of society as an artefact created by human beings'. New social movements within a reinvigorated civil society are playing a central role of reimagining political grammar in terms of active citizens in a struggle for autonomy. Arguably, this is the task of late modernity. As suggested by Dean, this is a citizen-led model of development, based in civil society and inspired by the civic republican tradition of democracy.

A new political imaginary requires a new grammar of democracy that is both emancipatory and sustainable. The challenge for civil society is to forge a new social and cultural grammar that can deepen democracy. That involves confronting global hegemonic forces 'by the initiatives of grassroots organisations, of local and popular movements that endeavour to counteract extreme forms of social exclusion and open up new spaces for democratic participation' (Ramírez, 2007, p 238). It also involves addressing Weber's 'iron cage of bureaucracy', which undermines democratic practice by subordinating the citizen to the bureaucratic state apparatus (Weber, 1919). In turn, that involves challenging the hegemonic conception of representative democracy (thin) by participatory democracy (thick) in a new synthesis that realigns politics to civil society in a project of demo-diversity (Barber, 1984). To put it concisely, the ideal of sustainable and emancipatory democracy is the late modern *agora*, where the citizen can democratically challenge oligarchies of wealth (capitalism) and power (bureaucratic state) (Geoghegan and Powell, 2009). De Sousa Santos (2007, p xli–xliii) concludes: 'thus, the knowledge held by social actors becomes a central element not appropriable by bureaucracies for the solution of management problems ... Democracy is the new historic grammar.' That, as Castoriadis argues, involves a fundamental shift in the political imaginary towards higher levels of creativity in our democratic discourse.

At the core of this analysis is the contention that civil society is this embodiment of 'strong' (participatory) democracy in contrast to the 'thin' (representative) democracy that characterises the age we live in. This makes civil society a highly political activity. The American social scientist Benjamin Barber (1984, p 117) has consummately encapsulated our democratic choices, advocating what he calls 'strong democracy', based on the civic republican tradition:

> Strong democracy is a distinctively modern form of participatory democracy. It rests on the idea of a self-governing community of citizens who are united less by homogeneous interests than by civic education and who are made capable of common purpose and mutual action by virtue of their civic attitudes and participatory institutions rather than the altruism of their good nature. Strong democracy is consonant with – indeed it depends upon – the politics of conflict, the sociology of pluralism, and the separation of private and public realms of action. It is not intrinsically inimical to either the size or the technology of modern society and is therefore wedded neither to antiquarian republicanism nor to face-to-face parochialism. Yet it challenges the politics of elites and masses that masquerades as democracy in the West and in doing so offers a relevant alternative to what we have called thin democracy – that is, to instrumental, representative, liberal democracy in its three dispositions.

Barber's advocacy of 'strong democracy' evokes the spirit of the father of democracy, Pericles, who admonished the Athenian citizenry 'we do not say that a man who takes no interest in politics is a man who minds his own business; we say that he has no business here at all' (cited in Held, 1996, p 17). Cohen and Arato (1994, p 17) assert that 'the idea of the democratization of civil society, unlike that of its mere revival, is extremely pertinent to existing Western societies'. They view civil society as a democratic process that is simultaneously expanding and protecting spaces for liberty and equality. This is its democratic mission.

Benjamin Barber laments the erosion of democracy from within, through the triumph of thin (representative) democracy – which in his view marginalises citizens from the decision-making process. He likens this process to 'politics as zookeeping', in which 'democracy is undone by a hundred kinds of activity more profitable than citizenship; by a thousand seductive acquisitions cheaper than liberty' (Barber, 1984, p xvii). Thin democracy shifts power to distant representative institutions, far from communities where citizens live. Instead of participating in decision making, citizens are reduced to a passive state, like animals in a zoo waiting for their keepers to decide their lives for them. Strong democracy envisages the participation of all the citizenry in at least some aspects of governance at least some of the time. Civil society opens up the public realm to the possibility of participative democracy.

Active citizenship, civil society and development

The renaissance of civil society is associated with the demands for greater participation in the welfare state through the involvement of the burgeoning third sector as a partner. In this reality, the third sector is perceived as an alternative to state bureaucracy and professional elitism and as a public space between government and market, where the spirit of altruism can flourish. Civil society in its reinvigorated form is presented as a democratic community-based alternative to the dependent status imposed by the social citizenship of the welfare state. In postmodern conditions, active citizenship is promoted as a more humane alternative to the Fordist 'one size fits all' philosophy of the welfare state. It is part of a wider critique of the modernist conception of citizenship that has in part been induced by the consumerist philosophy of neoliberalism but is also the product of a deeper social fragmentation connected to the rise of identity politics. Social politics, embodied in the institution of the welfare state, has consequently suffered in terms of public esteem. The growing disenchantment with this form of democracy and demands for greater public participation refocus attention away from the social to the active citizen. The core emphasis is on participation in the decision-making and service-delivery processes of the state, leading to the empowerment of the citizen.

Citizenship can be defined in T.H. Marshall's classic formulation as consisting of 'a three-legged stool'. First, there are fundamental civil rights, such as freedom of speech, thought and religion; equality before the law; the due process of the justice system; and the right to conclude contracts as equals – liberty in its broadest sense. Second, there are basic rights, including the right to vote, form political parties and contest elections – democratic pluralism in essence. Third, there are basic social rights: 'the whole range from the right to a modicum of economic welfare and security to the right to share to the full social heritage and to live the life of a civilised being according to the standards of the prevailing society' (Marshall, 1973, p 72). Social rights define the welfare state, according to the Marshallian thesis.

The development of social citizenship rights, according to the Marshallian thesis, is the product of class struggle incrementally promoting the decommodification of labour and an increasingly egalitarian society for the majority. The erosion of traditional social inequalities served to compress income differentials for the working population at both ends of the spectrum to create an increasingly popular and universalistic culture and to establish firm links between education and occupation, based on the meritocratic ideal. A universal status of social citizenship emerged in democratic pluralist societies encompassing the majority working population between the late 1940s and 1970s. It was known as 'the welfare state'. From the late 1970s the welfare state came under attack from a powerful conservative resurgence called 'neoliberalism'.

Active citizenship has emerged in this transformed social landscape. It was initially promoted by neoliberals 'as an exhortation to discharge the responsibilities of neighbourliness, voluntary action and charity' in the context of 'the rundown public sector services, benefit cutbacks and privatised programme in which it was advanced' (Lister, 1997, p 22). However, soon more radical democratic variants of active citizenship emerged in the form of community and service-user groups challenging paternalistic top-down relationships that disempower. These more democratic forms of active citizenship arguably indicate the emergence of new social movements among marginalised groups (a social Left?). In this transformed context, community is being reconfigured from its predominantly spatial orientation into communities of interest or alternative communities (what Hardt and Negri, 2004 call 'the multitude') with common social and cultural rights agendas that act as counter-publics. Simultaneously, the ecological citizen has emerged

Table 2.2: Models of development

Model	Ideology	Strategy	Goal	Location
Market led	Capitalism/ neoliberalism	Modernisation	Globalisation	Economy
State led	Social democracy/ Marxism	State planning	Social equality	Politics/ government
Community led	Democracy/civic republicanism	Citizen participation	Sustainable development	Civil society

Source: Powell and Geoghegan (2004, p 17)

as the fourth leg in Marshall's concept of citizenship, emphasising sustainable development. Three models of development exist in postmodernity and are set out in Table 2.2.

The market-led model has been the dominant discourse in the age of globalisation, shaped by neoliberal ideology. But its hegemony has been challenged by the financial crash in 2008 and the requirement that the state save the market from total failure. The state-led model largely disappeared in Europe with the waning of socialism after 1989. The community-led model currently offers the only politically acceptable alternative to the market-led model in the contemporary world. This does not mean that the state-led model of development won't work. Up to the 1960s there was a concern in the West that the planned economy was more effective than the market-led model. Social democracy was the dominant model of governance in post-war Europe. Furthermore, the Chinese party-state, based on state direction/ management combined with a market economy, indicates that the state planning model still exists in the form of 'socialism with Chinese characteristics'. However, as we observe in Chapter One, there are major strategic developments in China that are seeking to shrink the state. Arguably, there is a convergence taking place between economic neo-institutionalist models in both China and the West. In that sense the socialist model of development has reached its historic terminus. The community-led model emerges in post-socialist society as the alternative to the market-led model in an unequal struggle between democracy and capitalism. It seeks to protect 'the commons' (that is, a right to common use and ownership of public resources) against the encroachment of market forces – citizen power versus economic power.

Civil society, democracy and the 'third sector'

Civil society provides a space between the state and the market. It is an independent sphere where associational activity flourishes. Iris Marion Young (2000, p 158) has described this space as 'a third sector':

> Civil society refers to a third sector of private associations that are relatively autonomous from both the state and economy. They are voluntary, in the sense that they are neither mandated nor run by state institutions, but spring from the everyday lives and activities of communities of interest. The associations of this third sector, moreover, operate not for profit. Most participate in economic activity only as consumers, fund-raisers and sometimes employers. Even those activities of the third sector that involve providing goods and services for fees, however are not organised towards the objectives of making profit and enlarging market shares.

This is a helpful description, but there is a need to focus more clearly on what is meant by key terms, notably 'civil society' and its synonym, the 'third sector'. Clarity is important in understanding democratic inclusion. In this author's view, there should be a pivotal distinction between private and public spheres in understanding civil society. Families, social clubs, private functions and religious denominations are all located within the realm of civil society, but are circumscribed by their exclusivity and clearly belong to the private sphere. Some theorists of civil society, notably Robert Putnam in his influential book *Bowling alone* (2000), do not distinguish between the private and public spheres. Putnam (2000, p 27) includes in his definition of civil society clubs and community associations, religious bodies, unions, professional associations, card parties, bowling leagues, bar cliques, ball games, picnics and parties, as well as voluntary organisations, social movements and the internet. However, others differentiate between the public and private spheres and link civil society to the practice of participatory democracy in the public sphere (Cohen and Arato, 1994; Young, 2000).

What is at issue here is the question of whether civil society equals the sum of the whole of associational activity in society, outside the state and market, or whether it can be subdivided into private and public spheres. Private association (as noted above) is characterised by exclusivity. Civic association, on the other hand, takes place in the public sphere and is broadly inclusive, albeit that inclusion may be circumscribed by space (for example, residence in a local neighbourhood) or identity (gender, race and so on). However, it is defined by its orientation towards democratic participation. Private association comfortably coexists with thin conceptions of democracy based on the election of power elites and the rule of law. Civic association envisages a deepening of democracy through the creation of counter-publics – 'oppositional' organisations or discursive spaces beyond the control of the dominant political actors in the public sphere. These counter-publics create an interaction between civic association and political association that promotes democratic dialogue, but also conflict between representative and participative democratic forms.

Democratic inclusion finds a voice through civil society. However, there are real constraints. People living in poverty are often too preoccupied with survival to find the time to participate in their communities. There is no provision within our social and political order for the promotion of participation. Oscar Wilde's reported observation that 'the trouble with socialism is that it would take up too many evenings' goes to the heart of democratic participation and its limits. Putnam (2000) has characterised this phenomenon as a problem of 'civic engagement'. He attributes civil disengagement essentially to the impact of the postmodern lifestyle. This is a somewhat ahistorical view, since these debates date from antiquity. The civic republican tradition that originates in classical civilisation is based on an inclusive concept of democratic participation. This tradition connects the idea of civil society to the pursuit of civic virtue. There are also other views of civil society located in post-Enlightenment modernity: a conservative view, liberal view and radical democratic view. But the roots of civil society are in classical humanism and democratic participation.

Conclusion

The renaissance of civil society has occurred in a world where politics is experiencing a crisis. Civil society coexists in a triangular relationship with the state and the market. It is an uneasy relationship. Modernism resulted in a fusion between the state and civil society (as we shall see in Chapter Four). Postmodernism has refocused that relationship into a potential fusion with the market. Civil society struggles to maintain its autonomy as a public sphere where democratic association can flourish. It is a contested role in terms both of the internal ethical goals of civil society to promote virtue and of the external agendas of the state and the market to dominate society. Contestation defines civil society's role in the political order. Civic virtue rests on the idea of a virtuous state (for example, the welfare state) that, ideally, places equal value on the welfare of each of its citizens. This is the ideal. The reality invariably falls short of that ideal. Interests compete for the attention of the state, creating oligarchies of power and wealth. The more powerful the oligarchical interest, the more likely it is to succeed in its goal of influencing the direction of public policy. We have noted from the origins of governance in ancient Greece that policy has represented a deeper and more complex strand of governance than the art of politics, with all its venal associations. Civil society provides an ethical framework for good governance because it represents the active voice of citizens. Policy is deeply rooted in that ethical framework of society as the expression of the need for civic virtue in governance. Here we see the varying dimensions in citizenship interacting in the process of democratic governance. It is the legacy of humanism that is traceable back to ancient Greece. The distinction between 'welfare' and 'unwelfare' states, as raised by Veit-Wilson (2000, 2002), has seminal meaning if connected to this philosophical value base. Policy is the product of secularism, civic republicanism and socialism. While it has been shaped by modernity, its legacy is in humanism, giving democracy its distinctly Western character. In this fluid policy context a major debate has arisen about public policy and governance in which civil society has emerged as a key actor.

THREE

Modernity, civil society and civic virtue

The idea of 'making poverty history' did not begin with Bob Geldof, Bono or the commitment of rich countries to disburse 0.7% of national income in development aid. It goes back to the time of the French and American revolutions towards the end of the 18th century and to a transformation in outlook as momentous as that produced by the revolutions themselves. A small group of visionaries, the followers of Tom Paine in England and Antoine-Nicolas de Condorcet in France, ceased to regard poverty as a divine imposition on sinful humanity. It was seen as remediable in principle, since it was man-made in practice.

What this political pamphleteer and aristocratic administrator depicted for the first time was a planned world in which the predictable misfortunes of life no longer plunged people into chronic poverty. This plan was not a utopia. It was a template for a future reality; in the 20th century it came to be known as the welfare state.

Gareth Steadman Jones, in the *Guardian* (2 July 2005)

While the origins of civil society are in antiquity, civil society emerged in its modern form during the 18th century as a highly contested right to associate as free men and women. The connection with the realisation of citizenship as a basic political right, through the French and American revolutions at the end of the 18th century, is a close one. Civil society is by definition political. It is about men and women's struggles to become free and liberate themselves from oppression. Nowadays we talk about the role of civil society as a force against oppression in relation to the liberation of the former communist bloc from Stalinist tyranny in the political earthquake that convulsed Europe in 1989. The association with democracy is direct. But we often forget that democracy in the scale of human history has had a short life. It has flourished in Europe (not without interruption) since 1789 and in the United States since 1776. It had previously enjoyed a brief life in ancient Athens, only to be extinguished for two and a half thousand years. We are reminded that there are three possible forms of government: monarchy, oligarchy and democracy. In the United Kingdom, a democracy has been slowly established since 1832, but in the context of a constitutional monarchy. The United States is both a democracy and a republic, but with its wealth highly concentrated within a powerful plutocracy. Advocates of civil society have historically sought to promote the right to associate in the teeth of privileged opposition. Its first signs of life are detectable in Renaissance Italy, which became the cradle of modern humanism, subsequently evolving into the Reformation, the Scientific Revolution, the Enlightenment and, ultimately, the Age of Revolution, when democracy was reborn. This chapter charts the birth of civil society and its relationship to civic virtue. The argument will be that civil society is rooted in civic republicanism, secularism and socialism. But its origins are intimately connected to a much older tradition of charity that defined civic virtue, but not always in humanistic ways.

Power, virtue and humanism

Niccolò Machiavelli is widely regarded as the first genuinely modern thinker because of his denial of Divine Law. The custodian of Divine Law is the Catholic Church. Born in Florence in 1469, Machiavelli proved himself to be a consummate statesman, diplomat and writer. In the Age of Discovery he travelled widely, observing contemporary civilisation with a keen humanist eye. Yet, he learned to bend to the will of his political masters, surviving torture to end his life as a man of letters. His death in 1527 left a unique legacy. He is best remembered for *The Prince* (1961), based on the life of Cesare Borgia, Duke of Valentino and illegitimate son of the corrupt Pope Alexander VI. Originally published in 1532, *The Prince* has been condemned over the centuries as a diabolical work bordering on the sacrilegious. Pope Clement VIII was the first to condemn this study of the nature of elite politics as the naked pursuit of power. Since then, Machiavellianism has become a byword for the corrupt use of power. White (2004, p 79) describes Cesare Borgia as 'a master manipulator and strategist' who at the height of his powers 'took great pleasure in intimidation and political game playing'. His capacity for cruelty and deceit became legendary. The conventional interpretation of *The Prince* is evidenced in chapter XVII, titled 'Cruelty and Compassion and Whether it is Better to be Loved than Feared, or the Reverse'. Machiavelli declares with surrealistic irony:

Cesare Borgia was accounted cruel; nevertheless, this cruelty of his reformed the Romagna, brought it unity, and restored order and obedience. On reflection, it will be seen that there was more compassion in Cesare than in the Florentine people, who, to escape being called cruel, allowed Pistoia to be devastated. So a prince should not worry if he incurs reproach for his cruelty so long as he keeps his subjects united and loyal. By making an example or two he will prove more compassionate than those who, being too compassionate, allow disorders which lead to murder and rapine. These nearly always harm the whole community, whereas executions ordered by a prince only affect individuals. (Machiavelli, 1961, p 95)

In *The Prince*, 'virtue' is equated with the capacity of a person to achieve success and fortune as an individual, whether by justice or deceit and cruelty. Borgia learnt to his cost that fortune could be fickle and cruel ('the wheel of fortune'). *The Prince* is essentially a monarchical statement of power. Machiavelli regarded monarchy as an inferior form of government, only necessary when the people lacked the virtue to form a republic. In *The Discourses* (1518), Machiavelli sets out the requirements for good governance, the need for strong military defence and the role of religion as subordinate to the state:

But as regards prudence and stability, I say that the people are more prudent and stable, and have better judgement than a prince; and that it is not without good reason that it is said 'the voice of the people is the voice of God'; for we see popular opinion prognosticate events in such a wonderful manner that it would almost seem as if the people had some occult virtue, which enables them to foresee good and evil. (Machiavelli, 1970, p 255)

Machiavelli likens virtue in the body politic to a healthy lifestyle in the individual. These qualities of vigour and sacrifice equate with a virtuous political life that makes people free. It is this willingness to subordinate private egotistical advantage to the public good that defines the virtuous society.

The idea that power is divinely ordained is, therefore, rejected by Machiavelli. He reconfigures the exercise of power in purely secular terms, a view that enraged the pope but was the mark of his humanism and our intellectual liberation from the cosmic hegemony of Christian theology. In the Renaissance thought of Machiavelli is born the idea of human beings becoming moral actors in their own personal and political struggle to transcend fate as given – the external Christian view that 'God is in his heaven and all is well with the world'. Here the germ of the idea of civic virtue in modern life was born. Hope displaced fate. Virtue became a human quality and stratagem. As art freed itself from the celebration of the divinity of God to focus on the beauty of humanity, so human beings began to think differently about their world and how they could change it for the better. Gone was the illusion that power is divine.

Pocock (1975), in his monumental study *The Machiavellian Moment*, sought to examine the consequences of Machiavelli's politics for modern historical and social consciousness. Machiavelli's humanism affected our cosmological understanding, notably the comprehension of time. Christians denied cosmic recurrence – 'the wicked dance in circles' – as contrary to the doctrines of creationism and redemption (Pocock, 1975, pp 6–7). In the Christian mind, the world had a divinely ordained beginning and end. As Pocock (1975, p 7) puts it, in the Christian view 'movement in fallen man, if effected by his own depraved will and intelligence, was movement away from God and toward further damnation, away from meaning and toward deepening meaninglessness'. The connection with Dante's *Inferno* (Dante, c.1309–1320) is inescapable.

Machiavelli is first and last a secular thinker. Pocock (1975) celebrates his revival of the ideal of the classical republic as Machiavelli's 'moment' in history. He charts the expansion of Florentine political thought beyond the Alps to shape republican thought in Puritan England and across the Atlantic Ocean to the New World of the American colonies. He concludes that the American Revolution was the last great act of the civic humanism of the Renaissance. For Pocock, the seeds of the clash of ideas between the civic, Christian and commercial values of the 18th century that shaped the modern world were all present in Machiavelli's Florentine Republic, which he so valiantly sought to defend as its political servant and to critique as a humanist scholar.

What emerges from Machiavelli's humanism is the concept of *virtue*, which came to mean 'first, the power by which an individual or group acted effectively in a civic context; next the essential property which made the personality or element what it was; third, the moral goodness which made a man, in city or cosmos, what he ought to be' (Pocock, 1975, p 37). Virtue was linked to action in the humanist mind. The *vita activa* (active life) replaced the Christian concept of virtue located in the *vita contemplativa* (contemplative life). The belief in the *vivere civile* – the ideal of active citizenship – became the cornerstone of civic republicanism. Activism through association with others and participation in a common community of values were essential elements in the humanist worldview. Pocock (1975, p 68) concludes:

> Since this activity was concerned with the universal good, it was itself a good of a higher order than the particular goods which the citizen as a social animal might enjoy, and in enjoying his own citizenship – his contribution to the good of others, his relationship with others engaged in so contributing – he enjoyed a universal good and became a being in relation with the universal. Citizenship was a universal activity, the polis [Republic] a universal community.

Machiavelli, despite his poor press, had restored politics to earth by exposing its earthly qualities and the human capacity to alter our political and moral universe. He had also fundamentally questioned the moral basis of Christianity as a social philosophy. Charity symbolised the Christian capacity to engage in the pursuit of virtue, however paternalistic the form and egoistic the end. It is the original inspiration of social policy and reminds us of its basis in moral and social theory. We cannot unlock its meaning without understanding its history, which is ultimately about the welfare of our civilisation.

The theology of charity

Charity defines the care of the poor as a Christian duty. In its idealised form, charity is presented as an individualistic and altruistic act, as a private affair between two parties, the benefactor and the beneficiary. In Christian cosmology, redemption was possible through charity, however venal the life. Ontologically, charity balanced the venal and acquisitive in a moral and social compact with God. Justice was divinely ordained.

Modernity changed everything. Commentators detected a decline in charitable activity throughout Europe that has been associated not only with the Reformation but also with the rise of capitalism. It has been argued that the combined influence of these two forces undermined medieval ethics, 'wealth lost its mark of sinfulness, and the idea of voluntary generosity towards the poor as absolution for the sin involved in wealth became meaningless' (Rusche and Kirchheimer, 1939, p 36). Charity, apart from evangelical activities, ceased to be associated with institutional religion in the early modern world. Davies (1997, p 779) observes:

> This medieval system began to fracture in the Reformation period, particularly in the Protestant countries. The dissolution of the English monasteries (1540) had social consequences with which the hard-pressed Elizabethan Poor Laws could not cope. Modern Europe was obliged to seek new solutions. As the population grew, charitable institutions became much larger and more specialized. Purpose-built veterans homes, mental asylums, houses of correction, prisons, medical 'infirmaries', workhouses, labour colonies, and charity schools were multiplying fast in the eighteenth and nineteenth centuries. Liberal and humanitarian movements pressed for the abolition of slavery, torture, and of degrading conditions. The burden of funding and administration passed from the Church to parish and city councils, to private benevolent societies, and eventually to the state.

Charity in the modern era, in sharp contrast to the Middle Ages, when it had a genuine religious currency, represents a collective response to the existence of poverty in the wider social interest. Since the 17th century, secular values have informed charity discourse. De Swann (1988, p 23) has observed in this regard that:

> Charity was a form of altruistic behaviour par excellence: the sacrificing of money or goods for the sake of others; moreover, it was a form of action that profited not only the receivers, but also the collectivity of possessors as a whole. While this beneficence may therefore be conceived of as a bilateral relation between the giver and receiver, it must also be understood in the context of collective action on the part of the providers, for the sake of collective interests, such as defence against threats and the maintenance of labour.

This process of secularisation involved the delimitation of appropriate causes for charitable support, which reflected the main areas of social concern at the time, though the justificatory rhetoric of religious discourse was often retained. In the early 19th century, the poor depended to a large degree on the charity of the rich for their survival. Equally, the rich depended on the docility of the poor for theirs.

Paradoxically, as De Swann (1988, p 14) has observed, 'a moral order that encompasses the poor, whom it must persuade of the rightness of property, in justifying their exclusion also establishes their claim to part of the surplus'. The institution of charity in early 19th-century society existed in this moral paradox and was justified by contemporaries by reference to theodicy, a word coined by the German philosopher Leibniz in 1710 (Leibniz, 2006).

The theory of theodicy, in theological terms, asserts God's justice in the existence of a benevolent God. The Reverend Thomas Malthus, who combined the clerical role with the pursuit of the laws of political economy and demography, discussed the concept of theodicy in his *Essay on the Principles of Population*, published in 1798. He argued the case for a theology of scarcity: 'the Supreme Being has ordained, that the earth shall not produce food in great quantities, till much preparatory labour and ingenuity has been exercised upon its surface' (Malthus, 1798, p 360). The Malthusian ethic attributes an inherent indolence and sensuality to humanity that inevitably leads to distress. As Dean (1991, p 90) puts it, the Malthusian ethic amounts to a life-and-death choice for the poor: 'to obey or to transgress the dictates of the laws which are essential to divine providence, to choose a particular ascetic form of life or to perish'. Theodicy provided a theological justification for the limitation of charity to the 'deserving poor', that is, children and those disabled by old age and infirmity from working.

The rich in early modern Europe did not envisage a liberal distribution of charity to the poor. As Lis and Soly (1979, p 195) have put it, 'the charity of the elites centred almost exclusively on the respectable poor: children and the aged, sick and lame'. The impotent poor were differentiated from the 'able-bodied' poor, the former being considered deserving of assistance and the latter of punishment.

Medicine, charity and poverty

The new *mentalité* involved a much broader concept of charity. It was to crucially shape the nature of social policy in the modern world. The secular ideology that infused charity in early modern Europe was reflected in the emergence of public charity. The term 'public charity' was employed to describe a 'strategy for establishing public services and facilities at a sensitive point midway between private initiative and the state' (Donzelot, 1980, p 55). The regulation of the health of the population best exemplified this process in action. The emergence of the medical profession as a powerful interest group, coupled with the expansion of the apparatus of government, was essential to this development. The hospital symbolised the new *mentalité* and flourished in a variety of forms.

It is notable that these charitable hospitals were voluntary in inspiration, being frequently the initiatives of medical entrepreneurs who sought professional and social advancement as well as material gain. The poor provided the raw material for medical education and research. Richardson has demonstrated in reference to the United Kingdom during this period that 'patients in charitable institutions were generally regarded as experimental material, upon which practitioners would gain experience which would subsequently be turned to their own social and pecuniary advantage in private practice' (Richardson, 1988, p 47).

Medical patronage and incompetence became the subject of a crusade in the early 19th century by Thomas Wakley, surgeon, reformer and later MP, in the columns of the *Lancet*, which he founded. Wakley's revelations, which led to litigation, exposed the social relations between the medical profession and the poor, and ultimately the myth of medical charity as a humanitarian enterprise. The issue of dissection epitomised social relations between the medical profession and the poor.

The Burke and Hare case in 1828, which revealed that 'resurrectionists' in Edinburgh had turned their attentions to live victims in order to meet the anatomists' apparently insatiable demand for cadavers, brought dissection into the political arena. The resulting controversy produced the 1832 Anatomy Act, which transferred the penalty of dissection from the murderer to the pauper. Richardson (1988, p 266) has observed that this measure was 'in reality an advance clause' of the deterrent Poor Law of the 1830s; 'it was simultaneously an act of deference to the cash nexus, and instrumental and symbolic degradation of poverty'. She concluded that 'above all' the Anatomy Act 'served as a class reprisal against the poor' (Richardson, 1988, p 266). As a result of this measure, unclaimed bodies of workhouse inmates became the material of the dissection rooms of medical schools, contributing to the atavistic fear of the Victorian workhouse. In popular theology, a pauper's death had profound eschatological significance, since it could mean consignment to an eternal wilderness where body and soul were permanently separated. The dissection of the corpses of paupers was widely availed of by the medical schools.

Medical complicity in the sordid trade in corpses did little to enhance the profession's public esteem. Nonetheless, the fortunes of medicine prospered as the arteries of government spread outwards to embrace the health of the community. Public charity replaced private charity in the health sphere, involving a partnership between voluntary enterprise and statutory initiative.

The movement towards the segregation of the victims of physical diseases was paralleled by the development of facilities for 'lunatics and idiots'. The treatment of the mentally ill has been a major focus for the attentions of social control theorists. In 1967, the publication of Foucault's *Madness and Civilization* laid the groundwork for subsequent scholars. In this study, Foucault argued that the mentally ill were the archetypal outcasts, asserting that 'to inhabit the reaches long since abandoned by the lepers, they chose a group that to our eyes is strangely mixed and confused' (Foucault, 1967, p 45). The import of Foucault's argument was that madness in the Age of Reason came to be perceived as a fundamental social threat requiring the erection of a barrier between the mentally ill and the rest of humanity.

Foucault's work has been developed by other scholars. Doerner's (1981) European study has concentrated on the development of psychiatry in the context of 'the sequestration of unreason'. Scull (1979, p 30), in a study of the emergence of public asylums in England during the 19th century, has emphasised the importance of the transition to capitalism, which led to the 'ever more thorough-going commercialization of existence'.

Private charitable asylums were important because they pioneered the moral treatment approach associated with Tuke's Retreat, opened at York in 1792, and the appointment of Pinel as head of the Bicêtre in Paris in 1793. Moral treatment has been attributed with more 'humane' attitudes towards the mentally ill, 'aiming at minimising external physical coercion' (Scull, 1979, p 68). But Foucault has denigrated the reformism of the moral treatment movement. In reference to Tuke's new reformed asylum in York, which symbolised Quaker benevolence, Foucault remarked that 'the religious and moral milieu was imposed from without in such a way that madness was controlled, not cured'. With equal force he dismissed Pinel's Parisian asylum as 'an instrument of moral uniformity and of social denunciation' (Foucault, 1967, p 259). In Foucault's (1967, p 278) judgement, the transformation in the lives of the mentally ill that was attributed to the moral treatment movement represented 'a gigantic moral imprisonment which we are in the habit of calling, doubtless by antiphrasis, the liberation of the insane by Tuke and Pinel'. He averred that 'our philanthropy prefers to recognise the signs of benevolence towards sickness where there is only a condemnation of idleness' (Foucault, 1967, p 46).

A transformation in the treatment of the mentally ill poor had demonstrably begun. Whether this change can be regarded as a humanitarian reform has been seriously questioned by Foucault's penetrating critique. But in terms of classification and segregative control an important development had occurred. It was part of a wider process that was paralleled by the confinement and segregation of vagrants. The treatment of vagrants most poignantly evokes the regulatory nature of public charity.

Vagrancy, punishment and deterrence

Prior to the 17th century, the law had endeavoured to deter vagrancy through the application of corporal punishment in public places. Rusche and Kirchheimer (1939, p 21) have commented that 'the whole system was primarily the expression of sadism, and the deterrent effect of publicity was negligible'. The low value placed on labour in pre-modern society was replaced during the age of mercantilism by the doctrine of the utility of poverty. According to Lis and Soly (1979, p 117), this doctrine proclaimed that 'the national interest required ... the masses be held in a permanent state of poverty'. With regard to its more general regulatory import, Lis and Soly (1979, p 117) have observed in reference to the mercantilists' view of labour:

> In general, they considered labour as the source of all wealth, or even wealth itself. Hence they advocated not only demographic measures but considered it necessary to force the labouring masses to serve the nationalistic interests of the state. Deemed crude, ignorant, depraved, rebellious and, above all lazy, the wages of the lower classes had to be held as low as possible. Thus the poor were kept industrious, while the country gained a competitive advantage in international commerce.

Foucault (1967, p 46) characterised this policy change as evidence of 'a new sensibility to poverty and to ... new forms of reaction to the economic problems of unemployment and idleness, a new ethic of work, and also the dream of a city, where moral obligation was joined to civil law, within the authoritarian forms of constraint'.

Davies (1997, p 535) comments on the existence of a 'picaresque' literature dating from the 17th century that romanticised the lives of the vagrant poor, who, he records, had their own social order in a profoundly Saturnalian world, where poverty mocked wealth in a deeply *subversive* discourse:

Picaresque literature was clearly responding to a widespread social condition. Vagabondage and beggary filled a large social space, midway between the medieval forest outlaws and the regimented urban poor of the nineteenth century. It was spawned by the disintegration of hierarchical rural society, and encouraged by social policing that combined ferocious punishments with highly incompetent enforcement. Men and women took to the road in droves because they were unemployed, because they were fugitives from justice, above all because they longed to escape the oppressive, dependent status of serfs and servants. The *picaro* was wild but free.

Vagabonds sought protection in numbers, and in social hierarchies of their own. They travelled in bands with families and children, some of them mutilated to excite pity. They had specialised guilds of pickpockets, thieves, burglars, pedlars, beggars, cripples real and feigned, jugglers, entertainers, fortune-tellers, tinkers, whores, washerwomen, chaplains, and musicians – each with rules and guardians. They even developed their own secret language, known as *rotwelsch* or *zargon*. They gathered intermittently for meetings and 'parliaments', where they elected their 'kings' and 'queens'; and they shared the roads with gypsy tribes and gangs of unpaid soldiery.

In practice, most countries could only put vagrancy down by periodic military expeditions into the countryside, where exemplary hangings and press-gangings took place. In Eastern Europe vagrancy was conditioned by a harsher climate and by the persistence of serfdom. But fugitive serfs were a common phenomenon. In Russia the *yurodiv* or itinerant 'holy fool' was traditionally the recipient of hospitality and charity – proof too, perhaps, of more Christian social attitudes. (Davies, 1997, p 535)

This 'picaresque' world of poverty found its answer in repressive puritanism. Modernity and secularisation viewed vagabonds and vagrants with consummate harshness. In this climate of opinion, which reflected the need for labour in the flourishing domestic market and expanding colonial empires, the deterrence of vagrancy took on a new rationality manifested in the impetus to harness this source of manpower.

The politics of poverty

The English Poor Law reform debate flourished following the decline, after 1815, of the threat posed to English political stability by the French Revolution. The Old English Poor Law introduced in 1601, according to Piven and Cloward (1971, p 130), 'was based on several key principles: that relief should be a local responsibility; that relief allowances should be less remunerative than wages (the principle of "less eligibility"); and that "settlement" in the local community should be a prerequisite for aid'. By the late 18th century, the political climate had altered. In response to the challenge from the spread of revolutionary ideology and popular unrest, a more liberal administration of the Old English Poor Law had developed on the basis of local initiatives in the mid-1790s. This was known as the Speenhamland system. It permitted large-scale outdoor relief to the able-bodied poor, financed by the imposition of a labour rate.

The Speenhamland system was in essence a stop-gap response to a temporary political threat to the hegemony of the ruling order. It conferred on the poor a basic right to a subsistence living in the community. In the long term, it did not provide a viable scheme for capital because it was necessary to alter fundamentally the emphasis on settlement if the growing demand for a mobile reserve of industrial labour was to be met. A Poor Law system designed to curtail the mobility of labour had become increasingly anomalous in the age of the Industrial Revolution. Moreover, the Speenhamland system was believed to encourage population growth. This was anathema to the classical economists. Even before the political challenge posed by the French Revolution had receded, a debate about the fundamental principles on which the English Poor Law rested had commenced. In this debate the pessimistic theory of Thomas Malthus (1766–1834) that the multiplication of population always outstrips food production was to the fore. Malthus's pessimism was complemented by Adam Smith's theory of a 'wages fund', which asserted that there was a fixed percentage of the national income available for wages. It was also supported by David Ricardo's (1772–1823) 'Iron Law of Wages', which contended that wage payments above the market level in the long term operated to the detriment of the poor, since higher wages would encourage excessive population growth, leading to greater levels of misery.

While Malthus and Ricardo envisaged abolition as the ultimate goal of Poor Law reform, another exponent of classical economic theory, Jeremy Bentham (1748–1832), believed that the ideological position of this group could be reconciled with the concept of relief. He advocated in his *Pauper Management Improved*, first published in 1797 (Bentham, 1843), a system whereby England's 250 Houses of Industry would be brought under a system of centralised control and subject to rational administrative principles. These proposed penitentiaries for the poor were to prove decisive in shaping the government's response to the Poor Law reform debate in England.

The government reacted to demands for the reform of the English Poor Law by establishing the English Poor Law Commission in 1832, in which the classical economists, notably Edwin Chadwick (1801–90) and Nassau Senior (1790–1864), played a key role. It delivered its report in 1834. The English Poor Law Commission roundly condemned existing poor relief provision, citing the Speenhamland system as contrary to the spirit of the Elizabethan Poor Law. The Commission recommended a thoroughgoing reform of the English Poor Law, which swept away the restraints on the mobility of labour.

The new Poor Law (as it came to be called), which the English Poor Law Commission designed, was based on the concept of deterrence. This policy of deterrence was to be achieved through the rigorous application of the doctrine of 'less eligibility', that is, recipients of poor relief were to be exposed to conditions inferior to the lowliest labourer engaged in gainful employment. The able-bodied poor in England were henceforth to receive relief only in the carceral environment of the workhouse. The administration of poor relief was to be placed under the control of a central board with power to frame and enforce regulations for the governance of workhouses.

The debt to Bentham was evident in both the carceral ethos of the workhouse and the centralised control of the system. The discrepancy between the laissez-faire ideology that informed economic policy and the centralised control that underpinned social policy in England after 1834 exposed a fundamental paradox: that the economic freedom of the entrepreneurial class and the regulation of the poor by the state were complementary.

Richardson (1988, p 268) has commented that 'on a political level the affinities between Malthusian and eugenicist ideas are known', adding in reference to England that 'the New Poor Law "bastiles" seem to have prefigured some of the functions ascribed to the Nazi camps, such as breaking individuals into docility; spreading terror through the rest of society, and the destruction of individuality – for example in the way in which families were broken up and people were referred to by numbers instead of names'. This evaluation applies *pari passu* to the impact of the Irish Poor Law. But the severity of the social policy initiative taken against Irish poverty in 1838 merits even closer comparison with the Nazis' 'final solution' to the so-called 'Jewish problem'. It contained an essentially genocidal intent, however implicit this may have been (though if Senior is to be taken seriously, it was considered, in private, in eugenicist terms). In the second half of the 19th century, the poor began to find a voice and fight back against this terror. The poor were inspired by democracy and socialism, embodied in the Chartist movement, which demanded a charter of rights for the poor, similar to Magna Carta, which enshrined the rights of the nobility in 1215. Socialism became the voice of the poor, transforming them into a revolutionary subject – the working class.

Utopian socialism, mutualism and communitarianism

Utopian socialists, including Saint-Simon (1776–1825), Owen (1771–1858), Fourier (1772–1837) and Proudhon (1809–65), saw the great sources of evil in society as cut-throat competition, deceit, greed and inhumanity, and the great remedy as association and cooperation to restore harmony to human life. Fourierist communities, based on the ideals of association and cooperation, were established in New Jersey, Wisconsin and Massachusetts. Robert Owen established a utopian socialist community at New Lanark in Scotland during the early 19th century. Archambault (1997, p 32) has commented on the utopian socialist legacy: 'utopian socialism appeared before Marxism; in France it still has a deep influence on social economy organisations, co-operatives, mutual societies and a great many associations'. While Saint-Simon and Fourier advocated utopian models of association, in common with Robert Owen in Britain and William Thompson (1785–1833) in Ireland, Proudhon advocated mutualism. Archambault (1997, p 33) observes that 'mutualism stands between individualism and communism and restricts the rights of property'. Proudhon famously remarked: 'property is theft'. Mutualism was to create the philosophy that Europeans call the social economy, consisting of mutual insurance societies and mutual credit banks, credit unions, shared housing, trade unions, friendly societies and cooperatives, which all bear testimony to the fact that capitalism is not the only model of economic and social development. In a world where demutualisation has become the hallmark of contemporary capitalist acquisition, we are reminded of the rich legacy of the mutualist tradition. There is an increasing divide between the Anglo-Saxon world and continental Europe, regarding the value of mutualism, in the Age of Globalisation.

Utopian socialist principles translated to the New World, where a vigorous interest in communitarianism flourished during the 19th century. Many of these communitarians had a religious orientation: Hutterites, Doukhobors and Shakers, for example. Others, such as the Icarians, founded by Frenchman Étienne Cabet (1788–1856) and largely composed of French migrants, eventually settled in Iowa after many vicissitudes. A contemporary account by Charles Nordhoff, titled *The Communistic Societies of the United States: From Personal Observations*, originally published in 1875, paints a remarkable picture of these communitarian experiments. Nordhoff (1966, pp 337–8) recorded in relation to the Icarians that 'they live under a somewhat elaborate constitution, made for them by Cabet, which lays down with great care the equality and brotherhood of mankind, and the duty of holding all things in common; abolishes servitude and service (or servants); commands marriage, under penalties; provides for education; and requires that the majority shall rule'.

These idealistic experiments in communitarianism have not survived in substantial quantities into the 21st century, despite early proliferation. But as Holloway (1966, p x–xi) asserts, they have left a rich legacy. Kibbutzim in Israel became the glittering example of utopian socialism in practice during the 20th century. But it was 'a special case in a special place'. A succession of right-wing governments in Israel has weakened the kibbutz movement. On the other hand, in rural areas 'co-operative farm or farm colonies have proliferated – usually with government backing – in the United States, Canada, Mexico, Israel and Russia' (Holloway, 1966, p xi). However, even these remnants of utopian socialism in rural life have come increasingly under pressure from globalised agribusiness, driven by large subsidies in Europe and the United States.

In the urban world, the principles of utopian socialism have survived in mutuals, trade unions, shared housing, credit unions, retail cooperatives and so on. Predictably, even these benign forms of socialism are under attack from a rampant market determined to reshape the world uncompromisingly in the image of private enterprise. However, this is most pronounced in the Anglo-Saxon world. In France, the Socialist Party remains firmly wedded to the ideals of utopian socialism. Much of the battle within the European Union between the Anglo-Saxon model and the European social model devolves on a respect for the values of utopian socialism, expressed through mutualism, cooperativism and social protection. It is a tradition that is deeply rooted in the social life of Europe and, as we have seen, other parts of the world. In the Age of Globalisation, shaped in the Anglo-Saxon model of free enterprise, it faces a stiff challenge.

Marx: 'the Machiavelli of the proletariat'

Karl Marx (1818–83) and his political associate, Friedrich Engels (1820–95), personified the revolutionary socialist Left. Their legacy largely shaped the nature and structure of 20th-century politics. Marx advocated communism (that is, the abolition of private property) as 'the solution to the riddle of history' (cited in Wheen, 1999, p 73). He denounced communitarianism as 'a community of labour and equality of wages, which are paid out of communal capital, the community as universal capitalist' (cited in Wheen, 1999, p 74). Marx's socialism was 'scientific', guided by the laws of history, in contrast to the supposedly woolly utopianism of Proudhon, whom he particularly scorned. Marx has been described as 'the Machiavelli of the proletariat' by the Italian philosopher Benedetto Croce (1886–1952) (Joll, 1977, p 95). The Communist Party was to become 'the Modern Prince'. As the Italian Marxist theoretician Antonio Gramsci (1891–1937) put it:

> The Modern Prince, as it develops, revolutionises the whole system of intellectual and moral relations, in that its development means precisely that any given act is seen as useful or harmful, as virtuous or wicked, only in so far as it has as its point of reference the Modern Prince itself, and helps to strengthen or to oppose it. In men's consciousness, the Prince takes the place of the divinity or the categorical imperative, and becomes the basis of modern laicism and for complete laicization of all aspects of life and of all customary relationships. (Cited in Joll, 1977, p 96)

In this iconography, Joseph Stalin and his many historical imitators emerge as the Cesare Borgias of our times.

The Marxist theory of historical or dialectical materialism reversed conventional wisdom. The idea of the dialectic was borrowed from Hegel and turned on its head. It rejected idealism as the motor force in history, as Hegel had argued, and replaced it with materialism. According to Marx, the superstructure, consisting of the ideological make-up of society (that is, ideas, morality, culture and so on), was ultimately determined by the infrastructure shaped by economic relations. As Lee and Raban (1988, p 11) observed, 'Marxists employed a "catastrophic" theory of history'. Civic virtue was, therefore, simply a reflection of class interest. Social obligation was impossible in a society based on class conflict. History, for Marx, reflected a struggle between classes through a dialectical process that would ultimately lead to a proletarian state. Progressively, more modern forms of society replaced older ones. Capitalism replaced the feudal social order, which in turn had replaced ancient society, the successor of Asiatic civilisation. Each civilisation was characterised by a set of property relations that had been successfully challenged by a revolutionary class, thus giving way to a new social order. Marx predicted that the capitalist system in turn would perish as the result of its internal contradictions, leading to the emergence of a socialist society based on common ownership.

Marx set out his vision of the future in his magnum opus, which he called *Das Kapital* (Marx 1962). In this work and his many other publications, often co-authored with Engels, Marx believed that he had discovered the actual trends of 'real history'. Marx and Engels regarded their work as 'scientific', and in that sense it was mould breaking. What has turned out to be the lasting legacy of Marxism is not Marx's predictions and prescriptions for a socialist future, but his analysis of the nature of capitalism. His work is essentially a synthesis of European ideas, including German philosophy (notably Hegel and Feuerbach), French Jacobinism and English Ricardian economics. His intellectual contribution is comparable to that of Darwin and Freud, in the sense that it opened up a new perspective on the world that has reshaped human thought.

Fabian socialism, civic virtue and social policy

Fabians viewed socialism as the extension of democracy, from the political into the social and economic spheres of policy – social democracy. Social policy became the expression of the Fabian pursuit of civic virtue. Its four leading intellectuals, Sidney and Beatrice Webb, along with writers H.G. Wells and George Bernard Shaw, sought to reimagine British politics between the foundation of the Fabian Society in 1884 and the Second World War. Their legacy was the British welfare state. At the core of the *zeitgeist* of the welfare state was the pursuit of civic virtue through social policy.

Fabians were unshakably committed to the pursuit of the socialist goals of equality and social justice through exclusively democratic means. This created an unbridgeable gap between the Fabians and Marxists. The Jacobin–Marxist tradition was completely abhorrent to the Fabians' political thinking. For Fabians, evolution rather than revolution was the means to creating civic virtue. Named after the Roman general Fabius Cunctator (the delayer), whose patience in avoiding pitched battles secured ultimate victory over the Carthaginian general Hannibal, Fabians favoured a gradualist approach to political change based on the ideal of social reform. Fabians differentiated their approach from social liberalism by emphasising collectivism over individualism. In 1900 the Fabians joined the Independent Labour Party and the Social Democratic Federation trade unions to form the Labour Representation Committee, which grew into the British Labour Party. Fabians consequently viewed themselves as socialists, but with a staunch middle-class devotion to ethical socialism. This linkage between socialism and civic virtue became the value base of social policy. Society was to be collectively organised for the common good. But the power of the state was to be tempered by democracy. It was answerable to the people. In turn, the people were enjoined to embrace social obligation as the basis of a virtuous society.

Fabians are often associated with a dirigiste model of the state in which an enlightened elite of intellectuals tirelessly worked for the common good. This is a caricature. In reality, the Fabians advocated the idea of 'parallel bars' between the state and the voluntary sector. They regarded the state as a moral community that would provide against adversity, on the basis of mutual obligation. Here one can detect the influence of Continental utopian socialists. Inside the Fabian moral community, citizens would be expected to perform the duties of workers, parents and carers for the common good, which would benefit all in a democratic society.

The preoccupation of the Fabians with the concept of civic virtue became the guiding philosophical inspiration of the reformist tradition of social policy. Richard Titmuss, in his classic study *The Gift Relationship* (Titmuss, 1970), explained the philosophical roots of the discipline of social policy. This study, which takes the blood transfusion service as a microcosm of the British welfare state, devolves on the key role of altruism in society. Titmuss (1970, p 225) argued that 'the ways in which society organises and structures its social institutions – particularly its health and welfare systems – can encourage or discourage the altruistic in man'.

Because the Webbs disagreed with the voluntary sector regarding the recommendations of the Royal Commission on the Poor Laws (1909), writing a minority report in a markedly more radical tone, they are often perceived as being hostile to civil society. In fact, there was a high degree of consensus regarding the need for a system of unemployment insurance and the introduction of labour exchanges. The growing threat of socialism was to prove decisive, pushing the Liberal government, elected in a landslide victory in 1906, into a vigorous programme of social reform that laid the framework for the welfare state, while leaving the Poor Law intact.

Fabians were to put the alleviation of poverty at the centre of the social policy agenda. George Bernard Shaw, in a letter written to H.G. Wells in 1917, observed that 'we must reform society before we can reform ourselves ... personal righteousness is impossible in an unrighteous environment' (cited in Holroyd, 1988, p 27). This powerful Shavian rhetoric was matched by pioneering studies of poverty and its effects undertaken by Beatrice Webb in a monumental survey of London's poor between 1886 and 1902 on behalf of the philanthropist Charles Booth.

The Fabians' commitment to social research, which they believed would lead to scientifically based social legislation that would remedy the ills of society, was the hallmark of their intellectual approach. Fabians were committed to an empirically grounded view of social reality, which they tirelessly disseminated in an endless stream of facts and figures that became the hallmark of the social administration tradition. The foundation of the London School of Economics in 1895 provided an intellectual powerhouse where poverty and social conditions could be analysed, social ills diagnosed and injustice remedied. Social policy emerged as an academic discipline within this process of intellectual discovery. The legacy of the Fabians was to open the Victorian mind to the possibility of social reform. This did not put them at odds with civil society. They had a shared concern with poverty and social injustice.

Philanthropy, active citizenship and social reform

While political radicals sought to pursue collectivist solutions, voluntary organisations endeavoured to address the welfare of individuals, groups and families experiencing poverty and exploitation. Both shared a rejection of the 'ruling ideas' of the time, to the extent that they sought to counterpose 'the social question', challenging the prevailing individualist orthodoxy of political economy. Political economists rejected the concept of 'society' and the need for state intervention outside the deterrent Poor Law system. This was the discursive challenge that both voluntarism and social reform faced.

The emergence of active citizenship engaged in the arena of philanthropy needs to be set in the social context of the Victorian world. The urbanisation that characterised the emergence of capitalism in the modern world had created the perception of a social gulf between classes in the major cities. It was believed that the traditional hierarchies and social bonds of rural life had been fundamentally undermined, creating a social crisis. There was also a profound sense of political crisis as the spectre of social revolution engulfed Europe between the 1840s and 1880s. Socialism had emerged to challenge the inequalities of capitalism and to demand full citizenship rights from the ruling bourgeoisie for the disenfranchised proletariat.

In this uncertain landscape, dystopian images of the modern city began to emerge. The division between the prosperous West End of London and the impoverished East End provided a metaphor for the way the city was depicted and theorised in Victorian social commentary. Mooney (1998, p 56) observes: 'The East–West metaphor was among a number of images used at this time, which served to "distance" particular groups in the city, constituting them as a "social problem".' In this imagery of the poor, deprived urban areas came to be configured in the Victorian mind as 'dark' and 'hostile' places. The poor became the 'other' of Victorian society (Mooney, 1998, p 59). It has been argued that a form of domestic colonialism emerged in the *flânerie* of Victorian sociology and the active citizenship of philanthropists. These active citizens traversed a social terrain that was populated by the victims of rampant capitalism. It had created an outcast population evocative of imperial landscapes that challenged the mores of Victorian society (McLintock, 1995).

Samuel Smiles' *Self-Help*, published in 1859, epitomised the ethos of the times, enshrining the moral code of the dominant middle class in society and ensuring that firm limits were set against state intervention. Active citizenship, through voluntary work and social reform, represented twin strands of civic engagement directed against Victorian moral hypocrisy and social indifference. Beatrice Webb spoke also for voluntarism when she wrote in her diary in 1884: 'Social questions are the vital questions of to-day: they have taken the place of religion' (cited in Skidelsky, 1999, p 13). George Bernard Shaw (1856–1950) wrote in his play *You Never Can Tell* (1902): 'Let me tell you, Mr. Valentine, that a life devoted to the cause of humanity has enthusiasms and passions to offer which far transcend the selfish personal infatuations and sentimentalities' (cited in Skidelsky, 1999, p 12). Both social reformers and voluntary organisations shared a commitment to active citizenship through the promotion of a vibrant civil society. However, social reformers went a step further by insisting on the need to change the role of the state in the interests of the welfare of the population as a whole. For them, a healthy public domain involved an active state, as well as active citizenship. On the other hand, the London Charity Organization Society, founded in 1869, took a more individualised view of poverty and sought to remoralise the poor. Nonetheless, the 'social' was reconfigured as the responsibility of the public domain. As Dahrendorf (1994, p 27) has observed, 'in the twentieth century, the public domain was further enlarged to embrace health care and insurance against sickness, unemployment and old age, so as to guarantee social, as well as political and citizenship rights'. In the 19th century, volunteers, through their active citizenship, contributed to civilising social expectations and laying the foundations for social reform in the 20th century.

These volunteers were inspired by a new literary genre. The social novel emerged during the 19th century. Charles Dickens (1812–70) was to pioneer the social novel. *Oliver Twist*, published in 1838 (Dickens, 1984) in the wake of the harsh 1832 Poor Law Reform Act, revealed a deep sympathy for the poor and a personal hatred of social injustice. Dickens' ability to invoke intense feelings of horror in the reader left an indelible mark on society. The cruel Bumble, the spine-chilling Fagin and the Artful Dodger are unforgettable characters. They evoke the brutal and callous world of Victorian poverty. Later books, notably *Bleak House* (1853 [Dickens, 1971]) and *Hard Times* (1854 [Dickens, 2003]), demonstrate Dickens' very active social conscience. Social protest was also a core element in his work, but was obscured by his primary commitment to literature. Nonetheless, he was to inspire a generation of social activists in the Anglo-Saxon world who turned to voluntarism and reformism as the means to change a deeply unjust social order characterised by cruelty and indifference. In doing so, they were to re-forge civil society as an instrument of democracy and social justice.

In France, Émile Zola (1840–1902) was to prove a similarly powerful exponent of the social novel, as Dickens had become in the Anglo-Saxon world. But he is equally remembered for his political activism, epitomised by his campaign to secure a new trial for Albert Dreyfus. Zola's famous journalistic letter, *J'Accuse* (Zola, 1898), played a seminal role in exposing social hypocrisy and anti-Semitism in 19th-century France, earning him a fine, imprisonment and a period of exile in Britain in the interests of his personal safety. Captain Dreyfus (1859–1935) was a Jewish officer in the French army, who was accused of spying and court-martialled in 1894. He was degraded, and imprisoned on Devil's Island, off the coast of French Guiana. Despite clear evidence of a miscarriage of justice, Dreyfus' name was not fully cleared until 1906, when he was fully exonerated and restored to the army with the rank of major. The Dreyfus affair galvanised progressive democratic civil society in France as a counter-public that challenged the forces of conservatism: the army, the Catholic Church, the Royalists and the dark forces of anti-Semitism. In many respects, the anti-Dreyfusards were harbingers of the horrific events in the 20th century that culminated in the Holocaust (Arendt, 1958). Dreyfus' plight symbolised the repressive state regime of the Third Republic.

The divisions in French society remained, and re-emerged in the Vichy regime, established during the German occupation in the 1940s. The issue at stake in the Dreyfus affair, as Hannah Arendt was to point out in her monumental study, *The Origins of Totalitarianism* (Arendt, 1958), was not simply about a miscarriage of justice, but also a defence of democracy and civic virtue. Nicholas Halasz (1963, p 1) has described the Dreyfus affair as 'the story of mass hysteria'. Zola and his allies in defending Dreyfus were defending European democracy. The linkage between civil society, civic virtue and democracy had become a fundamental connection.

Social crusading, anti-slavery and civil society

The Dreyfus affair had highlighted the issue of race in modern European politics. Slavery was the dark side of European modernity. William Wilberforce (1759–1833) was one of a group of late 18th-century reformers that included Elizabeth Fry (1780–1845), who sought to highlight this issue. He devoted his public career to the abolition of slavery and the slave trade. When parliamentary interest flagged, Wilberforce founded the Anti-Slavery Society in 1821. Slavery was abolished in the British Empire shortly after his death, a belated recognition of his life's work. Wilberforce was a respected evangelical, being one of the leaders of the Clapham Sect, which promoted private philanthropy, missionary work overseas and reforms for the poor. The association between the anti-slavery movement and Christianity was a close one. Anti-slavery activists emerged as social crusaders challenging the inhumanity of slavery as an affront to democracy and civilised society.

The ideals of the Enlightenment had raised profound questions about the slave trade, which was clearly contrary to the values of the French Revolution (1789) of liberty, equality and fraternity. Montesquieu (1689–1755) had raised the justification for the slave trade in his *Spirit of the Laws* (1748) (Montesquieu, 1949), including the alleged subhumanity of blacks, and conclusively demonstrated that it had no basis in rationality. Long abandoned in Europe, slavery fuelled imperial expansion. Some Enlightenment rationalists sought to justify slavery on the basis of racial hierarchies. Evangelical Christians rejected slavery as both contrary to humanity and contrary to the will of God. They believed that we were all possessed of souls, making us equal in the sight of God. Spiritual equality was to become a major factor in the abolitionist cause that was pioneered by the Quakers (Fredrickson, 2005, p 40).

But there was also powerful evidence that the revolutionary spirit had inspired the black slave population. In 1791, under the leadership of Toussaint L'Ouverture (1746–1803), the Caribbean island of San Domingo (roughly the size of Ireland) experienced the world's first successful slave revolt. San Domingo (modern Haiti) was a French West Indian colony that supplied two-thirds of France's overseas trade and was the principal individual market for the European slave trade. Its economic base was dependent on the labour of half a million slaves. The slave revolt on San Domingo lasted for 12 years, defeating local whites, a Spanish invasion, a British expedition of 60,000 soldiers and a French expedition. This slave revolt has been celebrated in C.L.R. James' masterpiece, *The Black Jacobins*, originally published in 1938 (James, 1989). The final defeat of Napoleon Bonaparte's 1803 expedition resulted in the establishment of the black state of Haiti (Davis, M., 2006).

The American Declaration of Independence in 1776 was to put the issue of slavery firmly on the political agenda in the United States. If 'all men are created equal', why are some of them slaves? In the immediate aftermath of the American Revolution, there was widespread agreement that 'slavery was an unjust and harmful institution and that its days were numbered' (Fredrickson, 2005, p 40). Slavery, however, was not simply viewed as a violation of human rights. The slave rebellion in San Domingo (Haiti) during the 1790s made abolition an urgent and important political consideration. In the northern states, where slavery was limited, emancipation took place during the 1780s and 1790s. But in the cotton-picking states, south of the Mason–Dixon Line, slavery continued to endure because of its economic benefits for the white population. It was not until the Civil War in the 1860s that slavery was finally abolished.

During the first half of the 19th century, a genuinely interracial anti-slavery movement emerged. Quakers, once again, were in the forefront of the movement, disobeying unjust laws such as the Fugitive Slave Acts. However, John Brown's raid on Harper's Ferry in 1859, which was intended to inspire large-scale desertions from slave plantations, morally compromised the anti-slavery movement because of its violent tactics. It underlined a critical dividing line between civil disobedience and legitimate social protest (the hallmarks of civil society) and violent protest (the methodology of the terrorist). The fact that John Brown was driven by religious zealotry and the belief that God had given divine sanction to his deeds underlines the point (Fredrickson, 2005, p 42). The legacy of the anti-slavery movement in 19th-century America was to inspire the Civil Rights movement in the 20th century. It was a testament to the power of civil society to resist social injustice (see Chapter Six).

The anti-slavery movement was by no means confined to the Anglo-Saxon world. In Brazil a flourishing abolitionist movement in the late 19th century produced a large number of associations with strong urban support. These included the Caixas Emancipacionistas (Emancipationist Savings Bank), which supported campaigning, and Clubes and Associações Abolicionistas, which organised marches, rallies and support for runaway slaves. The anti-slavery movement in Brazil was also composed of clandestine groups, including the Caitazes in São Paulo, and an umbrella organisation called the Conferedação Abolicionista (Landim, 1997, p 327). The global scale of the anti-slavery movement is evidence of an embryonic global civil society emerging during the 19th century. But ideological divisions were already evident between those who favoured private philanthropy and supporters of more radical solutions involving the state.

The ideology of voluntarism: private versus public welfare

In the United States voluntarism took on an anti-statist political character of ideological proportions. Lester Salamon (1994, p 287) has observed in this regard:

> What is clear, however, is that a powerful ideology of voluntarism took shape that posited an inherent conflict between the non-profit sector and the State and put the non-profit sector forward not as a supplement to the State but as an alternative to it. In the process the ideal of voluntarism was thoroughly politicised, emerging by the late nineteenth century as the principal rallying-point for resistance to expand public aid to cope with the growing poverty and misery that rapid urbanisation and industrialisation were creating.

For Americans, poverty in the midst of plenty demonstrated a lack of virtue in the individual. While they were eager to help the weaker in society to avail of the prosperity that characterised the American dream, the state was widely rejected as the arbiter of human welfare, at least until the short-lived New Deal was introduced during the 1930s in response to the Great Depression. Franklin D. Roosevelt's social reformism was very much at odds with the American character. For Americans, charity and enterprise are two sides of the same virtuous coin. Voluntarism was compatible with capitalism.

This ideology of voluntarism represented an egoistic morality of wealth and a social Darwinistic view of poverty. The new 'gospel of wealth' that framed the American view of welfare was personified by the steelmaker-turned-philanthropist, Andrew Carnegie (1835–1918), who believed the capacity to amass wealth was a sign of superior moral virtue (Salamon, 1994). It spanned 'scientific' charity, which purported to be able to differentiate between the deserving and undeserving poor. Desert was the moral economy of welfare in the American mind. Charity organisation societies, modelled on the London Charity Organization Society, became the model for casework. The problem was that the social workers did not share the social Darwinism of the benefactors, quickly realising that poverty was the product of social injustice, rather than of moral failure (Powell, 2001, pp 32–44).

A different approach emerged in continental Europe. In Germany, the Elberfelder System was inaugurated in the city of Elberfeld in 1853. It became the model for cooperation between middle-class volunteers, the traditional role of the Church in charity and the state. Anheier and Seibel (2001, p 47) conclude: 'The model mobilised human resources, maintained governmental control over expanded services and avoided open conflict at local level.' We can see the beginnings of corporatism and social partnership in this model. By 1897, the Catholic Church had formed a national umbrella organisation for religiously run social services called Caritas. Its Protestant counterpart, Innere Mission, had already been established in 1848.

On the other hand, in France, the development of the voluntary sector was inhibited by the Jacobin distaste for intermediate organisations and ideological conflicts about *la question sociale*. The economist J.B. Say declared that 'society doesn't have to support its members' and 'to give the poor the right to alms is to destroy the ownership right and to favour communism; inequality does not mean injustice' (cited in Archambault, 1997, p 32). France was clearly the home of laissez-faire economics, even if the United States was its best ideological exponent. Nonetheless, France did have some authorised associations, such as the mighty Société Philanthropique, inspired by the Freemasons. It was to become the model for confraternities (for example, Lions, Elks, Roterians) around the world that combine the advantages of membership with good works. But, as Archambault (1997, p 30) concludes, the on-going conflict between a centralised state and civil society in 19th-century France was to historically retard voluntary activity.

Civil society, counter-publics and café society

Asen and Brouwer (2001, p 4) have explored the relationship between the emergence of counter-publics and civil society:

> As a historical concept, the bourgeoisie public sphere describes the emergence in civil society of a realm in which citizens came together as private persons to form a public that, acting in an advisory capacity, debated the activities of the state. Sustained through political pamphlets and coffee houses, the bourgeoisie public sphere flourished in Europe in the seventeenth and eighteenth centuries. The bourgeoisie public sphere was instantiated through critical discourse and presupposed a rational debating public. Bourgeoisie subjectivity arose from the world of letters to assume a political form. A political consciousness developed as the bourgeoisie opposed absolute sovereignty with demands for abstract and universal laws and ultimately asserted itself as the only legitimate source of these laws.... As a critical concept, the bourgeoisie public sphere signifies an open forum of debate and an egalitarian community of citizens implicit in the practice of the bourgeoisie and explicit in their justifications of the public sphere. Three qualities characterise this critical public sphere: access guaranteed to all citizens; citizens debate openly; and citizens debate matters of general interest.

The British coffee house of the 18th century and the cafés of the great European cities such as Paris and Vienna, during the 19th and 20th centuries, became a space between the private and the public spheres. In this convivial atmosphere, a conversational democracy took shape that sparkled with new ideas, driven by modernism's impatience for change. Whether these ideas came from artists, political radicals or writers, there was a shared sense of destiny being created in this social space, where democratic and revolutionary ideas took shape – of counter-publics, where seditious gatherings could discuss the detraditionalisation of society, politically, socially and culturally. Twenty-first-century society coffee-house chains, such as Starbucks, Caffè Nero and Costa Coffee, seek to mimic this Bohemian atmosphere, with a conspicuous lack of success. The debate has moved on to internet-café websites, chat rooms and noticeboards, where bloggers of the world unite in a vast debate in cyberspace. E-activism has added a new dimension to politics. But there are historic commonalities in challenging official versions of the truth and the suspicion of the authorities, which in some regimes (for example, China) have sought to impose censorship.

What soon emerged in modern society was that there were multiple publics representing a wide spectrum of views within civil society. Opposition was expressed not only towards absolutist rule. The right to democratic expression involved a plurality of viewpoints. Some of these viewpoints expressed in pamphlets and newspapers challenged popular support for anti-Semitism and the institution of slavery. A black public sphere opened up through the emancipation movement. Similarly, a women's public sphere found expression through engagement in civil society. Archambault (1997, p 37) notes the social engagement of feminists who created 'social houses' in deprived areas, fought for women's liberation and became heavily involved as medical auxiliaries in times of war. All of these counter-publics were united by a common desire for social justice.

During the 17th century the pamphlet emerged as a potent agitational instrument. John Milton's (1608–74) *Aeropagitica*, published in 1644 (Milton, 1868), was a powerful critique of censorship and a lofty defence of the freedom of the press. In the following century, the pamphlet became one of the most widely employed modes of political debate by political and philosophical commentators, including Joseph Addison (1672–1719), Jonathan Swift (1667–1745), Voltaire (1694–1778) and Jean-Jacques Rousseau (1712–78). As has been seen above, the French writer and social activist Émile Zola (1840–1902) was to revive the art of pamphleteering with powerful effect during the late 19th century.

The French Revolution in 1789 inspired the modern newspaper with both news coverage and discussion. Camile Desmoulins (1760–94) emerged as the greatest journalist in revolutionary France. In Paris alone there were 500 newspapers in 1792, and there were approximately 1,400 in France between 1789 and 1792. But after the 18th Brumaire and the advent of Napoleon Bonaparte, censorship and control of the press became systemic. In England, the flamboyant figure of John Wilkes (1727–97) became synonymous with the fight for freedom of the press, which he waged through his journal *North Briton*. For his relentless attacks on the government, Wilkes was sent to the Tower of London, but released on a writ of habeas corpus because he was a Member of Parliament. The abolition of stamp duty in 1855 was viewed as the ending of a 'tax on knowledge' in Britain. It was quickly followed by the emergence of a popular press. Mass circulation newspapers faced competition from a vibrant working-class press and other radical organs that gave expression to the views of a rich variety of counter-publics.

In Germany, the young Karl Marx was appointed editor of the liberal *Rheinische Zeitung* in 1842. He soon found himself embroiled with the local censor. Within a year, the government in Berlin had banned the paper. While the enforced closure of the *Rheinische Zeitung* was undoubtedly a great blow to its liberal-minded readers throughout the Rhineland – from Cologne, Dusseldorf, Aachen and Trier – Marx was more sanguine. He wrote to a friend:

> It is a bad thing to have to perform menial duties for the sake of freedom; to fight with pinpricks, instead of with clubs. I have become tired of hypocrisy, stupidity, gross arbitrariness and of our bowing and scraping, dodging and hair-splitting over words. Consequently, the government has given me back my freedom. (Marx, cited in Wheen, 1997, p 48)

Five years later, Marx and Engels were to publish the most incendiary pamphlet of all time, *The Communist Manifesto* (Marx and Engels, 1967). The year 1848 became the year when revolution engulfed Europe and inaugurated the right to associate.

Associative democracy, civil society and collective self-help

The year 1848 was to prove a defining moment in the emergence of associative democracy across Europe. Citizens rose up and demanded the right to form associations. The revolutions of 1848 were different in character to the French Revolution in 1789. They were often liberal in ethos, with utopian socialist influences. What was clear to the contemporary mind was the aspiration to build a society that emphasised both liberty and equality. The idea of associative democracy had been born. It challenged not only absolutism but the dictatorial tendencies inherent in Jacobinism and, subsequently, Marxism.

Archambault (1997, p 33) observes in relation to 19th-century France:

> The utopian socialists had a more direct influence on this [non-profit] sector during the short-lived Second Republic which voted for symbolic and ephemeral civil rights:

'universal' suffrage (for men only), freedom to associate, suppression of censorship for the press and of the death penalty, creation of huge workhouses for unemployed people. All of these civil rights and institutions lasted less than one year and died out with Napoleon III's coup. The aborted 1848 Revolution, however, left a deep impression and foreshadowed the evolution of the late nineteenth and twentieth century. More than 1,000 associations and over 400 mutual aid societies were created during the year 1848 alone.

In Germany, a rather different picture emerges. Anheier and Seibel (2001, pp 50–2) argue that associational life in 19th-century Germany was a force for faux stability that in reality undermined democratic participation in the Kaiserreich. They conclude that the 'flight into associational life' served to permit the continuance of authoritarian governance in Germany long after it was healthy to do so. The suppression of 332 social democratic associations between 1878 and 1890 indicates that civil society in Germany during the 19th century was politically skewed. The consequences were to haunt Germany during the 20th century.

Other European societies were more fortunate. The 1848 revolutions across Europe unleashed associational democratic activity in many countries. For example, in Denmark, Jonasen (2003, p 35) records:

> During the feudal monarchy until 1849, organising was forbidden unless the king had granted permission to establish the organisation. The liberalist trend in the 1848–1849 revolt claimed freedom of speech and organisation, and these freedoms were granted in the constitution. The feudal society had a number of (king-permitted) organisations, dealing with social work, but in the 1840s and after the 1849 constitution the number and diversity of organisations grew rapidly.

In Britain, the 1793 Rose's Act formally recognised the existence of friendly societies, a form of mutualism where artisans and skilled workers pooled their resources to cover contingencies such as old age, sickness and burial. Cooperatives, building societies and housing societies were all part of this mutualist development (Kendall and Knapp, 1996, p 251). However, trade unions were treated with less sympathy. A series of anti-combination laws sought to prevent unskilled industrial workers from organising into associations because of their perceived revolutionary potential. But mutualism was welcomed as community self-help.

After 1880, friendly societies and cooperatives flourished in Britain, Western Europe, the United States and many other parts of the world. In Britain, friendly society membership rose to 7 million in 1885, and nearly 10 million by 1920. Cooperatives in Britain had risen to nearly 1,400 by 1900 (Hinsley, 1962, p 14). As the 19th century progressed and demands for democratisation grew louder, trade unions began to be given legal recognition: Belgium (1866), Austria (1870), Britain (1870–76), Spain (1881), France (1884), Germany (1890) and Russia (1906). In the years between 1886 and 1900, union memberships rose from 1.25 million to 2 million in Britain, from 300,000 to 850,000 in Germany and from 50,000 to 250,000 in France. Union membership was to continue to climb steeply into a mass movement during the early years of the 20th century. Even in the United States, the American Federation of Labour boasted 1.5 million members by 1904 (Hinsley, 1962, p 15).

Necessity produced a flowering of civil society among the emergent industrial working class in cities across the world as a forum of collective self-help that was to transform social relations. We see the first signs of a social Left. Within the labour movement many workers identified with socialism. The rise of working-class political parties, often led by intellectuals who articulated the felt needs and democratic aspirations of their supporters, was one side of the associationalist coin. On the other side, many working-class people viewed their best means of protection as collective self-help. The link with the mutualist tradition that underpinned utopian socialism was clear. Many viewed their future needs as best resolved through civil society rather than through the state, with its totalitarian tendencies.

Conclusion

This chapter has sought to chart the rise of humanism as the cradle of democratic society. The renaissance of civil society and its relations to both prevailing political ideologies and movements have been discussed. We have examined the interlinkages and antagonisms contained within these multiple shades of modern political expression. What we see in common is a belief in progress and in humankind transcending its faith. This makes the renaissance of civil society a story of optimism and the hope of a more socially just future for an emancipated world. The chapter began with a review of the theological basis of charity and the role of the Church as the principal instrument of social provision. It has been argued that the collapse of religious society led to the emergence of civil society. Machiavelli proved a decisive influence in daring to think on a secular basis and challenge the venal authority of the Catholic Church. His espousal of civic virtue was to open the way back to the humanistic roots of Western civilisation. In the crisis that followed the collapse of the Church's moral authority, civil society filled a social void. New value systems grounded in democracy, socialism and secularity began to emerge. The civic republican tradition of democracy revived the notion of community. Conscience became an instrument of social action – 'doing good' replaced 'being good'. Despite Marx's catastrophic predictions about the future of bourgeois society, a new energy emerged, seeking social reform in the name of humanism. Social policy was to emerge as the instrument of this reformist agenda, linking social idealism to empirical reality. But the transition from charity to social citizenship was a process mediated by civil society. Instead of the relationship being antithetical, it was complementary. The Fabians provided the most eloquent intellectual expression of this altered world, where modernity became linked to the pursuit of civic virtue. Its social idealism was exported to many parts of the world. Civic virtue and social reform were at the centre of the political agenda of modernity in a debate that was to pit welfare against socialists committed to the overthrow of capitalism.

FOUR

Radical civil society, early social movements and the socialisation of the state

> The history of political and state theory in the nineteenth century could be summarized with a single phrase: the triumphal march of democracy. Progress and the extension of democracy were equated, and anti-democratic resistance was considered an empty defense, the protection of historically outmoded things and a struggle of the old with the new.
>
> Carl Schmitt, *The Crisis of Parliamentary Democracy*
> (1988, p 22)

The politics of radical civil society is the product of modernist utopian aspirations to create a more virtuous state. It is also the product of the capacity of citizens to employ their new-found political influence over the polity in an emerging democratic order. Democracy is the product of modernity: a belief in society's capacity to transform itself into a more just, egalitarian and caring form. This involved a rupture with the previous minimalist, 'nightwatchmen' state. What we are witnessing in modernity is the fusion of the state and civil society, through the process of social and political evolution that ultimately produced the welfare state. There were two elements underpinning this fusion. First, the statisation of society – state interventionism. Second, the socialisation of the state – the welfare state. The first of these processes is entirely compatible with an authoritarian state that disregards human freedoms and suppresses civil society. The second envisages a benevolent state committed to democracy and human welfare but with no clear role for civil society, which it tends to marginalise. A benevolent state has little obvious need for an independent civil society, since it has become the custodian of civic virtue. That is why it is known as the welfare state. Yet the resulting fusion had its critics, as this chapter will demonstrate. The idea of creating a 'Big Society' based on greater social equality was viewed by both liberals and conservatives with deep suspicion. But it came to epitomise the radical civil society agenda of social justice.

Modernism and the quest for social justice

Modernity gave birth to a movement called 'modernism', which was revolutionary in its impact. It was a disparate movement, in which emancipatory politics intersected with avant-garde literature and art. Modernism was a gamble with history and consciousness that was born of outrage at the state of human affairs. The activities of artists and writers geared to transform human consciousness by an appeal to sensation found a response among political agitators and social reformers. The publication on the eve of the 1848 revolutions in Europe of Marx and Engels' *The Communist Manifesto* (Marx and Engels, 1967) epitomised the impact of modernist ideas on politics. But while modernism sought to transform the world in the direction of greater equality and liberty, it found its mirror image in anti-modernism. The latter sought to pursue a counter-transformation, back to earlier social and cultural forms that are represented in an iconography of idyllic family and communal life. In other words, modernism, epitomised by the big city with its dangers of revolution, violence and permissiveness, is contrasted with the rural bucolic life of certainty and stability, where the seigneurial presence of God provides an anchor for enduring authority.

Modern protest movements have been very much an urban phenomenon. The relationship between ideas and action is a complex one. Socialists, trade unionists and feminists provided the intellectual impetus behind urban protest, but, at popular levels, the issues were not ideological. Rather, they were about wages, unemployment, tenants' rights and slum housing conditions, free school meals, poor relief and other practical issues that reflected the daily concerns of people living in poor communities. While the leadership hoped that their left-wing ideological perspectives would filter down, compromise was the political and social reality. Protest usually took the form of strikes, demonstrations and marches. Action was organised rather than spontaneous. The intellectual leadership sought to impose discipline, as well as ideology, on a natural sense of injustice felt by poor people.

The emergence of nationalism in the late 18th century coincides with the activation of citizens in the affairs of the state. This led nationalism to be perceived in Europe during most of the 19th century as a democratic revolutionary movement. However, in the latter half of the 19th century and in the early 20th century, the rise of radicalism, socialism, feminism and anarchism as popular protest movements pushed nationalism in a reactionary revanchist direction in Europe. On the other hand, nationalism became synonymous with anti-colonial liberation struggles against European colonisation in less developed parts of the world. Everywhere, cultural nationalism, with its emphasis on national languages, became a potent influence in the age of mass literacy. Territory, language and religion became the defining characteristics of nationalism.

Despite this dissonance between the leadership and the communities of protest, they shared a common belief in human progress. They both firmly believed that society could improve, if they could influence the state in the direction of social justice. Their modernist position stood in marked contrast to pre-modern protest movements. The latter were usually about agrarian use rights, or were religious in character and rooted in a belief that there had been a decline in the standards of the past, which needed to be restored. Similarly, there was a noticeable difference between modern protest movements and the later protest movements of the postmodern era, including the student rebellions in the 1960s, the environmental movement, the anti-nuclear movement and the Occupy movement, which have all questioned the consequences and moral basis of progress.

Modernity was a particularly Western phenomenon. Most of the world was shut out from this transformation. The nation-state was very much the product of development. Many of the European countries that were being modernised were simultaneously holding much of the rest of the world in imperial subjugation. This was to last until the middle of the 20th century, when colonialism was finally overthrown. Martin Jacques has argued in the *Guardian* (Jacques, 2005) that 'the defeat of colonial rule will come to be seen as the defining event of the twentieth century'. Before 1945, Africa, the Middle East, the Indian subcontinent and a substantial part of East Asia were ruled by Europe. China was also subject to a particular species of multinational colonisation. The Opium Wars during the mid-19th century against the iniquitous practice of drug trafficking by the invading powers epitomise the colonial relationship.

The American Revolution and unknown civil society: birthing social movements

The American Revolution was the opening event of modernity. Militant American colonists rose up against the British Empire. It was anticipated by the Great Awakening (the American Enlightenment) during the 1740s. But 1776 became the defining movement in liberal politics. The American Revolution was a national rather than a social revolution. Zinn (1999, p 77) calls it 'a kind of revolution'. Liberalism framed the event. However, it was also a story of the incipient emancipatory politics. Liberty did not mean equality. Revolution came to be defined by a campaign for independence by white men of means in the American colonies. For the rest of the population, there was no change. That did not mean that they did not seek change. They did. Their revolution was suppressed, but not without some positive gains. The American Revolution took on its own unique character that was to shape the United States. There was no obvious autocracy to overturn, albeit it was a plutocracy from the start. One group of oligarchs replaced another in an exchange of elite power. But there was a social struggle.

The disempowered did seek to take advantage of the revolutionary moment. Their struggle was to inspire later generations. Defeat was an ideological rejection of the doctrine of the *Rights of Man*, as experienced by the common people. Revolution in America was liberation of the few at the expense of multitudinous minorities defined by their powerlessness. The latter's story is a different one from the tranquil Tocquevillian version of America's associative democracy as a unique product of consensus and national self-belief. America in 1776 was a nation divided – divisions that have defined its modernity. The mythology of a classless society with an open-opportunity structure was constructed on the foundation that America had no feudal social order to constrain the growth of democracy. The reality of political life during the American Revolution was very different from the myth.

Gary Nash, in his ground-breaking book, *The Unknown American Revolution* (2005), casts this great historic event in a new light. This book deflates the popular mythology about America's glorious revolutionary birth. Nash provides a history from 'the bottom up', exploring the experience of slaves, Native Americans, women, and other social groups that contested for power, such as urban workers, tenant farmers and 'plebeian loyalists'.

Slaves were undoubtedly among the biggest losers. They rallied to the colours in the hope of emancipation. Nash (2005, p 33) comments on their massive participation in the American Revolution. He contends that the failure of the Founding Fathers of the American Republic to endorse the abolition of slavery led to the loss of 600,000 lives 80 years later, during the Civil War. While slaves fought bravely on both sides, most died (often from diseases, notably smallpox), neglected by those who had sought to exploit their bravery. Only in the northern states did small numbers of slaves gain their freedom and win the right to vote as equal citizens (Nash, 2005, p 209). For the rest of the slave population, the American Revolution was a lost opportunity (Nash, 2005, p 407). Nash concludes: 'Of black Americans who survived the war, the vast majority did not leave American shores but remained to toil and carry on the struggle to end slavery where most of them had been born.'

Native Americans fared no better. The Iroquois were crushed forever by the armies of the revolution. In the South, the Creeks and Cherokee were victims of 'genocidal state policy' at the hands of the revolutionary militia. To the west, the Shawnees had their villages destroyed and crops burnt. There was no question that the American Revolution was a white man's revolution. For Native Americans it was a defining event in their ethnic destruction. Resistance almost certainly meant death. For them, there was no liberation, just annihilation (Nash, 2005, pp 377–87).

Women played a part in the American Revolution, often seeking to draw parallels between political tyranny and the tyranny of gender inequality. Abigail Adams (1744–1818) was at the forefront of this campaign. She wrote to her husband, John (later President of the United States, 1796–1800), about the Code of Laws being written by the Founding Fathers:

> I desire you would remember the ladies, and be more generous and favorably to them than your ancestors. Do not put such unlimited power into the hand of the husbands. Remember all men would be tyrants if they could. If particular care and attention is not paid to the ladies, we are determined to ferment a rebellion, and will not hold ourselves bound by any laws in which we have no voice or representation. (cited in Nash, 2005, p 203)

While her husband dismissed her entreaties as 'saucy', Abigail Adams had cleverly linked civil and domestic governance at a time of revolutionary change. The genie was out of the bottle! Women had seized the revolutionary moment to demand equality. The seeds of the suffrage movement had been sown. The women succeeded in winning the right to vote in New Jersey, albeit on a limited and temporary basis. While women's suffrage only gradually evolved in the United States, there was no going back. Albeit, Zinn (1999, p 103) describes the position of women in post-revolutionary America as 'house slaves'. However, their influence over civil society was considerable.

Outside the arena of the struggle for constitutional rights, women reshaped civility in American society, setting new standards and expectations for their male compatriots. Nash (2005, p 421) comments:

Thus 'virtue' before the war a masculine quality that citizen-warriors demonstrated by sacrificing self-interest for the common good and sacrificing individual lives for the good of the whole society, had to be retooled and feminized in peacetime if the noble new democratic experiment was to succeed. In this rescue operation, the salvaging of the human traits upon which the republic could be built and sustained lay much in the hands of women. With virtue inculcated by women, the nation might overcome the decay of masculine virtue that brought war on. Women would be the moral bookkeepers and instructors in the new boisterous American society.

The campaign for equality had begun in America. That was the lasting legacy of the struggles of slaves, Native Americans, women and other oppressed groups. They were an unknown civil society but they did leave a significant historical imprint that was to shape America. They had also defined democracy in an alternative way. The Founding Fathers were committed to representative democracy as the embodiment of the liberal ideas of the American Republic. The struggle of America's unknown revolution has redefined modern democracy in associative terms. Theirs was a disparate struggle, isolated and disconnected in terms of mobilisation. But there was a shared idealism committed to the potential of associative democracy. It was, crucially, to influence more radical expressions of civil society that were to emerge as social movements in modern society. Furthermore, the divergence between representative democracy and associative democracy was to highlight a dichotomy between 'thin' democracy and 'thick' or 'strong' democracy.

Liberty, equality and civil society

The United States became the archetypal liberal society. Its identity and institutions were founded on classical liberal principles, what we call today neoliberalism. In many respects, this philosophy viewed human welfare as a private virtue to be pursued by the individual through self-help. Heywood (2003, pp 47–8) argues that classical liberalism rests on four core principles:

- egoistical individualism: human beings are naturally self-interested, with a pronounced enthusiasm for self-reliance tempered by charitable giving and a culture of philanthropy;

- negative freedom: human beings should be free to do what they want without state coercion;
- minimalist state: the state is a 'necessary evil' that imposes a collective will in society, constraining human freedom;
- civil society: in contrast to the state as the realm of coercion, civil society represents the 'realm of freedom; bringing balance and equilibrium to the body politic'.

These classical liberal principles equated with virtue in the minds of the Founding Fathers of the United States, albeit virtue etched in the pursuit of fortune. They were rich and powerful men who believed they were creating a utopia based on the unlimited natural resources of America. In many respects, their optimism was well placed. America was to grow into the wealthiest nation in the world. It was to forge a specifically Anglo-Saxon model of development, emulated across the English-speaking world and admired across the planet. It stood out in sharp contrast to Europe, which was to be shaped by the French Revolution of 1789.

Both the American and French revolutions were products of the 18th-century Enlightenment. However, they offered quite different interpretations of its meaning. For Americans (at least, those within the ruling orders), liberty defined virtue. On the other hand, Europeans became preoccupied with the pursuit of equality as the defining virtue of the good society. Europe was emerging from a highly stratified feudal social order. The belief that it was possible fundamentally to transform the ancien régime into a new democratic order only by revolutionary action was the motor driving European history. Social policy emerged as an instrument of an egalitarian will that slowly forged the welfare state. Even Americans were not entirely immune. The new political economy was taking shape.

Civil society: the right to associate

European notions of civil society devolved on the right to associate. Europeans' view of what that right meant went far beyond Alexis De Tocqueville's bucolic picture of Americans associating in a utopian world, where communitarianism flourished (De Tocqueville, 1956). For Europeans, the right to associate encompassed political, economic and social rights. In other words, association envisaged a robust democracy based on conflict, in marked contrast to the American consensus. European civil society grew out of clandestine Masonic lodges that sought to promote progressive political change, notably in France and

Germany (Archambault, 1997, p 52; Anheier and Seibel, 2001, p 36). Freemasonry emerged as the first substantive expression of this right to associate, building on medieval roots in guilds and brotherhoods.

This was not a uniquely European phenomenon. The radical influence of freemasonry was also evident in colonial societies, such as Brazil, where Masonic lodges became heavily identified with radical movements dedicated to revolutionary change (Landim, 1997, p 326). But the right to associate was not limited simply to the cultural and political concerns of elites. It also embraced the economic sphere, where workers sought to establish friendly societies, mutual associations, trade unions, working-class political parties, cooperatives and workers' educational associations (Archambault, 1997, pp 17–52; Anheier and Seibel, 2001, pp 30–52; Deakin, 2001, pp 152–5).

Pre-modern social policy was based on a combination of paternalistic charity and punishment offered in the name of religious virtue (Powell, 2010a, 2010b). The state was the enemy of the poor, whom it sought to coerce with cruel stratagems. Equality changed all that. During the 18th century people in Europe and America came to believe that they could transform their world by transforming the state. In Europe, that meant a secular, republican and socialist future based on the pursuit of equality for all people. Equality entailed greater social justice. At a practical level, people were politically redefined as citizens, with the entitlement to legal, political and eventually social rights. But there was also, at a deeper level, a sense that the world was being transformed and a moral community constructed, where life would be better. The ideals of human progress and social equality became intertwined in the popular mind. It was an irresistible force for change that was to transform political economy, sweep away the Dickensian world of poverty and build a new citadel – the welfare state.

The French Revolution, social policy and civil society

The 1789 French Revolution marked a great rupture in European social policy. It not only ushered in the era of modern democracy, it changed the course of social policy. Archambault (1997, p 29) comments from a French perspective:

> This period is truly a break in the development of the nonprofit sector. A drastic redistribution of respective responsibility in the private and public spheres, as far as social issues are concerned, took place. The most impressive work in this field was done by the Comité de Mendicité,

who considered it necessary to eradicate mendicity, which
had been punishable since the seventeenth century. Some
very important principles were set out by this committee.
'The extreme poverty is the fault of government', therefore
'public assistance to the poor is a sacred duty. Society owes
poor citizens a support and must either give them work or
if they are unable to work, secure them a livelihood'.

The revolutionary tradition in France meant that social policy was
not polarised around status and class, as it was in 19th-century Britain.
There was no pauper class. Both jurisdictions centralised poor relief:
one to promote punishment (Britain) the other to increase social
solidarity (France). Ashford (1986, p 155) comments: 'The French
centralized to achieve republican goals', adding that 'the debate over
the bureaux de bienfaisance and the bureaux d'assistance publique
makes this unmistakable'. Less than a year after the introduction of
public assistance in France in 1905, for the aged and disabled, 644,000
people were in receipt of state aid, with over 106 million francs being
paid out in benefits. Furthermore, by 1912, over a million citizens
were benefactors of the free hospital care (first introduced in 1893),
and following the introduction of a statutory pension scheme in 1910,
there were 103,000 pensioners. The local commune had a crucial
role in the administration of welfare, albeit that there were concerns
about the influence of the Catholic Church and 'outmoded forms of
charity', as well as the conservative influence of the peasantry, who
were instinctively hostile to state welfare. At a national level, aristocrats
protested but were usually dismissed as lacking in credibility. Ashford
(1986, p 137) notes in this regard: 'Maurice Sibille, the defender of
Catholic privileges and charity, objected to the basic formula, still
roughly adhered to in modern French aide sociale, of dividing costs
with about a fifth paid by communes, and two fifths by the departments
and the state respectively'. Conservative voices were seeking to defend
traditional forms of charity, based on paternalistic and egoistic traditions
of giving, whereas the post-revolutionary republican tradition had
redefined welfare as a right of the citizen and an obligation for the
state. On the other hand *sociétés de secours mutuelles* sought to harness
the mutualistic French tradition of social organisation (Palier, 2010,
p 35). This was a seismic shift.

Another seismic policy shift was taking shape in France in the form
of factory legislation. Émile Zola, in his novel *Germinal* (1885) (Zola,
1986), using social research undertaken 20 years before, exposed the
exploitative work environment that prevailed in French mines and

factories. This novel ignited public consciousness regarding the excesses of a burgeoning capitalist economy and the need to protect wage labour. Factory legislation existed on the French statute books from the 1840s. However, it was not until 1900 that sufficient resources, in terms of factory inspectors with adequate powers, were made available (Joll, 1976, p 27). Social and industrial legislation were forging a new sphere of public responsibility in France.

German civil society, the emergence of a public sphere

The conception of the public sphere in Germany was also undergoing redefinition. Hegel's ideas of the fundamental role of civil society were influential. So was the impact of the French Revolution. Anheier and Seibel (2001, p 33) conclude that 'the French Revolution of 1789 solidified the risk of attack from serfs and the poor on the one side and the increasingly powerful bourgeoisie on the other'. Germany was an uncompromisingly aristocratic political order backed by military power. But even in Germany the impact of the French Revolution forced some political movement. In 1794 the Prussian General Code was promulgated. It introduced formal legal equality and legalised 'private societies' (associations), provided that they served the 'general good' and did not pose a threat to the political order (Anheier and Seibel, 2001, p 34). The emergence of *hilfskassen* (friendly societies) provided not only protection against 'social risks' but also fora for political discussion (Palier, 2010, p 35).

Napoleon's defeat in 1815 was interpreted by the German aristocracy as the end of the *Franzosenzeit* (time of the French). In this regard they were wrong. The democratic spirit unleashed by the French Revolution of 1789 could not easily be suppressed. Young German soldiers who had fought against the French were influenced by their ideas and began to form associations with explicitly political agendas. The Karlsbad Decrees in 1819 responded by suppressing student associations, dismissing liberal-minded university professors, curbing free speech, censoring the press and establishing a central state intelligence service. The consequences of these anti-democratic political measures for German social and political development were disastrous. Civil society was forced underground and marginalised. Anheier and Seibel (2001, p 39) conclude:

> The period between 1819 and 1848 was decisive for the future development of associational life in Germany as

well as for the style of the country's political culture and discourse. The bourgeoisie's strong will to engage in the running of the nation's political affairs was harshly rejected by the aristocratic regime. For almost a hundred years after the Karlsbad Decrees, the great majority of the German bourgeoisie remained excluded from full participation and involvement in national politics. As a result, little political learning took place, and the bourgeoisie could not develop a sense of political burden-sharing and responsibility. This resulted in a widening gap between ambitions and achievement for the bourgeois involvement in public affairs.

The 1848 revolutions that swept across Europe failed to dislodge the grip of the German aristocracy on power. But the seeds of change had been sown in civil society. During the 1850s, civil society flourished in Germany. It was a process that produced several important outcomes. Political parties, liberal and socialist, found their feet in the associational life of civil society. At local level, civil society became an instrument for participation in governance through social engagement. It was based on public–private partnership principles and became 'the ideal-type of government–nonprofit relationship in Germany' (Anheier and Seibel, 2001, p 46). This meant that a welfare model was being shaped in Germany that was to involve a shared responsibility between the state and civil society for the poor. This process was augmented by German unification in 1871. Furthermore, it allowed Germany to begin the process of modernisation, providing a social structure within a rapidly growing urban industrial society (Anheier and Seibel, 2001, p 44).

The idea of an interventionist state determining the citizens' best interests was deeply embedded in German culture, notably in the Prussian tradition of paternalism. The German Chancellor, Otto von Bismarck (1815–98), observed in this regard: 'that the state should concern itself with those of its citizens who need help to a greater degree than hitherto, is not just a duty of humanity and Christianity, which should inspire all the institutions of the state, but also a conservative policy which has as its goal to encourage the view among the unpropertied classes of the population … that the state is not only a necessary institution but also a beneficent one' (cited in Joll, 1976, pp 27–8). The establishment in 1872 of the German Association of Social Policy (Verein für Sozialpolitik) proved instrumental in promoting public consciousness of the need for social reform. These German social scientists exposed the inadequacies of the social order in responding to the challenges of social change that arose from industrialisation and urbanisation.

Russia, modernisation and civil society

In Russia, an even more obdurate aristocracy existed. Change was occasionally attempted, for example, through the *zemstovs* in the 1860s that facilitated limited provision of healthcare and education. The overwhelmingly rural population was granted limited land reforms after the 1905 revolution, which mainly benefited the better-off kulak class of large peasant proprietors with significant land holdings. For the growing urban industrial class, there were limited social initiatives, including the restriction of working hours (1897), protection against industrial accidents (1903) and two laws limited to a small section of urban workers in larger industries that provided accident and sickness insurance (Thane, 1982, p 120). The resulting discontent was to prove fertile ground for Bolshevik organisation in the cities, which was ultimately to lead to the successful revolution in 1917.

In the final years of the tsarist regime, the government had forced employers to introduce sickness insurance organisations (kassy) operated by joint boards of management, including elected workers' representatives. State enterprises (including railways and steel plants in the Urals) had their own system of hospitals, clinics and midwife stations providing healthcare for 2.5 million workers and their dependants. The 1912 legislation resulted in a sharp rise in the number of kassy in St Petersburg and Moscow. While revolutionary activists sought to penetrate the boards of management of the kassy, they remained remarkably depoliticised, despite internal tensions between management and workers (Andrle, 1994, pp 116–17).

Civil society became a source of intense political rivalry between the regime and its opponents. The term *obschestvo* came to denote civil society or 'social public' in Russia. It was largely the preserve of the heavily radicalised intelligentsia. After the 1905 revolution, Peter Stolypin was appointed in 1906 to the new office of Prime Minister, until his assassination in 1911. He introduced an ambitious modernisation programme that included the replacement of feudal ownership of agricultural land in the countryside (where most Russians lived) by individual private ownership. Andrle (1994, p 7) notes that 'the novelty of Stolypin's reforms was their intention to create for the state a new and large social base by turning the peasantry into a class of private property owners and entrepreneurs, whose interests the state would make its business to uphold'. He argues that 'for the first time in the history of the Russian state, the government's legitimacy would consist not of a conceptual opposition between state interest and self-interest but a fusion of the state interest with the interests of a large property-owning class' (Andrle, 1994, p 7). Andrle concludes: 'Stolypin wanted to create a stable "civil society" for the Tsarist state' (Andrle, 1994, p 7).

The pre-modern fusion between the tsarist state and the dominant rural economy was in sharp contrast to developments in Western Europe. It resulted in a historic collision with modern Russia, led by the cities. The radical intelligentsia in urban Russia was irrevocably committed to modernisation along Western lines. It dominated social and political activism in the cities. But there were more primordial struggles at play in Russia. Underneath the level of political contestation was a deeper struggle for the soul of Russia. The westernisers (with their roots in the Enlightenment) and the Slavophiles, who sought to defend the Russian soul against what they perceived to be the individualistic materialism of Western modernisation, held diametrically opposed views of the future. The Russian Revolution in 1917 ended the debate and absorbed civil society within a totalitarian state apparatus.

Socialism and welfare: a Faustian bargain or utopian ideal?

Marxism envisaged revolution in the French Jacobin tradition. It invented the working class as a 'new political subject'. Abruptly, the teeming masses of urban poor were turned into the instrument of revolutionary change. *The Communist Manifesto* (Marx and Engels, 1967) became a clarion call of the revolutionary socialist movement. It contained a comprehensive vision and messianic belief in a better future. Sassoon (1996, p 7) asserts:

> By thinking of the working-class as a political class, ascribing to it a specific politics and rejecting the vaguer of categories ('the poor') of earlier reformers the pioneers of socialism thus virtually 'invented' the working-class. Those who define create. 'Democratic' politics, that is, modern mass politics, is a battlefield in which the most important move is that which decides what the battle is about, what the issue is.

What was distinctive about what Marx called 'scientific' socialism was its modern message. The socialist movement had a clear idea about the future. It was to be egalitarian. Social justice was the goal. The state was to be the instrument. It would bring the private sphere (capital) under the control of the public sphere (society). That was the theory.

But soon theory and action began to come into conflict. For Lenin, from autocratic tsarist Russia, the answer to the question 'what is to be done?', which he posed in 1902, was simple. The tsarist state must be overthrown and replaced by the 'dictatorship of the proletariat'. In reality, this meant dictatorship of the Communist Party based on the Jacobin revolutionary tradition, which was to unleash the monstrous terror of Stalinism. The 'Jacobin–Bolshevik model' has been described by Timothy Garton Ash as 'storming the Bastille or the Winter Palace; executing the king or the Tsar; a festival of popular liberation turning to terror, as the revolution devours its children' (*Guardian*, 1 September 2005). The violent model of change did not recommend itself to many Western socialists, who viewed democracy as the road to social justice based on equal citizenship. Social democracy was born. The mass working-class political party in tandem with trade unions was its voice. Russia was to follow its own path to violent revolution alone.

Germany became the fulcrum of the socialist debate about strategy between the Marxists and social democrats – between revolution and reform. Despite their endless rhetorical victories, Western European Marxists were constantly outmanoeuvred by the gradualist reforming politics of the social democrats. They offered a practical view of socialism that their impoverished working-class political subject could grasp. On the economic front, it meant the right to associate, to strike and to bargain for better wages and conditions. On the social front, it represented the pursuit of the social state based on progressive taxation, pensions for the old, insurance against unemployment and ill health, care of the sick, free education (including school meals) and a right to shelter in the form of social housing. These were the ingredients of the political manifestos of social democratic parties in Western Europe that enabled them to emerge as the collective voice of the working class. The birth of modern democracy and the rise of the mass working-class party are synonymous. What Marxists would view as a Faustian bargain was struck with capital. In reality, the deal struck between labour and capital was essentially based upon a utopian vision of the future, where classes could set aside their differences and peacefully agree the basis of a more socially just and egalitarian future. This was the model of democracy on offer, which was based on the belief that traditional elites could share power with the representatives of the organised working class in the interests of peaceful coexistence. It was a brave and noble ambition, but a profoundly utopian one – social democracy.

While Western Europe was the theatre where this project was formed, it soon percolated outwards to other parts of the developed world. New Zealand was an early and enthusiastic convert. Australia followed. Americans proved to be reluctant collectivists, eschewing socialism and only grudgingly granting welfare rights. Canada proved to be more fertile territory for welfare legislation. In South America's Southern Cone (Argentina, Uruguay and Chile), where European cultural influences are strongest because of the near elimination of the indigenous population, the idea of socialism also proved influential. Kirby (2003, p 24) asserts that Uruguay became the world's first welfare state. The legacy of the liberator of Latin America, Simon Bolivar (1783–1830), was to inspire a radical political legacy that has continued to the present day in the form of the 'new Bolivarianism'.

Socialising the state: welfare and social reform

German social reform led the way. In the 1877 election to the Reichstag, the new national parliament, the Social Democratic Party (SPD) won 9.1% of the vote – the same proportion as the conservatives. The Kaisereich was shaken to its foundations. It responded characteristically to this expression of democracy, with repression. In 1878 all forms of socialist activity were banned. Over the ensuing 12 years the anti-socialist legislation closed 332 social democratic associations. Repression proved to be a binding influence on the socialist movement in Germany. In adversity, socialists found unity. The Kaisereich capitulated. In the interests of national integration, the Bismarckian reforms were promulgated by Kaiser Wilhelm I in 1881. There followed a raft of social legislation, including:

- general health insurance (1883)
- occupational accident insurance (1884)
- a general pension scheme (1889).

These Bismarckian reforms have been described as a 'revolution from above' (Anheier and Seibel, 2001, pp 47–8). They proved to be the template for many other developed Western societies that sought to temporise with the ambitions of the rising socialist movement. Socialists opposed these welfare measures as an attempt to buy off the workers in a Faustian bargain (Thane, 1982, p 108). The Bismarckian welfare state rested on a political paradox. It was a conservative response to radical civil society's demands for social justice.

Other European nations followed Germany's example. In France, Archambault (1997, p 35) notes that the Third Republic discovered the virtue of solidarity, summed up by the slogan 'Everyone is indebted to his neighbour'. The sociologist Émile Durkheim (1858–1917) provided the intellectual inspiration for French social policy, based on the principles of solidarity and mutualism that during the 20th century became the cornerstones for the French welfare state. The utopian socialist legacy is clearly discernible. The socialists were split on the issue of social reform. The Marxists, led by Jules Guesde, abstained, 27 socialist deputies voted against and 5, led by the reformist socialist Jean Jaurès, a veteran Dreyfusard, voted for a series of welfare measures in the early 20th century. French socialism was disorganised and heavily fractionalised between utopian socialists, reformists, technocrats and insurrectionists (Sassoon, 1996, p 13). Consequently, social reform and welfare legislation developed more slowly in France, relative to Germany and Britain.

But by the outbreak of the First World War in 1914, considerable progress had been made in some areas of French social policy (as noted above). Democracy and war were key influences in propelling France along the road to improving child welfare. France had the slowest rate of population growth in Europe during the second half of the 19th century. Infant mortality rates were disturbingly high. France's military defeat by Germany in 1871 reminded the country of its vulnerability in terms of manpower to serve in times of war. By the beginning of the 20th century, France had developed an extensive system of child welfare clinics and free or subsidised milk supplies that was well ahead of the rest of the world. France led the world in its child-centred legislation, introducing laws regulating the exploitation of child labour as early as 1840, on compulsory education in 1882, on child protection in 1889 and on child courts and reformatory institutions in 1912. These measures were highly effective in reducing child mortality rates (Thane, 1982, p 119).

In the United Kingdom, radical civil society in the form of the Fabians' trade union and cooperative societies led to the electoral emergence of the Labour Party in 1906. It was to prove a watershed in British politics. An embattled Liberal government, elected on a landslide in the 1906 general election, introduced a series of social measures in parliament. These 'Liberal Reforms' included:

- 1906 and 1914 Education (Provision of School Meals) Acts
- 1906 Workmen's Compensation (Extension) Act
- 1907 and 1915 Notification of Births Acts

- 1907 Probation Act
- 1907 Matrimonial Causes Act
- 1908 Old Age Pension Act
- 1908 Small holdings and Allotments Acts
- 1908 Children Act
- 1909 Housing and Town Planning Act
- 1911 National Insurance Act.

The key elements in this impressive body of legislation were the introduction of statutory pensions and a system of national insurance. In 1909 the People's Budget introduced progressive taxation as a means of redistributing wealth between the rich and poor. While national insurance largely benefited white-collar male urban workers, pensions were open to all. There were four applications in Ireland, for every one in England, causing a torrent of racist indignation in the popular press. When the 1911 Census was published in 1917 it became clear that the reason was Ireland's skewed demographic structure, which had been produced by mass emigration. But the popular myth of the 'welfare scrounger' had been born (Powell, 1992, p 139).

The first wave of reforming legislation in New Zealand and Australia came with the Lib-Lab governments elected in the 1890s. Thane (1982, p 113) observes that 'although socialist and labour movements everywhere tended to be suspicious of public welfare provided by bourgeoisie and aristocratic parties, once in power they were prepared to promote welfare measures'. However, Australians remained highly dependent on self-help and savings. This delayed the introduction of statutory pensions and a national insurance system, widely discussed in Australia before the outbreak of the 1914–18 war.

In Canada and the United States, the impetus towards social legislation is also detectable. While North American elites did not experience the pressure of the rising socialist movement in the manner of their European counterparts, they were sensitive to the reality that the world was changing. Public expectation of government's becoming involved in regulating both the economy and society was growing. Civil society became the arena in which legislative reform was shaped. Jane Addams (1860–1935) became the embodiment of this flourishing civil society committed to social reform. Awarded the Nobel Peace Prize in 1931, Addams founded America's most famous settlement – Hull House in Chicago. It was modelled on London's Toynbee Hall. She tirelessly worked to promote social justice in housing, factory inspection and the treatment of immigrants, African Americans and women and children. She was elected the first woman President of the National Conference of Social Work in 1910. Jane Addams also served as President of the Women's International League for Peace and Freedom. Her most lasting legacy was the promotion of the social sphere as an integral part of the governance of the United Sates. The New Deal was to embody many of the ideals that had informed her lifelong struggle for social justice. Civil society was reshaping the American state by realigning the domestic and civil spheres.

The fusion of civil society and state

What we can conclude from this survey of initial attempts at social legislation that eventually led to the welfare state in industrial societies is that it was a humanitarian affair created in civil society. Some critics see it as too top-down change. As Novak (1988, p 125) puts it:

> Social reform is the product of class struggle; but it does not
> mean that social reforms reflect working-class demands. On
> the contrary, while working-class pressure has been decisive
> in determining the timing and scale of reform, the content
> and the control of social reform has often been determined
> within the ruling class. Social reform has more often served
> to undermine working-class politicization and pressure
> than to reflect it.

Novak's conclusion is a classic Marxist judgement on the value of the welfare state. It is undoubtedly true that ruling elites were terrified at the prospect of a socialist revolution. The Paris Commune in 1871, which evinced many political tendencies (for example, Blanquist, anarchist and Marxist), unnerved the bourgeoisie and aristocracy of Europe. They were ready to make concessions. However, it is pushing political paradox to the extreme to argue that this raft of social legislation was not in the objective interests of the working class. In Marxist epistemological terms, it began the process of 'decommodification', empowering working-class people to move beyond the status of commodities to be bought and sold on the labour market and into the status of full (if passive) citizenship in a new democratic political order. The world had shifted on its axis. Only orthodox Marxists failed to see it. For them, nothing but revolution would do. Social justice achieved through social reform that harnessed the democratic process amounted to political betrayal.

Marxism's failure to grasp the importance of civil society as a force for social justice in a democratic society was to prove a major blind spot leading to tyrannical regimes modelled on Stalinist Russia that professed to oppress in the name of social justice. Only the Italian Marxist Antonio Gramsci grasped the potential of civil society. Gramsci understood that a Russian-style seizure of power was not an option for socialists in the West. He believed that a strong civil society in the West protected the state from revolution based on the Jacobin-Bolshevik model that had dismally failed. Democracy and civil society had developed into barriers against violent social change. Power could not simply be seized at the top. The welfare state was creating a new democratic civility.

Gramsci addresses the socialist dilemma of choosing between 'reform or revolution' by going beyond it in a penetrating analysis of the nature of power. Drawing on military metaphors, Gramsci (1971, p 235) argues that 'among the more industrially and socially advanced states, the war of manoeuvre must be considered as reduced to more of a tactical than a strategic function; that it must be considered as occupying the same position as siege warfare used to occupy previously in relation to it'. He adds: 'The same reduction must take place in the art and science of politics, at least in the case of the most advanced states, where "civil society" had become a very complex structure and one which is resistant to the catastrophic "incursions" of the immediate economic element' (Gramsci, 1971, p 235).

Gramsci (1971, p 238) concluded in relation to the relevance of the Russian Revolution in 1917 that it was the product of a backward civil society that was without relevance for the West:

> In the East the state was everything, civil society was primordial and gelatinous; in the West there was a proper relation between the state and civil society, and when the state trembled a sturdy structure of civil society was at once revealed. The state was only an outer ditch, behind which there stood a powerful system of fortresses and earthworks; more or less numerous from one State to the next, it goes without saying – but this precisely necessitated an accurate reconnaissance of each individual country.

Gramsci had dilated the concept of 'political' so that it encompassed the entire public sphere. The Jacobin-Bolshevik belief that revolution could be secured by storming the citadel of power was redundant. It was impossible to alter the balance of power relations without persuading civil society. Sassoon (1996, p 78) observes:

Throughout civil society everyone has roles and functions, the crucial ones being held by a veritable army of intermediaries whose tasks it is to organize work, culture, religion and leisure (Gramsci called these – misleadingly – the 'intellectuals'). The ideological capture of this group is central to the conquest of power. No complex social system can survive or be constructed without them. They are the educators, the journalists, the clergy, the communicators, the artists, the advertisers, the disseminators of popular culture, the technical cadres, etc. In other words, all those who translate, modify and adapt and, therefore, constantly alter the dominant and accepted ideas of the existing order so that they can be understood, internalized and accepted by all. In this way, what is historically determined and hence transient appears just, natural and eternal. These intellectual 'functionaries' define what is normal and hence what is 'deviant'; they distinguish the acceptable from the unacceptable in all areas, including production and work, everyday life and the assumption of what is 'common sense'. And as everyone is, at least some of the time, an 'educator' or 'organizer' in this Gramscian sense, everyone is, some of the time, an 'intellectual'. Reciprocal socialization is the business of all humans.

Inherent in Gramsci's argument is the recognition that social change must be negotiated democratically. A virtuous society can be achieved only if deeply embedded in the body politic through a process of citizen participation. Social legislation is the product of enlightened compromise based on the aspiration for democratic progress.

Gramsci's ideas were later developed by Norberto Bobbio (1987, 1996). Bobbio presented civil society as the means to generate a framework for radical democracy. Going beyond the reform–revolution dualism, Bobbio argues that significant aspects of power, including the military, the bureaucracy and multinational corporations, are not subject to democratic control. These are democracy's broken promises. Bobbio sets out to establish procedural minima for democracy, including the value of toleration, non-violence in conflict resolution, enhanced social solidarity and the promotion of radical cultural learning experiences. At the core of his argument is the belief in democratising democracy on three levels: the exploration of direct democracy; the importance of alternative forms of representation; and the opportunity of expanding the space of democracy from the state to civil society (Cohen and Arato,

1994, p 167). These radical democratic ideas are similarly advocated by French political theorists Ernesto Laclau and Chantal Mouffe.

Marxists were not the only critics of social democracy. A penetrating critique emerged on the right of the political spectrum. Carl Schmitt (1888–1985) has been variously described as 'the Hobbes of our age' and as 'the philosophical godfather of Nazism'. These damning criticisms have obscured the contribution of Schmitt's role as a political theorist. His apologists have sought to rehabilitate his personal reputation, arguing that he has been politically misunderstood. But there is no doubt that Schmitt joined the Nazi Party in 1933, co-authored part of Hitler's early legislation 'synchronising' the states and rose to the post of Prussian State Councillor under the Third Reich. Holmes (1993, p 38) observes that 'his unsavory career between 1933 and 1936 is without doubt the main obstacle confronting his rehabilitators'. Schmitt's anti-liberalism – evident in his two most influential publications before he became a Nazi, *The Crisis of Parliamentary Democracy* (1988 [1923]) and *The Concept of the Political* (1996[1932]) – provided the intellectual foundations for his political support of the Third Reich. Tracy B. Strong (1996, p xii), in a foreword to a recent edition of *The Concept of the Political*, states that 'by virtue of the range of those to whom he appeals and the depth of his political allegiance during the Nazi era, Schmitt comes close these days to being the Martin Heidegger of political theory'. True. But Schmitt also had a profound intellectual impact on the political Left, no doubt drawn to his powerful critique of political liberalism, embodied in the weak Weimar Republic that struggled to govern Germany democratically between 1918 and 1933. Strong (1996, pp x–xi) notes Schmitt's influence over the political Left in Germany, France and Italy.

Heinrich Meier (1995), who explored the intellectual relationships between Carl Schmitt and Leo Strauss, sees the former as a 'political theologian', driven by religious revelation. However, the real source of Schmitt's political inspiration was undoubtedly the English philosopher Thomas Hobbes (1585–1679), who believed that humanity was unable to distinguish between 'good and evil'. According to Hobbes, humanity exists in a pre-social state of nature, in which life is '... nasty, brutish, and short', characterised by constant war of every person against every person. Hobbes' *Leviathan* (1651) became his philosophical testament to the world, condemning humanity to an authoritarian future. His dismal dismissal of the project of humanism was to shape Schmitt's two concepts of enmity that divided the world into 'friends' and 'enemies'. It fed the paranoid German right-wing belief that the Versailles Settlement of 1918 was a betrayal of Germany and the liberal Weimar Republic its bastard offspring.

In *The Concept of the Political*, Schmitt targeted the Weimar Republic, advancing a fusion theory of the *Sozialstaat* (social state). He argues that a fusion of the state and society had created a crisis of legitimacy:

> The equation state = politics becomes erroneous and deceptive at exactly the moment when state and society penetrate each other. What had been up to that point affairs of state become thereby social matters, and, vice versa, what had been purely social matters become affairs of the state – as must necessarily occur in a democratically organized unit. Heretofore ostensibly neutral domains – religion, culture, education, the economy – then cease to be neutral in the sense that they do not pertain to state and to politics. As a polemical concept against such neutralizations and depoliticizations of important domains appears the total state, which potentially embraces every domain. This results in the identity of state and society. In such a state, therefore, everything is at least potentially political, and in referring to the state it is no longer possible to assert for it a specifically political characteristic. (Schmitt, 1996, p 22)

Liberalism, in Schmitt's view, had been sacrificed on the altar of social democracy. It is notable that Schmitt viewed 'social democratisation' rather than state interventionism as the root cause of this crisis. The social democratic Weimar Republic was anathema to Schmitt. He argued paradoxically that the association that democracy creates between the state and society produces a totalising political system born out of weakness rather than strength, which is the antithesis of democracy: 'A pluralist theory is either the theory of state which arrives at the unity of state by a federation of social associations or a theory of the dissolution or rebuttal of state.... The state simply transforms itself into an association which competes with other associations; it becomes a society among other societies which exist within or outside the state' (Schmitt, 1996, p 44).

In Carl Schmitt's mind, social democracy and governance were mutually exclusive. He argued that President Hindenburg should establish a constitutional dictatorship under Article 48 of the Weimar Constitution to replace the fragmentation of pluralism with the force of order. These constitutional powers had already been invoked to put down Hitler's Beer Hall Putsch in Munich on 8–9 November 1923.

When Hindenburg appointed Hitler Chancellor in 1933, German democracy was at an end, but a racial welfare state emerged in the Nazi parody of 'Big Society' (see Chapter Five). Schmitt's critique of the purportedly totalitarian nature of social democracy was taken up during the post-war years by Fredrick von Hayek (1899–1992) and his American disciple Milton Freedman (1912–2006). It was to prove highly influential.

Conclusion

This chapter has charted modernism's quest for social justice. A titanic struggle took place between Marxists attempting to create a new subjectivity through the revolutionising of the working class, and anti-Marxists committed to social reform. The prospect of revolution drove the motor of history in the direction of a more collectivised society, where welfare began to emerge as a major political objective. The consequences were to change the nature of the state. As Carl Schmitt was to argue, a fusion began to take place between the state and society. In reality, the socialisation of the state was taking place. Social policy was emerging as the instrument of this transformation, providing content that turned the fusion into a dynamic reality. The foundations of the welfare state that was to become the archetypal political formation in the West were laid during this period. The politics of welfare is a modern utopian narrative of an attempt to create a more virtuous society. By socialising the state, democracy and civil society emerge as the generators of social change. But the more successful civil society proved at socialising the state, the more imperilled its own autonomy became. Inherent in the emerging welfare state was a fusion between state and society. The political transformation involved necessitated a reimagining of the state as a benevolent, all-encompassing institution. Could this armoury of violence simultaneously become the instrument for realising utopian dreams? Was progress inevitable? The answer proved to be 'no'. The first half of the 20th century witnessed the rise of totalitarianism, turning the state into a vast edifice of tyranny. Utopian ideals of human welfare were turned on their head in the new dystopian regimes that evolved into totalitarian societies based on fear. Democracy and civil society were eliminated. We must now turn to consideration of these matters, which highlight the fragility of civil society.

FIVE

Nietzsche's revenge: totalitarian big society

A doctrine is needed powerful enough to work as a breeding agent: strengthening the strong, paralyzing and destructive for the world-weary. The annihilation of the decaying races. Decay of Europe – the annihilation of slavish evaluations – dominion over the earth as a means of producing a higher type – The annihilation of the tartuffery called morality (Christianity as a hysterical kind of honesty in this: Augustine, Bunyan) – The annihilation of sufferage universal; i.e., The system through which the barest natures prescribe themselves as laws for the higher.

Friedrich Nietzsche, *The Will to Power* (1969, pp 458–9)

The legacy of Friedrich Nietzsche (1844–1900) is most often associated with the cult of violence and racial domination that convulsed Europe during the first half of the 20th century. A brilliant – if unstable – scholar, he held a chair in Greek at the University of Basle before turning to freelance writing, in a life characterised by a deep loathing of humanism as the secular expression of the Judaeo-Christian traditions. He despised democracy as a fool's errand. Nietzsche championed the strong and scorned the weak and vulnerable. His views resonated with those who opposed the cause of democracy and the pursuit of a more just and egalitarian world. In his conception, the philosopher was a 'stick of dynamite', an intellectual view that he championed in a series of books, including *Thus Spake Zarathustra* (1883–84) (Nietzsche, 1961), *The Genealogy of Morality* (1887) (Nietzsche 1994), *The Twilight of the Idols* (1889) (Nietzsche, 1968) and *The Will to Power* (1901) (Nietzsche, 1969). In these books, Nietzsche sought to detonate the humanistic basis of Western civilisation and advocate a return to barbarianism, as a strategy of cultural renewal. He added for good measure: 'Gott ist tot' (God is dead). Nietzsche was championing an 'end of civilisation' thesis, as his short poem *Ecce Homo* proclaimed: 'Insatiable as a flame, I burn and consume myself'.

Above all, Nietzsche detested the Jews. In one of his last pamphlets, *The Anti-Christ*, he declared that Jews 'have made mankind so thoroughly false that even to-day the Christian can feel anti-Jewish without realizing that he is himself *The Ultimate Jewish Consequence*' (cited in Lichtheim, 1974, p 86). Nietzsche cast a long shadow over the 20th century. Social Darwinism, anti-Semitism and the totalitarian state became the hallmarks of a world that had lost any idea of pursuing a virtuous life. These themes will form the core of this chapter, which will examine the corruption and destruction of civil society during a period when democracy was threatened by rampant totalitarianism and the scourge of racial politics. For a time, civilisation vanished, and with it, civil society. Yet, as Mishra (1977, p 10) has noted, 'the social and political significance ... of Nazi Germany has not featured to any great extent on the curriculum of social policy studies in Britain'. Götz Aly (2006), shockingly, argues that 'the Nazi welfare state' was built on the plunder of racial war, in which the German population was complicit in building a society that entirely abandoned the pursuit of civic virtue. This was the Nazi version of 'Big Society', in which civil society was totally subordinated to a totalitarian state.

The politics of totalitarianism

Totalitarianism is a product of modernity. The crises following the First World War created the conditions for the emergence of Fascist regimes, most notably in Germany, Italy and Vichy France. The totalitarian power exercised by these regimes was facilitated by modern technology, mass organisation and new technologies of communication. These regimes were distinguished from earlier absolutist states by their parody of democracy in staged plebiscites, the cult of leadership and such mythological notions as 'the master race'. In reality, they were one-party states, where the rule of law was subordinated to the power of the state, and ideology took place of freedom of thought and conscience. A notable characteristic of the totalitarian state, so brilliantly caricatured by George Orwell (1903–50) in his powerful political novel *Nineteen Eighty-four* (Orwell, 1949), is the subjugation of both private and public spheres to a 'new morality'. As noted in Chapter Four, Carl Schmitt had anticipated the fusion of state and society in his anti-liberal critique of the Weimar Republic. Totalitarianism envisaged a fusion not only of state and society but also of people and party, individual and collective, civil and political in a total unity. In this process, ideology becomes the means to justify or even glorify the violation and abolition of existing laws and morals in favour of higher goals of national, racist or social and class-oriented forms of community. For Orwell, this was the scientifically perfected servile state where even thought became a crime.

Adolf Hitler (1889–1945) was to emerge as the embodiment of the terrorist nature of Nietzschean philosophy. Nazi power was to prove both the antithesis and nemesis of civil society in Germany between 1933 and 1945. Anheier and Seibel (2001, p 65) remark that 'a comprehensive history of German voluntary associations during the holocaust remains to be written'. This may be true. But there is a body of historical literature addressing the social life of the Third Reich. Some historians have provided very detailed accounts of the quality of civil society in Nazi Germany. Nearly 50 years ago, William Shirer (1960) published his widely acclaimed and still influential book, *The Rise and Fall of the Third Reich*. Since then, there have been many publications that survey the terrors of Nazi domination and its serpentine grip on German social life. In 2000, Michael Burleigh produced *The Third Reich: A New History*. This superb account provides detailed evidence regarding voluntary associations and the abuse of civil society in Nazi Germany. In 2005, Richard J. Evans' book, *The Third Reich in Power*, added another important source of information.

William Sheridan Allen's *The Nazi Seizure of Power: The Experience of a Single German Town* (Allen, 1966) tells the story of the impact of the Nazi seizure of power (*Gleichschaltung*) in the context of the experience of a small German town. In microcosm, Allen's study shows how the Nazis subsumed associational life at local level into their vast system of power and propaganda. The possibility of opposition was simply erased. The dominance of the Third Reich over society was to become total in the plans of the Nazi leadership, right down to local clubs and societies in the smallest communities of Germany. It was not, however, simply a political project about the establishment of power to secure the regime. Power at every level was to become the instrument of a Nietzschean nightmare that was to engulf Germany and spread across Europe like a modern plague.

The French writer Albert Camus (1913–60) adopted plague as a metaphor for the Nazi occupation of France in his novel *La Peste* (*The Plague*), published in 1947 (Camus, 1960). In this work, Camus delivers a sermon in the form of a fable that tells the story of a city taken over by plague. Rats emerge as the main characters in the fable, which convincingly tells the story of an abstract destroyer that manages to depersonalise society as it consumes it with death and despair. As the plague subsides and the rats retreat, hope is restored to the city. But the moral in the tale is that the plague can return if society loses its virtue.

Totalitarian communitarianism and big society

The Third Reich, under the dictatorship of Adolf Hitler, became the embodiment of a Nietzschean ideological purification of German society through the destruction of the Weimar Republic. This it combined with *volkisch* populism to create a form of totalitarian communitarianism. Ian Kershaw (2008, p 133), in his monumental biography of Adolf Hitler observes:

> It was as a propagandist not as an ideologue with a unique or special set of political ideals that Hitler made his mark in these early years. There was nothing new, different, original or distinctive about the ideas he was peddling in the Munich beer halls. They were common currency among the various *Volkisch* groups and sects and had already been advanced in all their essentials by the pre-war pan-Germans. He voiced, and drew together, phobias, prejudice, and resentment as no one else could. What Hitler did was to advertise unoriginal ideas in an original way.

Hitler's speeches constantly intoned Germany's historic greatness and its current betrayal by the liberal Weimar Republic. The people's deliverance into the hands of Jews and communists and the nation's exploitation by Britain and France were all calculated themes to engender resentment and hatred. The publication of his *Mein Kampf* (Hitler 1938) during a spell in prison, following the abortive 1923 Munich Putsch, brought Hitler's thinking to a wider audience. *Mein Kampf* is part autobiography, part statement of *volkisch* philosophy, part political programme and part handbook for political action. Joll (1976, pp 332–3) notes that in *Mein Kampf* Hitler, apart from his paranoiac insistence on the Jewish danger, the international Jewish conspiracy and the Jewish infection of healthy Aryan society, outlined what his policy was to be – total control of education, sterilisation of the unfit and conversion of trade unions into organs for representing occupational interests, intended to increase the security of the national economy – in practice, this meant the end of the unions' role in negotiating better conditions for workers.

National Socialism becomes the defining political philosophy of the Nazi Party. Hitler spoke succinctly of the core of Nazi political philosophy: 'I had only to develop logically what social democracy failed in.... National Socialism is what Marxism might have been if it could have broken its absurd ties with a democratic order.... Why need we trouble to socialise banks and factories? We socialise human beings' (cited in Thomson, 1966, p 727).

Because National Socialism was in essence a deeply destructive philosophy bred on the political application of Nietzschean nihilism, it lacked the structure of social control that defined Stalinist Russia. In true Nietzschean style, violence became the defining paradigm of the Nazis' grip on power. As Davies (1997, p 975) put it, 'studied bestial ferocity had to compensate for structural weakness'. Germany was a 'fighting community' (Mason, 1997, p 7).

The idea of a 'national community' based on exclusionary ethnic politics emerged as essential to Nazi governance. Kershaw (2008, p 316) comments:

> Those who did not belong to the 'national community' – 'shirkers', 'spongers', 'parasites' and of course, those not deemed to be German at all, notably Jews – would be ruthlessly suppressed. But for the true 'comrades of the people' *Volksgenossen* – the term invented by the Nazis to replace 'citizen' (*Burger*) for those who did belong – the new society would be a genuine '*community*', where the rights of the individual were subordinated to the common good of the whole, and where duty preceded rights. Only on this basis could the German nation become strong again, recover its pride, cast aside the shackles unfairly imposed on it by its enemies in the Versailles Treaty. But only through the complete destruction of the hated, divisive democratic system could the 'national community' be accomplished at all.

The penetration of civil society became a vital structural instrument of Nazification in Germany. Anheier and Seibel (2001, p 67) comment:

> The breakthrough of Nazism was decisively facilitated by the Nazi Party's embeddedness in a rich set of quasi-associational satellite organizations that began to penetrate society. Associational life not only worked as a structural transmitter of Nazism in German Society, but failed to safeguard and support the legitimacy of the democratic state in general. The consolidation of the Nazi regime after 1933, and the acceptance of racism as an unquestioned pattern of discrimination, would have been unthinkable without the penetration of society by Nazi associations of all kinds.

> Nazi satellite organizations such as the NSV [Nazi People's
> Welfare Association] were explicitly in charge of enforcing
> racist principles. These associations and quasi-associations
> played a supportive role in the preparation of genocide in
> the context of mass deportations during the Holocaust.

Hitler's seizure of power as German Chancellor in January 1933 was to inaugurate a chapter of unparalleled violence in world history. But the self-styled *Führer* was, above all, leader of the German nation, which he reconstituted through a policy of totalitarian communitarianism. Within one month, civil liberties were abolished. Within two months, political opponents were in prison or exile. Within four months, Germany's trade unions were abolished (Kershaw, 2008, p 435). The Nazi victory was total. All political parties, except the Nazis, were banned (Anheier and Seibel, 2001, p 60).

Hitler appointed Bernard Rust, an *Obergruppenführer* in the SA (Nazi militia), as Nazi Reich Minister for Science, Education and Culture. A fanatical Nazi in his twenties, Rust had previously been dismissed from his teaching post in a Hanover school on grounds of mental instability. Rust was in charge of schools, universities and youth organisations, as well as German science. His anti-intellectualism was rampant. He boasted that in his previous capacity as Prussian minister for the same brief, he had succeeded in 'liquidating the school as an institution of intellectual acrobatics' (Shirer, 1960, p 309). Hitler's own views on education were consumed by an ambition to create a nation of Spartan warriors in the service of the Third Reich. He proclaimed that 'the whole education by a national state must aim primarily not at stuffing with more knowledge but by building bodies which are physically healthy to the core'. The total loyalty of the youth of the nation was regarded as essential by Hitler: 'When an opponent declares, I will not come over to your side, I calmly say, your child belongs to us already. What are you? You will pass on. Your descendants, however, now stand in the new camp. In a short time, they will know nothing else but this new community.' He added: 'This new Reich will give its youth to no one, but will itself take youth and give to youth its own education and its own upbringing' (cited in Shirer, 1960, pp 309–10). The family had been superseded by the state in the Nazi conception of governance (Ayçoberry, 1999).

The school curriculum was thoroughly Nazified, with *Mein Kampf* as its 'infallible pedagogical guiding star'. Teachers were given special training in National Socialist principles and racial dogma. All teachers (including university professors) were required to join the National

Socialist Teachers League. No male was permitted to teach unless he had previously served in the SA, the labour service or the Hitler Youth. Jews were banned from the teaching profession. Mason (1997, p 280) asserts: 'race thinking and racial policies in the wisest sense were to be the foundation, or goal, of a new social order on a national and continental scale'.

Germany's august universities were not exempt from this process of Nazification. The University of Berlin instituted 25 new courses in racial science. The application of racial mythology to history produced ludicrous results in the interests of ideological orthodoxy – German physics and German mathematics produced equally ludicrous results. Great scientists, including Einstein and Franck in physics, and Haber, Willstaetler and Warburg in chemistry, were dismissed or resigned. Einstein was denounced by fellow academics as an arch-villain. Professor Wilhelm Müller, in a book entitled *Jewry and Science*, perceived a world Zionist plot to undermine science and destroy civilisation. He attacked Einstein's theory of relativity as 'directed from beginning to end toward the goal of transforming the living – that is, the non-Jewish world of living essence, born from a mother earth and bound up with blood, and bewitching it into spectral abstraction in which only an unsubstantial diversity of geometric dimensions survives which produces all events out of the compulsion of its godless subjection to laws' (cited in Shirer, 1960, p 312). Ironically, between 1905 and 1931, 10 German Jews had been awarded Nobel Prizes for Science; such was the irrationalism of Nazi racial dogma.

The tentacles of Nazi ideological hegemony stretched into the cultural life of Germany, which had prospered under the liberal Weimar regime. On 10 May 1933, one of the most infamous events in modern history occurred: the mass burning of books on the Unter den Linden, opposite the University of Berlin, under the watchful eye of the Nazi Propaganda Minister, Dr Goebbels. The books burnt included works by some of the greatest German authors: Thomas and Heinrich Mann, Lion Feuchtwanger, Jakob Wassermann, Arnold and Stefan Zweig, Erica Maria Reinarque, Walther Rathenau, Albert Einstein, Alfred Kerr and Hugo Preuss. Non-German authors whose books were tossed into the flames, amid joyous celebrations, encompassed many of the greatest writers of modern times: Jack London, Upton Sinclair, Helen Keller, Margaret Sanger, H.G. Wells, Havelock Ellis, Arthur Schnitzler, Sigmund Freud, Émile Zola, Marcel Proust and André Gide. A student proclamation declared that any book was consigned to the flames 'which acts subversively on our future or strikes at the roots of German thought, the German home and the driving force of our people' (Shirer,

1960, p 301). This act of symbolic violence constituted a statement of total hegemony of the state over civil society.

The Reich Press Law of 4 October 1993 made journalism a 'public vocation'. Newspaper editors were ordered under Section 14 of the Press Law 'to keep out of the newspapers anything which in any manner is misleading to the public, mixes selfish aim with community aims, tends to weaken the strength of the German Reich, outwardly or inwardly, the common will of the German people, the defence of Germany, its culture and economy ... or offends the honour and dignity of Germany' (cited in Shirer, 1960, p 305). The media was totally politically and racially cleansed. Censorship was complete. Similarly, film and radio became instruments of propaganda in advancing Nazi ideological goals and the project of constructing a totalitarian communitarian society. Kershaw (2008, p 591) concludes that by the mid-1930s Hitler's 'mastery over all other power groups within the regime was by now well nigh complete, his position unassailable, his popularity intense'. The Nazification of charity provides an illuminating example of this process of totalitarian communitarianism in practice.

Nazi charity, national community and communicative power

Nazi charity sounds like an oxymoron. In reality, charity became a key instrument of totalitarian communitarianism. The Nazis simply co-opted civil society, replacing its ethical principles and turning it into an agency of communitarian totalitarianism. Burleigh (2000, p 219) observes:

> If faith and hope were integral to National Socialism, so too surprisingly enough, was charity. This ceased to be an uncomplicated reflection of human altruism, still less something individuals do discreetly for the good of their souls, or to reap tax exemptions and titles. Instead, it becomes a favoured means of mobilising communal sentimentality, that most underrated, but quintessential, characteristic of Nazi Germany.

Anheier and Seibel (2001, p 62) conclude that the Nazis' co-option of civil society enabled them 'to eventually conquer the state from below'. They view this process as a form of 'disruptive continuity'.

Characteristically, the Nazi incorporation of civil society was shrouded in the language of propaganda. Hitler, speaking at the opening of the Winter Aid campaign for the poor in 1935, spoke of the Nazis' 'socialism of deed', asserted:

> We hold that, by such visible demonstrations, we are continually stirring the conscience of our *Volk* and making each of you once more aware that you should perceive yourself as a national comrade, and that you should make sacrifices!...We want to show the whole world and our *Volk* that we Germans regard the 'community' not as a hollow phrase, but as something that for us really does entail an inner obligation. (Cited in Domarus, 1992, p 717)

Hitler further elaborated on his view of charity in relation to 'one-pot' Sundays, in which the population was encouraged to save on more elaborate meals every second Sunday during winter and donate the savings to the Winter Aid campaign. Hitler declared:

> Don't tell me, 'All right, but it's still a bother to do all the collecting'. You have never known hunger, otherwise you would know what a bother it is to be hungry....And if the other then says: 'But you know, all these stew Sundays – I would like to give something, but it's my stomach. I have stomach problems all the time anyway, I don't understand it. I'd give ten Pfennigs just the same'. No, dear friend, there is a reason behind everything we do. It is particularly useful for you, someone who does not understand, if in this way at least we can guide you back to your *Volk*, to the millions of your national comrades who would be happy if they only had that stew all winter long that you perhaps eat once a month. (Cited in Domarus, 1992, pp 716–17)

The emphasis on community and the importance of *Volk* solidarity was fundamental to Hitler's thinking regarding charity. But behind this philosophising was the reality of a totalitarian strategy to undermine and incorporate German charity into the apparatus of the Nazi regime. The Nazis needed to control civil society as an instrument of communicative power and a means to ensure that their hegemonic ideology was triumphant.

Like all aspects of Nazi political thinking, charity presented a propaganda opportunity. Goebbels had already grasped the importance of the Nazi People's Welfare Association (NSV) before the party came to power in 1933. Under the leadership of Eric Hilgenfeldt, the NSV soon established itself as an autonomous organisation independent of other Nazi civil society organisations, including Ley's German Labour Front, which supplanted free trade unions, Schirach's infamous Hitler Youth and Scholz-Klink's NS Frauenschaft (National Socialist Women's Association) (Burleigh, 2000, p 219).

The NSV soon emerged as a very aggressive player in the field of civil society, knocking out three of its seven 'rivals' at an early stage by absorbing the socialist welfare organisations, disbanding national councils, marginalising Jewish charitable organisations and dividing the resources of the Christian workers' welfare organisation with confessional charities (Burleigh, 2000, p 220). The two main confessional charitable organisations, as already noted in Chapter Three, were the Protestant Innere Mission and the Roman Catholic Caritas association. The other two big players were the German branch of the Red Cross and the German League for Voluntary Welfare.

Through what Burleigh (2000, p 220) describes as 'the black arts of co-ordination', the Nazis gradually subsumed German charitable organisations. Initially, Hilgenfeldt strengthened the NSV by absorbing smaller charities, such as self-help groups for the blind, deaf, dumb and distressed gentlefolk. This was followed by a forced amalgamation with the German League for Voluntary Welfare. The German Red Cross adapted by including Nazis in key positions and adopting the Hitler Salute and Nazi songs as part of its public face.

Charities were not atypical of civil society organisations in Germany. Kershaw (2008, p 435) notes that by mid-1934: 'Almost all organizations, institutions, professional and representative bodies, clubs and societies had long since rushed to align themselves with the war regime. "Tainted" refinements of pluralism and democracy were typically removed, nazified structures and mentality adopted. This process of "co-ordination" (Gleichschaltung) was for the most part undertaken voluntarily and with alacrity. The Christian churches were the exception to the process.'

This was not simply an evangelical question, albeit that the battle for the hearts and souls of the German people was fought. It was about power. The position with the confessional charities was resultantly complex in terms of 'coordination'. The Protestant Innere Mission more easily accommodated the Nazis than did its Roman Catholic counterpart. It had resented the domination of the Roman Catholic Zentrum Party over the social part of the national agenda during the Weimar Republic, in place of previous Protestant dominance during the Kaiserreich. Moreover, many conservative Christians disliked the state welfare policies of the Weimar Republic, which were dominated by social democratic politics based on secular humanist values. Protestants were not ethically opposed to eugenics. Anti-Semitism was deeply rooted in the German Protestant tradition. Their founder, Martin Luther, had been an ardent anti-Semite. He had wanted to rid Germany of Jews, advising that they should be deprived of 'all their cash and jewels and silver and gold', and furthermore 'that their synagogues or schools be set on fire, that their houses be broken up and destroyed … and that they be put or stabled like the gypsies … in misery and captivity as they incessantly lament and complain to God and us' (cited in Shirer, 1960, p 294). Protestants were, therefore, able to share common ground with the Nazis on key moral and social issues, although it is important to acknowledge that many smaller sects did not share this view. The Jehovah's Witnesses courageously resisted legal repression, with 10,000 imprisoned, of whom 950 died (Evans, 2005, pp 254–5). But the resistance of this sect was the exception. In reality, most Protestants were oblivious to the moral and theological issues at stake.

The Nazis were quick to seize the propaganda advantage in Nazifying religion from below. For example, Pastor Martin Niemöller, a staunch Nazi supporter, described in his autobiography titled *From U-boat to Pulpit* (1937) his conversion to the cause. Pastor Niemöller was picked out for public praise as a model of Christian virtue in the Third Reich. The use of the German Christian movement became a strategic step in the goal of Nazifying Protestantism with 3,000,000 members. A new Reich church was recognised by the Reichstag on 14 July 1933. 'German Christians' supported a policy of 'one people, one Reich, one faith'. The Nazis produced a 30-point programme for a 'national Reich Church', which included several defining principles that sought to politicise religion.

However, it would be quite wrong to link Protestantism with Nazism. Most Protestants were detached from the fanatical German Christian movement 'designed to revive religion through intense engagement with *volkisch* politics, creating a people's church as a community of care and blood' (Burleigh, 2000, p 257). The pseudo-religious cult was of little interest to the majority of Protestants. This was a source of great frustration to the Nazis, who sought to dominate the minds of the population and turn their attention away from Christianity with its Judaic roots, supposed effeminacy, other-worldliness and life-affirming values. Hitler betrayed this frustration when he expressed his contempt towards Germany's Protestants (who composed two-thirds of the population) in a telling comment: 'You can do anything with them. They will submit…. They are insignificant little people, submissive as dogs, and they sweat with embarrassment when you talk to them' (cited in Shirer, 1960, p 296).

But in reality, the Nazis viewed Christianity as a major threat. Burleigh (2000, p 256) concludes that, in Nazi thinking, 'Christianity was "foreign" and "unnatural", or what has been described as the Jews' "posthumous poison", a notion the Nazis picked up from Nietzsche. Viewed pseudo-historically, it was an eastern Mediterranean "servant ethic" imposed upon the credulous ancient Germans by force and subterfuge. Christianity had obliterated their values and traditions, sapping their "racial" vitality.'

Some Protestant clergy heroically resisted the Nazis. Ironically, a disillusioned pastor, Niemöller, was to become the leader of the minority resistance among the Protestant clergy. He was arrested in 1937, tried and sent to Dachau Concentration Camp, where he spent seven years until his liberation by Allied troops. The theologian Dietrich Bonhoeffer became the symbol of moral resistance to the Nazis. During 1937 an estimated 807 Protestant clergy were arrested, and in the ensuing years many more arrests occurred. But the majority of Protestant pastors, in common with the rest of the German population, submitted to Nazi terror. In 1938 the highly respected Bishop Marrens of Hanover ordered the clergy in his diocese to take an oath of allegiance to the *Führer*. This symbolic act bound the Protestant Church in Germany to the Nazi regime (Shirer, 1960, p 298).

The Nazis had even greater problems with Roman Catholics than with Protestants. There was an ideological chasm that divided the Nazis from Roman Catholicism. The lack of regard of the Nazis for human life was an affront to Catholic values, which revered the sanctity of life. Eugenics was wholly contrary to Catholic doctrine, but anti-Semitism was not. The Nazis moved quickly to dissolve potential ideological tensions. They signed a concordat with the Vatican on 20 July 1933 that promised to respect freedom of religious worship and the right of the Catholic Church 'to regulate its own affairs'. This was the spiritual equivalent of the Nazi–Bolshevik pact of 1939. The lack of sincerity on the German side was total. The ink was hardly dry before the Nazis proceeded to break the agreement. On 25 July 1933, the German government promulgated the sterilisation law, which was profoundly offensive to Catholics. Open persecution of Christian worship began in 1936. These acts of persecution were accompanied by acts of desecration of religious symbols. Attempts to remove religious images from schools encountered public opposition, notably in Catholic Bavaria. Some Catholic clergy spoke out, most notably the aristocratic Bishop Galen of Munster, who was to become one of the most inveterate critics of the Nazis. He publicly denounced their burlesque displays as neo-paganism.

The goal of Nazifying religion was not simply an evangelical issue. For the Nazis, wresting control of confessional charities was of fundamental importance. Given their relative structural weakness, compared with the communists in Russia, civil society became a major site where the Nazis contested for power. In their project, they proved highly successful.

The success of the Nazis in penetrating civil society organisations and undermining their autonomy pushed Germany's charitable organisations into a marginal existence. Burleigh (2000, p 221) concludes:

> Having corralled the confessional charities and Red Cross within a new national steering body, Hilgenfeldt replaced collegial deliberation with the Führer principle, employing various sleights of hand to marginalise his rivals. In 1934, legislation was introduced to restrict the confessional charities' ability to solicit funds outside the Churches. Mailshot campaigns were prohibited, and a state permission had to be sought for charitable campaigns in general. The confessional charities were obliged to collect on behalf of the Nazis' own 'Winter Aid' programme, in return for a proportional share of the proceeds. Various Nazi organisations took the lion's share, leaving the combined religious charities and the Red Cross with a diminishing remnant as each year passed. Since the 1923 hyperinflation, they had received top-up subsidies from the state. Now disbursement was subject to the agreement of People's Welfare. In 1938, the Inner Mission requested 2.84 million Reichsmarks and the Caritas Association 1.2 million Reichsmarks; they received 15 and 12 per cent of what they needed. Their turnover was also subject to sales tax. In 1939, these payments were terminated, on the ground that People's Welfare itself had assumed enhanced responsibilities in Austria and the Sudetenland. Hilgenfeldt argued that the Churches were secretly collecting funds for a confessional sector whose days were numbered. He also struck at the already self-coordinated Red Cross. Civilian welfare responsibilities it had developed in peacetime were relinquished to People's Welfare, while it was 'encouraged' to revert to its original paramedical military remit. In 1937, the deputy presidency of the Red Cross went to the SS

Reich Doctors Leader, Robert Grawitz. Three years later, the total co-ordination of the voluntary charitable sector was symbolised by the abolition of the steering committee on which they were notionally represented.

Anheier and Seibel (2001, p 61) report that Nazification was highly successful, with 12.5 million citizens enrolling as members of NSV by 1939. NSV boasted 80,000 salaried staff and over one million voluntary staff members. It was engaged in the domestic life of 56% of German households. By 1943, membership of NSV had risen to 17 million, with other charitable associations truly marginalised and the social service role of municipal authorities challenged.

The Nazis soon applied their strong-arm tactics to volunteering and fundraising, turning the ideal of charity on its head. Fear and extortion became the defining elements in the Nazis' approach to charity, coupled with propaganda spectacles. Burleigh (2000, p 226) comments in this regard:

> While they marginalised the confessional welfare agencies, the Nazis reinforced voluntarism with compulsion. Posters reading 'I am a member of the NSV – and you?' appeared on buses and trams. Novel collection methods, such as co-opting zoo elephants to draw crowds, or horsemen holding tins aloft on sticks to reach upper-storey windows, soon palled. Contributions to Winter Aid were deducted at source from wages – anticipating levies for Nicaraguan or Vietnamese comrades in the later German Democratic Republic – with worker consent to this extortion negated by enrolling everyone into the People's Welfare at works assemblies, and asking anyone who dissented to make this publicly known. Workers were then surprised to find People's Welfare pamphlets in their wage packets, for which further deductions had already been made. Schoolteachers handed out large quantities of Winter Aid badges to children in the knowledge that they would never be able to dispose of them, indirectly pressurising parents to make up the deficit to spare their offspring shame at school. Some schools introduced display boards showing which pupils had or had not succeeded in offloading their People's Welfare badges. Passengers on buses and trains morosely suffered conductors who withheld their change for charitable purposes. Winter Aid became a form of licensed extortion.

Strong-arm tactics became part of the Nazis' repertoire of skills in reshaping the ethical base of charity into an instrument of state terror:

> The ratchet of charitable coercion went beyond having a box or tin aggressively rattled under one's nose, a minor nuisance in the bigger scheme of things. The issuance of badges and flags enabled collectors to hone in on those not evincing the appropriate commitment. So did special forms which householders were obliged to complete, detailing what they had donated. Further forms involved a 'moral' assessment of the donor. Next came empty Winter Aid bags, suggestively deposited outside the front door. The use of Hitler Youth, SA and SS men as collectors only enhanced the impression of being mugged on behalf of charity. Overt threats followed, for not fulfilling one's sacrificial duty implied a hostile attitude towards the collective educational goals of the National Socialist state. A choice had become a potential political crime. Not playing the game had dire consequences, which were often couched in terms of 'protecting' erring individuals from the righteous anger of the people, an insight into the perversions to which the far from inherently benign concept of 'community' was subject. (Burleigh, 2000, p 226)

Jacobin-style terror was applied to the human virtue of charity. Those who did not comply with Nazi propaganda were in danger of being 'named and shamed'. That did not simply mean public embarrassment. The threat of the mob through the institutionalised violence of the SA and SS was very real. Compliance was essential for survival. The ethical base of civil society had been destroyed by the Nazis. For them, the idea of welfare was contrary to their social Darwinist view of the world. The weak and those not of Aryan blood did not have a right to exist in the Nazi scheme of things.

'Community aliens' and populist authoritarianism

After their seizure of power in 1933, the Nazis immediately engaged in a populist campaign against those who were perceived as 'asocial' members of the community. Several hundred 'professional criminals' were arrested, in a strike against Berlin's criminal gangs, shortly after the Nazi takeover. In September 1933, to coincide with the launching of their first Winter Aid programme, the Nazis arrested 100,000 vagrants and beggars as part of a 'Reich beggars' week. By late 1937 a decree ordered the arrest of everybody whom the Reich deemed to be 'asocial', including gypsies, prostitutes, pimps, tramps, vagrants, beggars and hooligans (Evans, 2005, p 88). Unemployed people were targeted as 'work-shy', since the official view was that nobody needed to be unemployed in the Third Reich. During raids ordered by Reinhard Heydrich, head of the SS Security Service, in June 1938 across all police districts, 10,000 arrests were made. Evans (2005, p 89) notes that 'people classified as asocial now swelled the depleted concentration camp population across Germany, causing massive overcrowding'. Their treatment in the concentration camps, as Evans (2005, p 90) records, was particularly harsh: 'The asocials were the underclass of camp life, just as they had been the underclass of society outside. They were treated badly by the guards, and almost by definition they were unable to organise self-help measures of the sort that kept political prisoners going. The other prisoners looked down on them, and they played little part in camp life. Death and sickness rates among them were particularly high.'

Among these groups of 'community aliens', Germany's 26,000 gypsies were singled out as particularly dangerous. Historically, gypsies had been the object of persecution. Persecution was heightened by the Nazis, who viewed them as a threat to racial purity. In 1938, a decree ordered gypsies and itinerants to undergo racial-biological examination. A system of registration and identity cards was introduced. These measures were widely supported by social workers, criminologists, police and authorities, municipalities and public opinion at large (Evans, 2005, pp 524–7). Similarly, Germany's Afro-German population was selected for exclusionary treatment, including sterilisation. Homosexuals were also targeted as 'asocial' and punished. The price of racial and biological purity was high. Germany's Jewish population was picked out for exemplary punishment in the form of extermination – the Nazis' final solution to the challenge of cultural difference. Hans Fallada's novel *Alone in Berlin*, originally published in 1947 (Fallada, 2009), narrates the story of a working-class couple's resistance to Nazi domination through circulating postcards and leaflets, only to be caught, tried and executed. Resistance was futile but, for the participants, meaningful.

Pogrom, civil society and anti-Semitism

Adolf Hitler became an anti-Semite as a young man in Vienna, reacting to the city's multicultural environment. He felt deeply alienated and resented Jews. Hitler observes: 'Gradually I began to hate them.... For me this was a time of the greatest spiritual upheaval I have ever had to go through', concluding: 'I had ceased to be a weak-kneed cosmopolitan and became an anti-Semite' (quoted in Shirer, 1960, p 43). While in Vienna, he became obsessed with Jews, reading about them and observing the 'phenomenon' closely in the manner of a sociologist. However, his conclusions were expressed in the highly unacademic language of a violent racist:

> Where ever I went, I began to see Jews, and the more I saw, the more sharply they became distinguished in my eyes from the rest of humanity.... Later I often grew sick to the stomach from the smell of the caftan-workers....Was there any form of filth or profligacy, particularly in cultural life, without at least one Jew involved in it? If you cut even cautiously into such an abscess, you found, like a maggot in a rotting body, often dazzled by the sudden light – a kike! (Cited in Shirer, 1960, p 43)

The shocking language and atavistic hatred expressed by the young Hitler towards Jews presaged the pogroms of the 1930s that were to culminate later in the Holocaust. The violence of later deeds had become embedded in Hitler's mindset long before he acquired power. While Hitler's rhetoric might be written off as the ranting of an insane mind, it was to unite a large section of the German population in a race war that defined innocent civilians as legitimate targets on the basis of their ethnicity.

Civil society, as reshaped by the Nazis, became an essential instrument for prosecuting the race war. Anheier and Seibel (2001, p 67) assert:

> The breakthrough of Nazism was decisively facilitated by the Nazi Party's embeddedness in a rich set of quasi-associational satellite organizations that began to penetrate society. Associational life not only worked as a structural transmitter of Nazism in German society, but failed to safeguard and support the legitimacy of the democratic state in general. The consolidation of the Nazi regime after 1933, and the acceptance of racism as an unquestioned pattern of discrimination, would have been unthinkable without the penetration of society by Nazi associations of all kinds. Nazi satellite organisations such as the NSV were explicitly in charge of enforcing racist principles; these associations and quasi-associations played a supportive role in the preparation

of genocide, in the context of mass deportations during the Holocaust.

Shortly after the Nazis seized power, a national boycott against Jews was held on 1 April 1933. It met with mixed success and was called off after one day. But in 1935 anti-Semitism was once again orchestrated by the Nazis across the country; offensive signs were daubed on walls and shop windows, with arrows painted on the pavement indicating Jewish business premises (Burleigh, 2000, p 28). In September 1935 the Nuremberg Laws were introduced, which deprived Jews of German citizenship and outlawed marriage and sexual intercourse between 'Aryans' and Jews, the employment by Jewish households of female 'Aryan' housemaids under 45 years of age and the raising of either of the German flags by Jews. This combination of social and economic exclusions by boycott and street-level propaganda, in tandem with mass-media manipulation and licensed discrimination, reduced Germany's Jewish population to the status of victims of state terror. Burleigh (2000, p 315) notes: 'Legalized discrimination, mob violence and the "dejudaisation" of the German economy were ultimately designed to force Jewish people to emigrate – thus it was felt, exporting anti-Semitism.... The crucial concern, however, was to eject the Jews at no cost to the nation's finances – that is, how to strip these people of their capital before they left, while knowing full well that foreign countries would not look kindly upon impoverished would-be immigrants.'

The Nazis set about a systematic campaign of ousting Jews from the German economy and forcing their emigration from Germany. This was not an easy task because the Nazis' anti-Semitic campaign had failed to convince key sections of the German population, including supporters of the former Left, rural Catholics, landowners and army officers, who continued to have social and economic interactions with Jews (Burleigh, 2000, p 317). The German population had not been completely Nazified. There were approximately half a million Jews living in Germany in 1933, and 200,000 in Austria. The marginalisation of Jews was not enough for the Nazis. Their removal became a core Nazi objective, which was achieved by 1941.

The Nazis decided to resort to a national pogrom, known as the *Kristallnacht* (or night of the broken glass) on 9 and 10 November 1938. In a sense, this was the culminating event following five years of localised pogroms. The scale of the event makes it remarkable. It has been estimated that 7,500 Jewish businesses were damaged or destroyed in a night of unrestrained mob violence, vandalisation, looting, rape, assault and murder. In response, 20,000 Jews were arrested, collectively fined one billion marks as punishment, forced to pay for the damage to their properties and had their insurance monies expropriated by the German state (Shirer, 1960, pp 526–7; Burleigh, 2000, pp 322–42).

There is evidence that significant sections of German society reacted with disgust towards the pogrom. Roman Catholics in the south and west of Germany regarded the pogrom as an affront to the Christian virtue of 'love thy neighbour'. While Protestants were more sanguine, individual pastors protested. The liberal middle classes were disgusted by the pogrom, and in some instances were active in support of Jewish people. For example, Robert Bosch, a businessman, and formerly active in the Association for Defence against Anti-Semitism, transferred one million marks to a Dutch bank in order to fund the illegal emigration of Jews. Other German citizens (including senior civil servants) did likewise, hiding Jews in their homes and assisting them to escape abroad. Some citizens had the courage to speak out against the pogrom. But in a climate of totalitarian communitarianism, those who expressed humanitarianism and supported Jewish people risked ritual denunciation by the authorities, or worse. What they did prove was that the Germans in the Third Reich were not universally anti-Semitic, and clandestinely a residue of democratic civil society did exist in resistance form, defending humanitarian values in the face of state terror and media propaganda (Burleigh, 2000, pp 332–3). However, a series of books – notably Daniel Goldhagen's *Hitler's Willing Executioners* (1997) and Christopher Browning's *Ordinary Men* (2001) – argue that the German population was overwhelmingly complicit in the Holocaust.

The *Kristallnacht* became a tipping-point in the Nazis' campaign against the Jews. Burleigh (2000, p 338) concludes: 'Murderous violence was still at this stage a means to another end, enforced emigration, but in some circles the very fine balance was appreciably tilting, making murder – not as yet conceived as a continent-wide bureaucratic mission – an end in itself.' The final solution was taking shape, in which 6,000,000 European Jews were exterminated in ghettos and concentration camps across the continent. The Holocaust, as it came to be called, questioned the basis of social progress and secular moral values in Western civilisation, which was shaken to its foundations.

Events in Germany were echoed in other European countries. In Poland and Russia, which the Nazis invaded, the extermination of Jews was carried out with unparalleled brutality. In France, the Vichy regime, under the leadership of the former First World War French general Marshall Philippe Pétain, pursued anti-Semitic policies, but less vigorously than Germany did (Webster, 1991; Jackson, 2001). Burleigh (2000, p 473) states: 'Vichy anti-Semitism was designed to force foreign Jews out of France, and indigenous Jews to assimilate to vanishing point, with no distinctive identity or socio-economic profile.' The French approach was different to the Nazi policy of driving all Jews out of Germany between 1933 and 1941. Nonetheless, the Vichy regime was deeply racist.

Edith Archambault (1997, p 39), in an assessment of civil society under the Vichy regime, notes that the right to associate, enshrined in law since 1901, was overturned in 1941. As a result, the Freemasons (historically associated with the French Left), along with many political organisations, were dissolved. Like the Nazis in Germany, the Vichy regime established a pro-government associative network, especially among youth organisations. Unlike Germany, a strong underground civil society emerged in opposition to the Vichy regime:

> Many forbidden associations were clandestinely reorganized. This clandestine network was a basis for the Resistance Movement directed by De Gaulle. At the end of World War 2, the 1901 Act was re-enacted and all restrictions, with the exception of foreigners' associations, were abolished. The [1901] Act would never be seriously questioned again. (Archambault, 1997, p 39)

The Vichy regime in 1941 offered France 15 'Principles of Community' as its answer to the Declaration of the Rights of Man of 1789. A national revolution was declared by the Vichy authorities that opposed liberal individualism and sought to return France to the 'natural' communities of the past. The plan was to reorganise the population into hierarchically based organic communities, where duties would take precedence over rights and class struggle would be assigned to history. At the centre of the community would be the family, defined as the 'essential cell', standing above both the individual and the state (Jackson, 2001, p 149).

Associationalism, dis-welfare and genocide

Anheier and Seibel (2001, pp 62–5) have made a significant assessment of the relationship between associationalism, racism and genocide: 'The structure of associationalism and the welfare state were instrumental for the ideological adaptation of a society to policies resulting in genocide.... Extreme discriminatory policies included Rassehygiene (racial cleansing) and eugenics.... Associational life became instrumental to the penetration of civil society by racist and Social Darwinist ideology.'

As a contemporary social policy commentator, Hermann Althaus, put it in 1936: 'For the sake of the healthy nation, national socialist welfare has to reject or to reduce to a minimum care for those of minor value while simultaneously throttling down the strength of sick genes' (cited in Anheier and Seibel, 2001, p 64).

The Hereditary Health Courts in Nazi Germany amounted to 220 in number and were overseen by an appellate system of 18 higher courts. These arms of the judicial system consisted of a judge, a public health doctor and another medical 'expert', not necessarily from a relevant branch of medicine. Sterilisations were carried out by 140 doctors on a fee-per-item basis, involving, in the case of females, ligation of the fallopian tubes and, in the case of men, vasectomy. Some 5,000 people died from complications after surgery, mainly women. Others committed suicide (Burleigh, 2000, p 358). But this was only the beginnings of a policy of 'medicalised mass murder' or 'the realisation of Nietzschean ideas'.

Burleigh (2000, pp 382–404) records that eugenics led to euthanasia, a policy at odds with German law. Aktion T-4 was to become the instrument of the Nazis' euthanasia campaign, starting with the children's euthanasia programme. The policy quickly moved on to include adult psychiatric patients. The euthanasia programme was carried out in intense secrecy. But public disquiet began to grow at the alarming rate of unexplained deaths among those in the care of the state or voluntary health services. Professionals including doctors, judges and pastors began to object on behalf of members of the public. Bishop Galen of Munster became the regime's most inveterate critic of sterilisation, touching a humanitarian chord in the German population. The euthanasia programme was halted in 1941, after it achieved its projected target of 70,000 victims. The death machine moved on from hospitals and asylums to extermination camps, where 'pseudo-medical killing finally became an integral aspect of racial mass murder, with doctors in SS uniforms on the selection ramps of Auschwitz' (Burleigh, 2000, p 404). There were no ethical restraints 'in the business of commodifying and destroying people – although we should not over-industrialise or over-medicalise the Holocaust, which included direct violence of a primitive kind' (Burleigh, 2000, p 404).

The social Darwinism of the Nazis was expressed through a policy that started in eugenic sterilisation, moved on to the use of euthanasia for vulnerable citizens and ended in extermination. It was an exercise in 'political biology', as one academic commentator, Hans Bucheim, has put it:

The National Socialists considered that their own people, and during the second world war the people of Europe, had squandered their substance; they looked on them as a plantation overgrown with weeds, which must at all costs be cleared by isolating the 'incorrigible', cutting out the 'canker of decay', propagating the worthwhile elements and letting the less valuable wither away, sterilizing the sick, and either transplanting or suppressing the unstable varieties. The end-product of this policy would be a new, biologically sensible, well-ordered European community.... This programme would be carried through by means of euthanasia, deportation, Germanisation and, last but not least, the 'extirpation of all those classes of people considered to be worthless or dangerous'. (Cited in Krausnick and Broszat, 1968, p 31)

What was clear was that modern German society was faced with profound moral choices. It chose to pursue policies that led to the deaths of millions of people based on ethnic and hereditary cleansing, including Jews, gypsies and those judged genetically vulnerable on the basis of their genes, behaviour or simple need for care. This was the social Darwinist route. It was characterised by dis-welfare, in which the vulnerable were singled out for extermination. Civil society in Germany reacted. Professionals protested. But not before the Nazis had achieved their targets in clearing hospital beds for 'healthy' citizens. The suppression and co-option of civil society was the secret of the Nazis' domestic success in turning Germany into a totalitarian state.

Conclusion

What are we to conclude about the role of civil society during these cataclysmic events? The reality was that civil society had been penetrated and co-opted by the Nazis in order to create their version of big society. Its resulting Nazification meant that it ceased to be an effective voice. Nazification had encompassed all aspects of civil society: charities, churches, cultural life and so on. The ethical basis of German society had been undermined. It was notable that, while many within the Protestant community were sanguine or indifferent, a large number of pastors had the moral courage to object, and paid the price. Some joined the resistance, of whom Pastor Dietrich Bonhoeffer is the most famous example. He became a martyr in the German resistance movement. But Germany ceased to be a society where the pursuit of humanistic virtue was possible. Instead, the Nazis offered a parody based on building a super-race. What we learn from Nazi Germany is that there exists another side to modernity, in which the state becomes an instrument of terror and civil society is co-opted into its apparatus. This is the statisation of society, referred to at the outset of Chapter Four. It is the obverse of the socialisation of the state. Without the ethical compass of civil society driven by the humanistic goal of promoting civic virtue, the modern state has the capacity to turn itself into a vast, Nietzschean dystopia. The lessons for those who believe in a social policy driven by the principles of social justice are clear. There can be no civilised modern society without welfare. It defines human rights and human dignity. In this chapter, we have seen how the Nazis turned charity into an instrument of their power. Even the system of donations was infused by the exercise of terror, backed by the SS and SA. Race emerged at the centre of Nazi social policy, seeking to build a super-race through the application of eugenic principles in hereditary courts. For those determined to be of the wrong race or the wrong genes, Nazi social policy inexorably led to death. It was the antithesis of life, liberty and democracy. Social justice had become undone in this vast experiment of human violence.

SIX

Rights talk, new social movements and civic revolts

It was terribly dangerous to let your thoughts wander when you were in any public space or within the range of the telescreen. The smallest thing could give you away. A nervous tic, an unconscious look of anxiety, a habit of muttering to yourself – anything that carried with it the suggestion of abnormality, of having something to hide. In any case, to wear an improper expression on your face ...; was itself a punishable offense. There was even a word for it in Newspeak: facecrime.

George Orwell, *1984* (1989, p 65)

There is a battle to be fought, not only over which universals and what rights should be invoked in particular situations but also how universal principles and conceptions of rights should be constructed.

David Harvey, *A Brief History of Neoliberalism*
(2007, p 179)

It is true, the reasons to get angry may seem less clear today and the world may seem more complex. Who is in charge; who are the decision makers? It's not always easy to discern. We're not dealing with a small elite anymore, whose actions we can clearly identify. We are dealing with a vast, interdependent world that is interconnected in unprecedented ways. But there are unbearable things all around us. You have to look for them; search carefully. Open your eyes and you will see. This is what I tell young people: If you spend a little time searching, you will find reasons to engage. The worst attitude is indifference.

Stéphane Hessel, *Time of Outrage* (2011, p 11)

The term 'rights talk' has been invoked by distinguished commentators to describe the post-war world (Judt, 2005, p 567; Harvey, 2007, p 177). But what does it mean? What is its connection to democracy, if any?

Does it simply represent a retreat from democracy into jurisprudence? Is it possible to construct a universal concept of human rights? Are we addressing individualised rights of oppressed people, and if so do we do this individually or collectively? Are human rights the modern expression of humanism in the face of a bureaucratic state with the capacity to behave with totalitarian characteristics? Or is 'rights talk' something different that draws on the post-war intellectual tradition of humanism that has linked 'rights talk' to democratic action – in the form of new social movements within the broad framework of civil society? Stéphane Hessel's *Time of Outrage* has found a response during 2011 because it is a passionate statement of rights and the need for their defence.

In this chapter we will move beyond liberal notions of human rights based upon the protection of the individual. The UN Declaration of Human Rights (1948) was a landmark in protecting citizens from tyranny. Its importance cannot be overstated. But there is another tradition of human rights, going back to Tom Paine's *Rights of Man* (1791–92) (Paine, 1969), that links human rights to moral protest and democratic struggle to create a 'civilised society'. In this chapter it will be argued that dissident struggles and social movements have become the collective expressions of 'rights talk', in which citizens (1) have created an alternative democratic space (to parliament, as a top-down model of democracy), (2) have created a bottom-up forum based upon multiple counter-publics, continuously seeking to renegotiate power relations (Asen and Brouwer, 2001) and (3) have changed the democratic narrative, through the influence of civic insurrections in 1989 and 2011. This is a vital manifestation of civil society in terms of the collective expression of human rights in the tradition of radical humanism.

Human rights and existential humanism

In the post-war climate, the paradox of enshrining human rights at a historical moment when the idea of moral universalism was deeply compromised, was evident. Hannah Arendt (1906–1975) argued in her influential book, *Origins of Totalitarianism*, published in 1958, that, stripped of civic and political rights, human beings lose their essential humanity. The significance of the 1948 Universal Declaration of Human Rights, which has now survived for over half a century, has been summarised by Michael Ignatieff (1999, p 58): 'Human Rights has become the major article of faith of a secular culture that fears it believes in nothing else... the drafters put their hopes in the idea that by declaring rights as moral universals, they could foster a global rights consciousness among those they called "the common people".'

The promotion of human rights has largely been carried out by the United Nations and civil society through a variety of voluntary or non-governmental organisations (NGOs). Amnesty International, Human Rights Watch, the Anti-Slavery Society and others have revitalised voluntary endeavour. It is possible to dismiss NGOs, dedicated to promoting human rights in the age of economic globalisation, as simply representing the interests of a new global middle class, liberal-minded and committed to doing good globally. David Harvey (2007, p 177) argues: 'this amounts to privatization by NGO. In some instances this has helped to accelerate further state withdrawal from social provision. NGOs thereby function as a Trojan Horse for global neoliberalism.' He invites us to discursively move beyond 'rights talk' as an exercise in the defence of 'bourgeoisie virtues' (Harvey, 2007, p 181). While Harvey's strictures are somewhat overstated, his point is clear. The defence of human rights ultimately resides in the exercise of citizen protest.

Modern humanism developed during the 18th, 19th and 20th centuries. Its development was closely linked to Enlightenment rationalism and the scientific revolution that undermined traditional Christian beliefs. Humanists view the human condition in progressive terms, as a striving, evolving process toward higher states of being. They believe that human beings are endowed with the creative potentialities to solve problems confronting individuals, communities and governments. Humanists promote international cooperation, human rights and the protection of the planet from the destructive forces of war and modernity. The humanist ethic is based upon a commitment to the realisation of both individual and social possibilities within the context of mutual responsibility. In the post-war world humanism became linked to the pursuit of democracy.

The defence of democracy has taken on a new urgency (Keane, 2009). Existential humanism developed out of the experience of occupation during the Second World War. It is particularly associated with French resistance and Nazi occupation. The French existential school was embodied in the works of Jean-Paul Sartre (1905–80), Simone de Beauvoir (1908–86) and Albert Camus (1913–60). It argued for a future based upon greater human freedom, in which inauthenticity or 'bad faith' is rejected by a philosophical movement that adopts as its central premise the fact of individual human existence. Saul (2010, p 26) characterises this existential humanist perspective as 'one that saw alienation as a tragic fact of modern life, large bureaucracies as the machinery of quiet death and individual rebellion as a profound form of self-fulfilment'. The student movement that emerged during the 1960s challenged modern human destiny as living death in a project of 'hyperdemocracy as only the young could practice it' (Saul, 2010, p 30). The Free Speech movement (FSM) at University of California, Berkeley, erupted in 1964, challenging the liberal ideals of freedom of speech and association to their very limits. In May 1968 French students revolted on the streets of Paris, turning Sartre, Camus and de Beauvoir's existential humanism into an attempt to replace representational democracy by a participatory model forged in the purist ideals of human freedom and social justice that would transform human subjectivity by de-alienating the self as the revolutionary subject. As resistance survivor Stéphane Hessel (2011, p 8) puts it: 'the responsibility is that of the individual who will rely neither on a form of power nor a god. You must engage – your humanity demands it.' Hessel attributes his philosophical perspective to his teacher, Jean-Paul Sartre.

Albert Camus' book *L'Homme Révolté*, first published in 1951, argues that revolt is one of the essential conditions of humanity. In the modern world Camus views protest as a metaphysical revolt. He differentiates between revolution and revolt. For Camus the former, in the tradition of Jacobianism and Leninism, leads to further accretions of power on the part of the state and, ultimately, terror. On the other hand, he views revolt as a natural form of protest with its own in-built restraints. Camus (1962, p 261) concludes:

> The revolution of the twentieth century claims to base itself on economics, but is primarily political and ideological. It cannot, by its very function, avoid terror and violence done to reality. Despite its pretentions, it begins in the absolute and attempts to modify reality. Rebellion, inversely, relies on reality to assist it in its perpetual struggle for truth. The former tries to realize itself from top to bottom, the latter from bottom to top. Far from being a form of romanticism, rebellion, on the contrary, takes the part of true realism.

Camus' disavowal of violence makes him a seminal figure in the intellectual history of post-war civil society and the birth of new social movements primarily concerned with cultural and existential issues.

Civil society and revolt: the velvet revolutions

In this eloquent analysis of revolt Camus links the act of rebellion to democratic participation in changing the conditions of human existence. It is as much an act of the mind (metaphysical) challenging existing political fictions with the realities of their social and moral hegemonies. Rebellion is ultimately located in the terrain of human subjectivity, informed by an existentialist humanism that invites us to consider what Zygmunt Bauman (2000) describes as 'liquid modernity' and its potential for change.

Zygmunt Bauman (2000, p 8) argues that we have reached a turning-point in our historical experience of modernity:

> It would be imprudent to deny, or even to play down, the profound change which the advent of 'fluid modernity' has brought to the human condition. The remoteness and unreachability of systemic structure, coupled with the unstructured, fluid state of the immediate setting of life-politics, change that condition in a radical way and call for a rethinking of old concepts that are today simultaneously dead and alive. The practical question is whether their resurrection, albeit in a new shape or incarnation, is feasible; or – if it is not – how to arrange for their decent and effective burial.

In this reconstituted modernity (or 'liquid modernity'), social institutions such as family, class and neighbourhood had become zombiefied (Bauman, 2000, p 6). The glue that had held modern civilisation together has dissolved, leading to calls for the reconstitution of civil society. The 1968 Student Revolution proved to be a seminal movement in ushering in a new era of moral protest that redefined politics. It represented the beginning of new social movements, in contrast to more traditional forms such as trade unions.

A new vocabulary of human rights began to emerge from the mid-1970s. 'Rights talk' became fashionable among progressive intellectuals in both East and West. But it was the Stalinist monolithic hold on power in Eastern Europe that became the key theatre in the ensuing struggle. The Orwellian exploitation of language as power by communist regimes began to be interrogated by 'rights talk'. Intellectuals, who developed this critical new language of 'rights talk', became 'dissidents'. The Czech playwright Vaclav Havel (1936–2011) became the archetypal dissident. But the main challenge to communism came from civil society – a popular movement that challenged the hegemonic control of Stalinism. Judt (2005, p 567) observes: 'the significant efforts to reconstitute civil society – a nebulous phrase describing an uncertain objective but one widely espoused by the intellectual opposition in Eastern Europe from the mid-seventies onward'. Civil society became the counter-public that overthrew dictatorships in a series of 'Velvet Revolutions' in 1989. They were peaceful revolutions, based entirely on moral force: communism in Eastern Europe in reality turned out to be a series of zombie states, held together by the grip of fear but totally lacking in popular support. Anheier et al (2012, p 15) have concluded that 'the revolutions of 1989 could be viewed as the culmination of the post-1968 movements'. Like a house of cards, these regimes collapsed in the face of democratic revolt across Eastern Europe. But, arguably, these events need to be set in the wider context of what Lester Salamon (1994) perceived as 'a global associational revolution' that was shifting the planet on its axis. However, it is important to add a historical qualifier here. The suppression of the largest urban protest in Chinese history, at Tiananmen Square in Beijing, resulted in the loss of hundreds of lives and martial law being imposed by the party-state.

The impetus for the global associational revolution has come both from the bottom up and from the top down. Eastern Europe provides the most dramatic example, with organisations such as Solidarity in Poland and the Civic Forum Movement in Czechoslovakia capturing the imagination of the world. Vaclav Havel emerged as its iconic leader, mocking totalitarianism with absurdism. Less well reported were the environmentalist movements in Eastern Europe during the communist era: the Danube Circle in Hungary, and Arche, the environmental organisation that campaigned against acid rain in East Germany by tying thousands of bed sheets to apartment roofs and then recording the pollution accumulated. These activists in Eastern Europe (including the Soviet Union) described 'their efforts as the creating of a "civil society", a society in which individuals have the right not only to speak out as individuals, but also to join together in organisations' (Salamon, 1994, p 5). The meaning of the global associational revolution is that it represents the globalisation of norms of civic engagement that has the power to change regimes, but also the power to change policy. The internet has empowered activists to share ideas and tactics and coordinate their campaigns, rather like the pamphleteering and coffee house society of the 18th century. Political debate no longer depended on the traditional media of newspapers and television, largely owned by the wealthy or controlled by the state.

This pressure for bottom-up change through civil society was perhaps most dramatic in Eastern Europe because it brought down the communist form of government and its hegemonic system of control. However, the 'global associational revolution' was, by definition, a global movement touching most continents. The Zapatista movement in Mexico, and movements elsewhere in Latin America, such as the Brazilian Landless People's movement (MST), were characteristic of grassroots political activities against government oppression in the Americas. These postmodern rebellions eschewed the seizure of state power in favour of 'a radical transformation of civil society and culture – with particular emphasis upon communications, globally as well as locally' (Mayo, 2005, p 119). In Africa a 'new wind' of change has given rise to grassroots political and environmental organisations, notably in Nigeria, usually of a non-profit voluntary nature. Chopko, the Indian environmentalist movement, arose from a spontaneous effort by rural residents to protect an endangered forest by literally linking their arms around it.

Support in the West for the expansion of voluntary organisations was distinctive because of its top-down character and its association with the scaling back of the welfare state. Neoconservatives were at the forefront of this process, notably Margaret Thatcher in Britain and Ronald Reagan in the United States. Reagan opposed 'Big Government' per se. Thatcher took a more fundamentalist conservative line by calling for the dismantling of not only the welfare state, 'but also the organised voluntary sector and leave social care wholly to volunteers' (quoted in Salamon, 1994, p 8). She described volunteers as 'the heart of all our social welfare provision' (quoted in Salamon, 1994, p 8). In her conservative vision both the state and civil society curtailed the virtuous individual. Support for volunteerism has not been unique to neoconservative governments. The Socialist president of France François Mitterand (1916–96) sought to liberalise taxes on 'social economy organisations' during the 1980s. However, social economy organisations in France (like Germany) are 70% supported by public funding, creating a symbiotic relationship between the state and the voluntary/community sector. During the 1990s and 2000s we have witnessed the growing influence of neoliberalism in a conservative restoration and the shrinking of the state. Stéphane Hessel (2011, p 5) in reference to France, encapsulates the retreat from the post-war welfare state and the feelings of injustice and indignation it has aroused:

> We are told, shamelessly, that the state cannot bear the costs of certain civil measures any longer. But how can we lack the funds to maintain these programs when our nations enjoy greater wealth than at any time since the Liberation, when Europe lay in ruins? How else to explain this but by the corrupting power of money, which the Resistance

fought so fiercely against, and which is now greater, more insolent, and more selfish than ever.

The Wealthy have installed their slaves in the highest spheres of the state. The banks are privately owned. They are concerned solely with profits. They have no interest in the common good. The Gap between the rich and the poor is the widest it's ever been; the pursuit of riches and the spirit of competition are encouraged and celebrated.

He concludes with a call to youth to mobilise in defence of democracy and social justice:

> The basic motive of Resistance was indignation. We, veterans of the French Resistance and the combat forces that freed our country, call on you, our younger generations, to revive and carry forward the heritage of ideals of Resistance. Here is our message: It's time to take over! It's time to get angry! Politicians, economists, intellectuals, do not surrender! The true fabric of our society remains strong. Let us not be defeated by the tyranny of the world financial markets that threaten peace and democracy everywhere.

George Monbiot (2012), in an article on neoliberalism, similarly laments the decline of democracy and its replacement by 'totalitarian capitalism in which no one may dissent from the will of the market'.

Critics of civil society point out that the real emphasis is on dutiful citizen engaged in self-help. In the context of the atomised individualism and fragmented social order that we live in, there is an element of unreality about the larger claims made for the concept of civil society as an alternative to state welfare. As Kramer (1981, p 283) puts it:

> Voluntarism is no substitute for services that can best be delivered by Government, particularly if coverage, equity and entitlements are valued ... there is a danger that those who have jumped on the bandwagon of the era of limits, signalling the end of the Welfare State by advocating more voluntarism, are being co-opted by others who share less concern with social justice than with tax reduction.

Clearly, it is quite unsustainable to suggest that the needs of the most disadvantaged can be met by the voluntary sector. Civil society based purely on the principle of private altruism would not be a civilised society. Indeed, there is no essential link between civil society and civilised society – contrary to Paine's view. The Tea Party in the United States is illustrative. Civil society has had a chequered political history. It can be both progressive and reactionary: radical and conservative. The Nazi party undermined the Weimar Republic in Germany by infiltrating local organisations. It should not be forgotten that the Mafia is an intermediate institution that involves a vast criminal network. Its 19th-century origins were in popular resistance to the French occupation of Italy. According to legend, the acronym MAFIA means *Morte Alla Francia, Italia Avanti* (Death to France, Italy Forward). Today, Mafia means many different criminal networks across the world. It has become a global crime network and represents the antithesis of civil society. The acronym MAFIA is, in the public imagination, synonymous with evil and death – the embodiment of incivility.

Closer to home, paramilitary organisations in Northern Ireland have exerted considerable influence in their communities by establishing a significant presence within some voluntary and community organisations. At a more general level some small local groups have been thoroughly illiberal in their responses to drug abusers and HIV victims. Pseudo-religious cults, with their internal cultures of intimidation, psychological domination of the individual and sometimes violent agendas, further highlight the dark side of associational life, most notably in Japanese culture (Murakami, 2011; Kirino, 2008). In a climate of increasing ethnic conflict – manifested in Europe by communal hostility towards the Roma, asylum seekers and refugees – intermediate institutions located within the community can be anything but civil. Anders Behring Breivik's shooting of 69 members of a socialist party youth organisation in Norway during 2011 captures the incivility of the racist right. Owen Jones (2012, p 223) has attributed 'the rise of the far right to the marginalisation of working-class people'. He has, furthermore, pointed out that the British Nationalist Party (BNP) 'has cynically manipulated mainstream multiculturalism with its focus on inequality as an issue of race' (Jones, 2012, p 234). The rise of the Far Right in Europe is the product of the politics of austerity: a lack of affordable housing, low wages and job insecurity. In these circumstances 'rights talk' can be challenged by xenophobia, vigilantism and racialised evictions and deportations. Both Camus and Havel would be appalled!

The peace rebellion and existential rights

In the wake of the Second World War the issue of peace became a dominant paradigm of politics during the Cold War period (1945–89). The peace rebellion posed a fundamental challenge to Cold War politics, questioning its moral purpose and legitimacy. The peace rebellion was an extra-parliamentary social movement based upon moral protest. The defining characteristics of social movements is their location within a tradition of moral protest. At least this is true of Europe. There is a view that American social movements are more likely to temporise with power politics (Byrne, 1997, pp 160–5). The Campaign for Nuclear Disarmament (CND) epitomised the public perception of the peace movement in the United Kingdom. In reality, the peace movement was a much broader social movement. It dates from the 1950s, when the British Peace Committee obtained over one million signatures against nuclear weapons, despite its links with the 'communist' World Peace Committee. CND was formed in 1958, when the first Aldermaston march against the manufacture of nuclear arms in Britain took place (Mayo, 2005, p 194). From the mid-1960s to the mid-1970s the peace movement across the Western world was dominated by the anti-Vietnam war campaign, which was to bring down US President Lyndon Johnson's administration in 1968. The Vietnam War, waged by the world's most powerful democratic state against a poor communist nation in the Far East, became a touchstone moral issue for many young people during the turbulent 1960s, which also witnessed the student movement. But not all idealistic young people flocked to the peace movement to express their moral concerns. Some joined the Peace Corps, an organisation established in 1961 by the US government to raise living standards in the 'Third World' countries. It epitomised the youthful idealism associated with the 'Camelot' presidency of John F. Kennedy. Volunteers, after an initial period of training, spent two years working alongside the citizens of the 'host' country in local development organisations, training the indigenous population to take over their jobs when they returned home to the US. The Peace Corps were volunteers, who received their living costs and expenses but otherwise offered free labour. The peace movements and the Peace Corps represent the radical and liberal faces of civil society. Both were committed to a humanistic view of the world, but their approaches were very different, underlining the variable meanings of civil society.

Parallel developments to the Peace Corps took place in other Western countries involved in emergency relief or development aid. In France, Médecins Sans Frontières and Médecins du Monde are the most famous of what Archambault (1997, pp 1–2) calls 'a voluntary homologue – without borders', that embraces pharmacists, architects, agronomists and many others motivated to respond to world poverty. While critics may dismiss these organisations as a Western movement towards the 'NGOisation' of the planet, the authenticity of their participants' social idealism is beyond doubt. Volunteering to promote world peace through international aid and development became one of the highest forms of expression of social idealism in the post-war world.

The peace movement was to achieve its apogee in 1980s Britain, with many parallel organisations in continental Europe. The Women's Peace Camp at Greenham Common, started in 1981, exemplified the cross-cutting influences between social movements. Even political parties were drawn into the Peace Campaign – splitting the British Labour Party, with disastrous electoral consequences in 1983. The events of 9/11 in 2001 put the peace movement on the defensive. The Peace Movement already weakened by the collapse of communism in Eastern Europe, the 'War on Terror' redefined the issues in terms of a defence of the 'Christian West' against the Islamic world in what was widely presented in terms of a 'just war' doctrine. Nonetheless, the Stop the War Campaign united peace protestors (including Muslims), who were given fresh voice by the Iraq War of 2003. But there was no clear European parallel to the anti-war movement in the US, led by Cindy Sheehan and Gold Star Families for Peace. Grieving relatives have a particular moral purchase on the right to protest, even in a country in the throes of war. The *Nation*, 12 June 2006, asserted: 'Sheehan emerged as a middle-aged, middle-class "Everymom" who raised her voice in a time honoured shout to defend her kid!' She epitomised a broadening of participation in peaceful social protest. Older generations were becoming involved – parents and even grandparents.

The social composition of the peace movement underlined the growing political influence of a humanistic intelligentsia, expanded by mass third-level education during the second half of twentieth century. It is possible to define a direct connection with the student movement during the 1960s. Many were radicalised by their participation. Hardt and Negri (2000, 2004) have pointed to the emergence of a 'new world order' characterised by global military intervention. This 'military humanism' directed against tyrants such as Slobodan Milosevic, Saddam Hussein and Colonel Gaddafi, with or without UN sanction, has divided Western populations concerned with the mortality arising from such interventions. The war in Afghanistan is being scaled down in response to American public opinion, which does not view it as a just war.

Planetary citizenship and environmental rights

Unconstrained economic development and the sustainability of life on the planet were also issues that were to capture the imaginations of idealistic citizens during the post-war era. The environmental movement, dominated by green politics, raised the issue of human survival in a different but no less urgent context – the other side of the nuclear debate. Nuclear power became the target of public protest in Western societies. Pollution also became a focal concern, highlighting a postmaterialist culture in which the redistributionist politics of the modern age, which divided the political Right and Left, was challenged by a new agenda that put sustainability before economic development. This development has been likened to a 'silent revolution' (Byrne, 1997, pp 80–1). It was a new agenda that evolved in civil society. The change of political focus was to become the inspiration of André Gorz's *Farewell to the Working Class* (1982), which postulated that a new subjectivity was transforming progressive planetary politics. Organisations like Friends of the Earth (FoE), originally founded in San Francisco in 1969, and Greenpeace, formed in Vancouver in 1971 by protestors against nuclear testing off Alaska, became global symbols of resistance to perceived planetary degradation. The formation of these organisations was to radically transform public consciousness regarding the sustainability of life on planet Earth. Greenpeace adopted a strategy of high media visibility based on direct action-tactics, which sometimes backfired, as in the campaign against Shell to stop it from dumping its *Brent Spar* oil rig into the North Sea (Byrne, 1997, p 141). The bombing by French agents of the Greenpeace flagship, *Rainbow Warrior*, in Auckland harbour in 1985, with loss of life, highlighted the dangers of direct-action tactics and the political constraints within which civil society organisations operate. Non-violence is the cultural and ideological hallmark of what has been called 'the New Left', as symbolised by social movements (Tarrow, 1998, p 97). Its impact is global. The Rio (or Earth) Summit in 1992, attended by 108 heads of state or government, suggested that environmentalism was shaping public policy. Products of the Rio Summit included the Kyoto Protocol on climate change in 1997 and Agenda 21 on sustainable development. But the achievements of the Rio Summit, under the aegis of the United Nations, resulted in conflicts between the developed and developing nations.

For example, in China the Three Gorges Dam became the symbol of modernisation from the time of Sun Yat-Sen (1866–1925), who was regarded as the founder of modern Chinese society. Objections by environmental opponents to on-going attempts to dam the Yangtze river have been described as a human rights issue (Hutchings, 2000, p 420). China is the world's fastest-developing economy. China dialogue seeks to promote open discussion of the environmental consequences of rapid development. Globally, official resistance to curbing growth is strong. The Rio + 20 Earth summit in 2012 was a failure because of a lack of consensus on the scale and pace of global development. The global economic crisis was blamed for this policy failure.

Environmental activism touches a primeval cord. It is a campaign about sustainable development that goes to the core of the citizen's right to existence on the planet. Issues of regulation and deregulation of development status pose fundamental existential problems for the citizen. The German Wutbürger ('angry citizen') campaign in Stuttgart against an underground railway station is emblematic. It failed (Römmele and Schober, 2012). The powerlessness of place and the placelessness of power underline the challenge that environmental activists face. Sometimes the environmental movement is driven to the adoption of direct-action tactics that create major ethical issues. While the ultimate guarantor of state power is force, civil society is based upon the democratic ethical ideal of non-violent persuasion, what Jurgen Habermas (1984) calls 'communicative ethics'. The influence of green thinking is challenged by the global economic crisis and the emergence of business-friendly neo-environmentalism that is designed to adapt subjectivity to the idea that technological development and environmental protection are, after all, compatible objectives (Kingsnorth, 2012). Or so the revisionists would have us believe.

Moral voices, new subjectivities and reflective citizenship

The world that Alexis de Tocqueville wrote about in *Democracy in America* (1835) was one in which the citizen cultivated the 'art of association'. In the political vocabulary of the times, association was the defining paradigm of citizenship. Emerging political parties were part of this movement towards associative democracy. Kirp (1999, p 26) observes: 'newly powerful political parties were themselves a kind of association, a bridge between the private and public spheres'. That was before political parties discovered the power of patronage and the pragmatism of political office, shaped by the influence and financial contributions of powerful interests. Not that the 18th-century town hall meeting was the essence of good democratic inclusive practice. It was quite the contrary. Women, blacks and those from 'the wrong side of the tracks' were excluded. This was a white-man-of-means world. Postmodern politics has changed all that by putting culture on the agenda and liberating human subjectivity from the tyranny of tradition.

Feminism emerged as a powerful voice in this new politics seeking to alter human subjectivity by challenging the historic dominance of patriarchy. Women's lives in modern society had been dominated by *Kinder, Küche, Kirche*. The 3 Ks, which as a phrase dates from the 1890s, sought not only to impose domesticity upon women but to exclude them from public life. Given its Germanic associations, some added a fourth K to the phrase – *kinder, küche, kirche, Kaiser* – symbolising the patriarchal values that informed the architecture of this social thinking. Feminism emerged as a response to this repression of women. Connolly and Hourigan (2006, p 58) have observed: 'the women's movement is one of the most globalised forms of protest that continues to operate in contemporary society. Its importance, therefore, as a global social, political, cultural and intellectual project cannot be underestimated in the field of social movements.' The feminist slogan 'the personal is political' captures the complex cultural agenda of what came to be known as 'second wave feminism'. It didn't simply seek to mobilise around political and legislative change. The women's movement was as much a project of deconstruction as it was a revolutionary struggle for equality. It therefore sought to transform public discourse regarding women's position in society. There were divergences between radical feminists favouring direct action and liberal feminists who advocated a more hierarchal approach to institutional reform. The combined outcomes of this second wave of feminism as a counter-cultural project were undoubtedly significant both in terms of tangible elements (for example, participation in the labour force and equal pay) and in terms of altering subjectivities regarding women's role and place in society.

The French sociologist Alan Touraine argues that sociocultural conflict has replaced the socioeconomic conflict that dominated industrial capitalism in the modern era. Touraine contends that society is characterised by a permanent struggle between those who determine the rules (including cultural norms) and those who seek to redefine the social order in the shape of their own values and principles – what he calls 'historicity', the 'overall system of meaning which sets dominant rules in a given society' (Touraine, 1981, p 81). Power and meaning making are inextricably linked. New social movements contest for power in postmodern society by challenging dominant assumptions and sometimes changing their meaning. The feminist movement has undoubtedly been a most successful social movement, weakening patriarchy and redefining citizenship in an act of cultural deconstruction.

The main focus for transformation has not been the state but civil society and culture. Women became the ultimate exemplars of Camus' metaphysical revolt by literally changing their social identity, albeit many feminists continue to feel that equality remains an elusive goal.

Postmodern political consciousness has changed our understanding of what it means to be a citizen. Various strands within postmodern political life, such as feminism and queer theory, have challenged the precepts of liberalism and social democracy. The private spaces of social life, first opened to public scrutiny by pioneer social activists in the Victorian era, have become the battleground of cultural politics. Radical democrats espousing participation through the fragmented causes of identity politics have been joined by neoconservatives in challenging the hegemonic influences of liberalism, social democracy and the nation-state. The great metanarratives of the pursuit of human emancipation through social politics, and of pluralism through diversity and individual choice, have lost their persuasive force in postmodern discourse. The politics of postmodernity has reshaped political discourse into an interplay between human subjectivities and the state. This reflexive process is continuously reinventing political issues into new forms, new debates and new subjectivities. Postmodern consciousness has transformed established meanings and relationships between the family, civil society and the state into an anti-bureaucratic and anti-clientist form, based upon the democratic value of the citizen's rights to participate. Citizen journalism has opened up new communicative spaces through the exploitation of new media technologies that broaden inclusion and political diversity and that are having 'far reaching political implications' (Blaagaard, 2012, p 73).

Vaclav Havel (1993, p 54) has powerfully captured the challenges to both civic life and the concept of citizenship posed by postmodern society:

> The dictatorship of money, of profit, of constant economic growth, and the necessity, flowing from all that, of plundering the earth without regard for what will be left in a few decades, along with everything else related to the materialistic obsessions of this world, from the flourishing of selfishness to the need to evade personal responsibility by becoming part of the herd, and the general inability of human conscience to keep pace with the interventions of reason, right up to the alienation created by the sheer size of modern institutions – all of these are phenomena that cannot effectively be confronted except through a new

>moral effort, that is, through a transformation of the spirit
>and the human relationship to life and the world.

This observation underlines the importance of civic life in formulating a future in which 'the only kind of politics that makes sense is a politics that grows out of the imperative, and the need to live as everyone ought to live and therefore – to put it somewhat dramatically – to bear responsibility for the entire world' (Havel, 1993, p 54).

Globalisation, sans movements and emancipatory rights

Postmodernity has witnessed a cultural shift in attitudes towards the poor and oppressed that has been evident since the 1970s. Social policy, under the influence of the New Right, is increasingly being used not for the benefit of those who are thought to be citizens in need, with a view to their inclusion, but against those who are increasingly regarded as non-citizens, to punish and exclude them. Refugees and asylum seekers are the designated 'community aliens' of postmodern society. But the traditional working class has also been 'demonised'. As Owen Jones (2012, p 249) puts it: 'smearing poorer people as idle, bigoted, uncouth and dirty makes it more difficult to empathize with them'. Their shared working-class experience is part of the historical narrative that Piven and Cloward (1979) have called poor people's movements. But as we shall see below, poor people's movements, what the French call 'sans' (without) movements, do contest for emancipation – social movements are not simply the preserve of the radical intelligentsia. This is a world in which disadvantaged citizens resist or protest against inequality through new collectivities.

In France the sans movements were to become a vibrant part of post-war political life, reflecting a neglected aspect of globalisation – migration from poorer to richer regions. Touraine (2001, p 51) comments that 'the positive goal of today's social movements, which oppose both the reign of markets and the domination of communitarian-inspired movements, is the defence of the cultural and social rights of individuals and minorities'. Take, for example, the beur movement, founded by young Franco-Algerians who feel culturally disrespected by the society that they were born into as French citizens. Its campaigns have focused on the need for French society to address the cultural identity and need for respect of its immigrant population. Kedward (2005, p 504) notes that 'the Beur movement developed an inner pluralism through its identity with place and freedom of association', a contested issue in France. *Les exclus* raised fears about culture. The debate about girls from Islamic backgrounds wearing the *hijab* (headscarf) in school, which led to a ban, is symbolic of deeper concerns about cultural recognition. The *sans papiers* (immigrants without residence rights and associative status) are also campaigning for homes, jobs and citizenship rights. In France, the homeless have fought hard for the *droit au logement* (right to housing) since the 1950s, paving the way for other *sans* movements. France was somewhat taken by surprise by the emergence of an unemployed (*chômeurs*) movement. Pierre Bourdieu called it a 'social miracle'. Speaking of the occupation of the École Normal Supérieure in Paris by the *chômeurs* on 17 January 1998, Bourdieu declared that 'the first conquest of the movement is the movement itself, its very existence. It pulls the unemployed, and with them all insecure workers, whose numbers increase daily, out of invisibility, isolation, silence, in short out of non-existence' (cited in Kedward, 2005, p 569).

Bourdieu's remarks were prompted by a lack of support from the traditional trade unions, the CGT and the CGDT, albeit the former did make some attempt at limited accommodation. But 70% of public opinion supported the *chômeurs* and 78% of the French population said that they were closely acquainted with at least one unemployed person. Political recognition through negotiation became unavoidable (Kedward, 2005, p 569). Inevitably, there has been a political reaction in the form of Marine Le Pen's openly racist platform that has attracted more than one in five French voters to the cause of the Front National (National Front).

In Britain, the squatters' movement was reborn in 1968. It represented a historic campaign for the right to shelter. Bailey (1973, pp 21–2) records that the squatters' movement began as a protest against summer homes being abandoned for most of the year and 'developed into an attack on the right of landlords to do as they wished with *their* property, particularly if the exercise of these rights entitled leaving houses empty while other people were homeless'. The squatters' movement had identified an embarrassing contradiction in British housing policy – mass homelessness despite significant housing stock remaining unused – with the state being a significant social owner of unused properties. Despite the movement's hope for mass action, there was a reluctance to trespass on the part of the disadvantaged public, regardless of their need for shelter (Bailey, 1973, p 184). A new offence, introduced under clause 144 of the Legal Aid, Sentencing and Punishment of Offenders Act 2012, will make squatting punishable by up to six months' jail and a fine of up to £5,000 in England and Wales. One London squatter mused 'is that what the Big Society is all about?'. But the squatters' movement did succeed in putting pressure on local authorities with significant stocks of unoccupied social housing. Squatting movements also developed in Germany and Denmark. Colonies like Kreuzberg in Berlin and Christiania in Copenhagen symbolised this squatting movement, which appeared to have more to do with radical autonomist politics than poverty.

Poor people's movements emerged in other parts of the world. Kirby (2001, p 163) comments: 'Over the final decades of the twentieth century, Latin America saw the emergence of a vibrant civil society as new collective actors such as shanty town organisations, human rights movements, Christian-based communities and various forms of self-help groups made their presence felt in the social and political life of their countries.' These movements can be dated from the 1960s, partly as a survival strategy for the poor against state tyranny, but latterly as a critique of neoliberalism, which has been largely rejected by electorates in Latin America since the turn of the 21st century. They have 'restored social actors in modern society to fully conscious life' (Kirby, 2001, p 164). What is clear is that Latin America has recently become a theatre in which civil society from 'the bottom up' has flourished. Similarly, in the Arab world over the past decade there has been a major expansion in organisations championing the interests of homeless people, human rights and women in police states (Dreamo, 2012, p 50).

The concept of active citizenship through social movement participation opens up a new site for democratic practice. The pursuit of inclusive citizenship provides new space for social activism. In this context the traditional conflict between capitalism and socialism is moved on to new ground. In essence, this is a struggle for both recognition and a redistribution, which can be defined as the absence of social, economic, cultural and political rights. Poor people's movements have become the embodiment of this new politics of emancipatory rights.

Pierre Bourdieu, in a witty polemic against globalisation, *Acts of Resistance* (1998), contextualises these political changes. According to Bourdieu's analysis, the crisis of politics and the rise of street protests in France and other countries is due to the hollowing-out of the state, which has undermined the public sphere. He argues that citizens who are rejected by the state in turn reject the state: 'in the same way, one has the sense now that citizens, feeling themselves ejected from the state (which, in the end, asks no more that obligatory material contributions, and certainly no commitment, no enthusiasm), reject the state, treating it as an alien power to be used so far as they can to serve their own interests' (Bourdieu, 1998, pp 4–5).

The Arab Spring

The 2011 uprisings in the Maghreb–Mashreq region are widely referred to as the Arab Spring, symbolising an emancipatory agenda realised through a series of civic insurrections. On 17 December 2010, a Tunisian street vendor called Mohamed Bouazzi set himself on fire as an act of moral protest. His protest was to ignite rebellion during 2011 across the region. Tahrir Square in Cairo became the public face of the revolt that overturned dictatorial regimes in Tunisia, Egypt, Yemen and Libya. It is the latest example of the global associational revolution in the age of the electronic media, where tyranny finds it difficult to hide from the scrutiny of the public gaze. Anheier et al (2012, p 18) assert; 'the mobilisations of 2011 appear typical of the early stages of new social movements; the involvement of a new generation, experimentation with forms of organisation, new and sometimes inchoate ideas, and, above all excitement'.

The successful civic revolts have been accompanied by civil uprisings in Syria and Bahrain that have been met with violet suppression. Other protests have taken place in Algeria, Iraq, Jordan, Kuwait, Morocco, Lebanon, Mauritania, Saudi Arabia, Sudan, Western Sahara, as well as a rebellion in Mali. The scale and depth of the Arab Spring indicates deep-seated concerns about human rights and dictatorial regimes within the region.

While the Arab Spring has elicited widespread support in the West, there are major emerging questions about the political meaning and outcomes of these revolts. Will they lead to democratisation, women's rights and more individual freedom? The electoral success of the Muslim Brotherhood and Salafi Nour parties in Egypt does not suggest that the Arab Spring will lead to greater Westernisation. Islamic values have widespread support, particularly in rural areas. This would appear to be due to the fact that religious civil society was the only form of civic expression untouched by long years of authoritarian repression. Roula Khalaf and Heba Saleh (2011) help to explain this democratic paradox:

> In Egypt, secular groups with leftist and pan-Arab ideologies ossified under the weight of repression by successive regimes determined to abolish all potential challengers. The [Muslim] Brotherhood, with its message rooted in Islam and spread through mosques and charities, proved harder to eradicate. When Mr Mubarak fell, the organisation – with its long-standing structures and networks – remained

the country's most organised political force, even as new secular and liberal groups scrambled to form parties under the chaotic watch of the ruling military council.

Their brand recognition and history of victimisation by the previous regime made them the logical choice for many voters, who saw them as strong and credible agents of change.

Gustave Massiah, speaking at the Solidarity Meeting with the Revolutions in the Arab World in Paris on 2 May 2011, has taken a more complex view of events in the Maghreb–Mashreq region. He argues that five lessons can be learnt from the Arab uprisings:

1. The first lesson is that the situation can indeed perhaps qualify as revolutionary.
2. The second lesson is the assertion of major demands: for freedom, for independence, and for the end of corruption.
3. The third lesson is that by rebelling in its own way, a new generation has taken up the revolutionary torch.
4. The fourth lesson is that the issue at stake is the democratisation of the whole Maghreb–Mashreq region.
5. The fifth lesson is that this new era opens up the possibility of a new phase of decolonisation. (Massiah, 2012)

This analysis compellingly evokes the vital human rights struggle that is on-going in the Maghreb–Mashreq region. It is a political struggle against repressive police states, a social struggle by workers, peasants, women, youth and others for emancipation and also an anti-colonial struggle against the attempts of the old colonial powers in the form of the G7 by a passionate civil society seeking liberation. Bernard Dreano (2012, pp 42–53), in a review of Arab resistance to colonisation over many decades, similarly takes a positive view of the events in the Maghreb–Mashreq region, noting the emergence of cyber-dissidence linked to youth networks. He also comments on the active role taken by women and workers, and the peaceful protest of civil society in the struggle for change. Dreano (2012, p 52) concludes: 'whatever happens in the coming months and years, things are not going to go back to what they used to be, and the 2011 awakening of the Arab people will be harvested in the coming decades'. It is premature to pass judgement on the Arab Spring. The hope is that it represents a progression towards greater democracy, stronger civil society and more freedom.

The Occupy movement and zombie capitalism

In the zombiefied world described by Bauman (2000), zombie banks have emerged as the most visible manifestation of zombie capitalism, following the 2008 financial crash. Yet within Europe the bailing-out of zombie banks has taken precedence over sovereign states. Even if the banking system is dead, it must be kept alive! This is the world of 'liquid modernity', where 'all that is solid melts into air' (Marx and Engels, 1967). In order to revive capitalism from the dead a major redistribution of wealth from the citizens to the rich has become necessary – in the view of the dominant conservative political elite. This is a life-and-death struggle for the survival of capitalism, which may be saved at the expense of democracy. Žižek (2011, p 69) asserts: 'the marriage between democracy and capitalism is over'. In this conflict, civil society finds itself the last and best hope for democracy. The renaissance of civil society has coincided with the new technology of the internet, creating a communicative revolution in which digital activism has transformed moral protest and fragmented media communication, with citizen journalism rivalling the established media in the search for truth.

The Occupy movement has emerged in this chaotic context as the voice of democracy in the form of a radical civil society. It is a discombobulating mix of the theatrical and theoretical. In a global village, the local camps of the Occupy movement stand out as symbols of protest in a world of zombie criticism. The internet provides the information that the official media suppresses. A Pinteresque truth is emerging, in the sense that our world is composed of 'many truths that challenge each other, recoil from each other, reflect from each other, tease each other' (Pinter, 2005). It is difficult to separate truth from fiction in this virtual reality. The Occupy movement has sought to contest official versions of the truth in the interests of public enlightenment.

The Occupy Wall Street movement was inspired by the Arab Spring (Greenberg, 2011; Van Gelder, 2011). However, while the occupiers of Tahrir Square had a single and unifying demand of regime change, the Occupy movement sought to create a more metaphysical revolt, by addressing the mind. It viewed its protest as an antidote to 'the pollution of our minds' by 'infotoxins … commercial messaging and the … financial and ethical catastrophes that loom before humanity' (Greenberg, 2011). The link to Camus' existential humanism is direct. What the Occupy Wall Street movement and the protesters of Tahrir Square shared was a common mastering of technology through online networking sites that enabled them to manage their protests in a unique new way.

The Occupy movement became a global phenomenon. While the Occupy Wall Street movement has been the centre of attention, it was preceded by camps in Madrid, Athens, Santiago and Malaysia. The Occupy movement's unifying theme is economic and social injustice – encapsulated in the slogan that 99% are being expropriated by the 1%. This is a powerful message that has attracted popular support: 'polls have shown almost twice as many Americans agreed with Occupy Wall Street than disagree with it. Far from alienating middle America, the movement captured the public and political imagination' (Younge, 2012). This popular success is no doubt directly linked to the suppression of the movement through the closure of camps, suggesting that the law is harsher on protesters than on bankers. In an evaluation of its legitimacy Gary Younge, writing in the *Guardian*, opined:

> The relationship between the physical space that the occupation movement has held and its political efficacy has not been settled – and perhaps never will be. Its importance doesn't lie in what it means, but what it does. It started by changing how people think about the world they live in; now it's strengthening their confidence to change it. (Younge, 2012)

The political legacy of the Occupy movement has been to reinsert 'inequality' into the public debate in post-socialist society. This is a considerable achievement.

The outraged: los indignados and Aganakismenoi

Stéphane Hessel's *Time of Outrage* (2011) found its answer on the streets across European cities during 2011. The Outraged movements date from anti-austerity protests. Greece and Spain became the main theatres of protest. In Spain *Democracia real ya!* was the slogan of Spanish *indignados* who occupied the Placa del Sol in Madrid and Placa de Catalunya in Barcelona and hundreds of squares across the country from 15 May 2011, calling for changes in social and economic policies and greater participation by citizens in decision-making (della Porta, 2012, p 66). In Greece the *Aganakismenoi* movement occupied Syndagma Square in Athens on 29 June 2011 and engaged in public debate about the consequences of the harsh austerity measures being imposed on the country. Costas Douzinas (2011) observed: 'the parallels with the classical Athenian *agora*, which met a few hundred metres away, are striking'. The daily occupations of Syndagma Square often draw crowds of 100,000 citizens to protest. In many other European cities similar protests took place organised by outraged citizens. Their sense of injustice was very real.

As hundreds of millions of euros are expended on saving banks many citizens are reduced to poverty. Donatella della Porta (2012, p 66) has observed that this has led to a public perception of profound social injustice – encapsulated in the metaphor 'the abduction of democracy'. The neoliberal solution to the economic crisis is generating a political crisis that is undermining trust in democratic institutions. Della Porta (2012, p 66) argues that the crisis is delegitimising the elitist model of democracy (based on political parties) because the locus of decision making has moved elsewhere (Brussels, Berlin, New York) and is no longer responsive to popular concerns. The influence of lobby groups and shadowy powerful interests over politicians has led to perceptions of corruption at the heart of government. Political party-funding systems have heightened this distrust because of the influence of oligarchs. The concentration of media ownership in the hands of wealthy media moguls has further exacerbated public anxiety.

The response to austerity economics has been two-fold. The traditional Left has mobilised around strikes, street protests and orchestrated responses to the public expenditure cuts and erosion of labour rights. New social movements have broadened the struggle into a debate about the nature and meaning of democracy – *Democracia real ya!* Their approach seeks not only policy change but greater public participation in the formulation of policy, which digitalisation makes possible. They have put Claus Offe's 'meta-question' of democracy at the centre of the debate (della Porta, 2012, p 66). Della Porta (2012, p 66) observes: 'the *indignados* discourse on democracy is articulated and complex, taking up some of the principal criticisms of the ever-decreasing quality of representative democracies, but also some of the main proposals inspired by other democratic qualities beyond electoral representation. These proposals resonate with (more traditional) participatory visions, but also with new deliberative conceptions that underline the importance of creating multiple public spaces, egalitarian but plural.' The issue is the quality of democratic experience and the need for political elites to actively engage with citizens' voices. The Outraged movement is reportedly supported by 90% of citizens in Spain and Greece (Della Porta, 2012, p 67). Trust in European institutions will not be fully restored until democratic engagement takes place around the question of what it means to be a citizen in the twenty-first century.

Pussy Riot and Russian punk anarchism

The democratic crisis in the European Union is overshadowed by the open repression of Putin's Russia. There is no legacy of democracy in Russia. Tsarist autocracy was followed by Stalinist tyranny, after a brief revolutionary moment. It seems to be Russia's destiny to suffer 'the Machiavellian Prince' as ruler. But there are democratic undertones within the creative world of Russian artists and musicians.

Out of this anarchic cultural vortex sprang Pussy Riot, a feminist punk rock collective that performs concerts critical of church and state. On 21 February 2012 Pussy Riot staged an impromptu protest in Christ the Saviour Cathedral in Moscow. In their brief, 51-second performance they sang a song, 'Virgin Mary, Redeem Us of Putin'. It was essentially the theatre of the absurd – an anarchist protest against political and cultural repression. But it appeared on YouTube, under the title 'Virgin Mary Chuck out Putin', and became a major focus of public interest. The head of the Russian Orthodox Church proclaimed the song to be 'blasphemous' and declared that the Church was 'under attack' and that 'the devil has laughed at us'. The Putin regime responded by arresting, imprisoning and putting on trial three members of the Pussy Riot collective on charges of public hooliganism. An intense media campaign has been launched by the Russian state, which controls the broadcasting system. The Pussy Riot trial has divided Russian society. It has been called Russian's Dreyfus affair. The sentence of two years in a penal colony handed down to the three members of the punk band collective has been described by Amnesty International as a 'travesty' (*Observer*, 19 August, 2012).

The Pussy Riot struggle is, arguably, not about individuals; it is essentially about an idea – democracy. It is a Pinteresque narrative of art against power, drawing on the anarchist tradition of Mikhail Bakunin (1814–76) and Emma Goldman (1869–1940), both of whom challenged uniformity and repression. These punk rockers have made a political statement that has galvanised Russian civil society in its campaign for real democracy. Their protest poignantly evokes Camus' rebel, as the spirit of Russian resistance to repression.

The psychopolitics of crisis: apocalypse now?

Francis Forde Coppola's 1979 epic war film *Apocalypse Now* (an adaption of Joseph Conrad's novella *Heart of Darkness*) depicts modern war as a descent into primal madness. Set in the Vietnam War it tells the story of war-weary Captain Willard's (Martin Sheen) being dispatched to assassinate AWOL Renegade Colonel Kurtz (Marlon Brando) – secreted in the Cambodian jungle, where he is rumoured to have established himself as a local godhead. Kurtz's genocidal dictum 'Drop the Bomb: Exterminate them all', graphically illustrated by human heads mounted on stakes outside his compound, provides a hallucinatory Wagnerian quality to a film in which the insanity of the individual mirrors the insanity of the Vietnam War. The director struggled to find an ending to the film. This became a metaphor for the film itself, in which reality and fantasy are merged. There is no purpose. Consequently, there can't be an end – at least not an end with a point, since futility on a grotesque scale has no point!

In a sense, *Apocalypse Now* reflects the contemporary crisis following the collapse of the neoliberal project in 2008. It is hard to see an end to the crisis. Austerity (which makes recovery very difficult, if not impossible) is the officially supported policy in Berlin and Brussels, as well as in the Western media. Yet, it doesn't seem to have a point – other than an ideological point. All of the escape routes have been closed off by the markets. The crisis has become political paralysis. There is no obvious fix

Slavoj Žižek argues in his book *Living in the End Times* (2011) that global capitalism is fast approaching its terminal crisis. As noted in Chapter Two, he identifies the Four Horsemen of the Apocalypse as: the worldwide ecological crisis; imbalances within the economic system; the biogenetic revolution; and exploding social divisions and ruptures. He characterises public reaction to this economic Armageddon in psychological terms as stages of grief: ideological denial, explosions of anger and attempts at bargaining, followed by depression and withdrawal.

In post-2008 financial crash reality, we are experiencing what Žižek calls 'The *real* real', which he likens to the horror in a horror film. The line between politics and fantasy has become blurred in our contemporary reality. This presents citizens with a series of questions:

- How can we overcome being subjects?
- How do we restore content to our democratic imaginary?
- How do we deal with the legacy of the 2008 financial crash?

The answers must be based on an attempt to reclaim political reality. First, we must discover the difference between truth and falsehood. Second, we are challenged to explore new democratic models and narratives, in the search for answers. Third, we need to reinvent politics in the form of a critical citizenship based upon inclusion and participation, in which the self and other interact in a new narrative of the republic. Finally, we need to rediscover society in the forum of sustainable communities, populated by *real* people.

How can this be done? The Irish President, poet and intellectual, Michael D. Higgins, in his book *Renewing the Republic* (2011, p 21), has set out an agenda:

> I believe we must now promote a positive vision of what it means to be a citizen in Ireland. This citizenship should be based on equality and respect, with a basic level of rights and participation – a citizenship floor – below which no one should be allowed to fall. We need to move away from radical individualisation towards a radical kind of inclusion.
>
> Inclusion means valuing diversity in all its forms and challenging exclusion wherever it occurs. No one in our society should experience the destructive effects of discrimination, isolation or rejection.
>
> Inclusion means celebrating solidarity by recognising the aspirations, concerns, creativity and potential of every citizen, regardless of the age, orientation, capacities or means. Inclusive citizenship also brings shared responsibility – a life that goes beyond the self to include those around us and, indeed, the generations yet to come.

The Irish President advocates a creative society constructed from the bottom up:

> the creative society cannot be imposed from above; it is built on creativity made possible by sustainable communities. Properly respected, the cultural space can be an invitation to push the boundaries of the possible – enfranchising us all in our capacity for living, and enriching the social and economic life of the nation. (Higgins, 2011, p 22)

He argues that the alternative is Žižek's Apocalypse:

> Should the adjustment in economic and social assumptions prove to be incapable of being made, we probably face an unmediated confrontation between the excluded and those who chose to be unconcerned. Such a point is the one at which the dark prescriptions of Slavoj Žižek become relevant. Around the world there is evidence that such

an outcome is achieving momentum, and some support. (Higgins, 2011, p 62)

President Higgins (2011, pp 16–17) concludes with his own apocalyptic warning:

> We are drifting to a final rupture between the economy, politics and society. If it happens, the ensuing conflict will not be mediated through trade unions, political parties or social movements. It will be a naked confrontation between, on the one side, the wealthy getting wealthier, and the poor getting poorer; between the excluded and the powerful; between the technologically manipulated. It will be a conflict as raw as any in history of private accumulation between, on the one hand, consumers, and, on the other, the excluded poor, who no longer have any norms of citizenship that they share or which would mediate their conflict.
>
> Public participation is now falling in every institution of civil society. The norms of a shared life have little opportunity of being articulated. That is the inescapable other side of the coin of globalisation, which is the unaccountable economy on a world scale. That is why it is necessary for the Left to outline the case for a new and vibrant citizenship that can vindicate such values as solidarity, community, democracy, justice, freedom and equality. These values can be achieved by giving them a practical expression in a new theory of citizenship.

The challenge that President Higgins has presented is essentially about the need for a new political fiction to take the narrative of democracy forward. It is very clearly framed within the language of civil society: community, inclusive citizenship and sustainability.

Arguably, President Higgins' vision of a political rupture generated by bottom-up forces within civil society points to the social Left, as opposed to the political Left, as the driver of change in post-politics society. The Occupy movement (now suppressed in New York, London and Dublin) is the most visible contemporary manifestation of the social Left as an actor in post-politics. In response to the eviction of protestors from the grounds of St Paul's Cathedral, the *Guardian* (29 February 2012) declared on its front page:

> You cannot evict an idea. Such is the message of defiance from Occupy. But it is not entirely true. For the whole point of Occupy is that it's not just an idea bouncing around the internet. Occupy is stubbornly about the physical reality of space. Others may write books and organise seminars. Occupy puts up tents. It takes up space. It is there.

The Occupy movement represented 'the commons' in postmodern society, that is, a right to common use and ownership of public resources, symbolised by public space. Sarah van Gelder (2011, p 1) likens the Occupy movement to the Arab Spring and argues that its name identifies the cause of the current crisis: 'Wall Street banks, big corporations, and others among the 1% are claiming the world's wealth for themselves at the expense of the 99% and having their way with governments.' What is refreshing about the Occupy movements is their determination to link their political critique of capitalism to practical welfare initiatives aimed at the socially excluded. Despite their chaos, they genuinely represent a search for truth. However, there are clear weaknesses, as well as strengths. As Anheier et al (2012, p 19) put it, 'the movements of 2011 appear to be committed to "thick" democracy as a method but they have not to date articulated clear substantive aims: for instance, in relation to the regulation of the global economy, social justice or sustainable development'.

Rights talk and the defence of the commons

Rights talk now has the ring of a funeral dirge for a dead political project. The grief reaction among the citizens for their lost sovereignty varies from denial through anger to despairing acceptance. There is a rupture with the past, but with no clear vision of the future that isn't apocalyptic. In the circumstances, the Irish president has gently reminded citizens that they have the power to construct their own future. His democratic vision is for a bottom-up renewal. He wants us to forge our own political fiction, in which we once again become actors in making our own history. We are invited by President Higgins to deepen our democracy, think for ourselves and shape our own destiny. Oddly, this sounds strangely counter-intuitive. Like Benjamin Barber's caged animals, we don't like to leave the comfort of the cage. Somehow, we remain mesmerised like the characters in Haruki Murakami's novel, *IQ84*. But there are voices of protest: the Arab Spring, Pussy Riot, *Los Indignados*, *Aganakismenoi* and the Occupy movement. The Occupy movement has attracted public support because its members dared to step outside their personal cages and enter the public sphere. But we are told that it is private space and they must be moved on. They were making democratic noises, which the authorities judged to be an unreasonable provocation of the citizens. Despite their public support, their protest was suppressed. The Occupy movement resembles those campaigns for the right of association that gave birth to democracy during the 18th and 19th centuries. That resulted in the 20th-century welfare state, the good society that benefited citizens. It too is being suppressed, however successful and compatible it is with a burgeoning economy. Social justice is a forbidden language in the 21st century.

Despite the constraints, participatory democracy continues to flourish as elites palpably fail to defend the democratic legacy of modern democracy by imposing neoliberalism in the form of privatisation, cuts in services and reduced employment rights on reluctant electorates. The voices of moral protest will continue to be heard in defence of democracy and the values that underpin it: liberty, equality and solidarity. Why? Because democracy is the voice of 'the commons', for example, the House of Commons in the UK.

The concept of 'commons', as already noted, refers to common use or ownership by the public. It is a historic term that pre-dates modern communism. E.P. Thompson (1975), in his classic book *Whigs and Hunters*, examines the Black Act (1723), which created 50 additional capital punishment offences. The law was aimed primarily at persons 'armed with sword, firearms, or other weapons, and having his or their faces blacked', who shall appear in any forest, chase, park or enclosed ground 'wherein any deer have or shall be usually kept' 'or in any warren, or on any high road, heath, common or down ...' (Thompson, 1975, p 21). Ironically, this draconian piece of legislation was passed by the British House of Commons without dissent, on the basis that it was 'emergency' legislation. The beneficiaries of the Black Act were the rising capitalist class, known as the Whigs, who successfully expropriated 'the Hunters' – ordinary people exercising customary agrarian rights, not for sport but for survival.

In postmodern society the meaning of 'commons' is much broader. Commons can refer to local use rights: for example, parks, access to beaches, libraries, post offices, schools, hospitals and so on. But it also refers to many services delivered in common by the welfare state (health, education, social protection, social housing, culture, arts and heritage). With the advent of globalisation the internet has become a universal (if contested) commons. Peter Barnes (2006), in his book *Capitalism 3.0: A Guide to Reclaiming Commons*, argues that the concept of the commons is based on shared ownership, gifted to the public.

But, arguably, its social meaning is deeper than simply gifted shared ownership. Commons is a set of existential rights that extend from air, water, ecosystems and food as the basic necessities to sustain life, through quality-of-life issues such as income, shelter, knowledge and security, to the contested issue of sustainable development – based upon protecting the planet for the use of future generations, as advocated by the Bruntland Report (1987), titled *Our Common Future*.

Conclusion

In the post-war era the world was initially silenced by the magnitude of events associated with the Holocaust, and their sheer horror. But it didn't last. Rights talk began. Human rights defined moral choices. New social movements emerged. Soon contradictions of modern democracy began to emerge. The quest for equality was incomplete. The lesson that a rising humanistically minded intelligentsia learnt was to become social actors on their own behalf. New social movements became the vehicles that gave expression to this new politics. Issues ranging from safety of the planet through to identity politics reshaped the debate about equality and justice. Human rights had become an overarching discourse, which new social movements used to benchmark their campaigns for greater democracy and social justice. The dominant motif was for change based on social justice for all. A radical civil society had taken shape during the post-war years. Much of its agenda was culturally oriented. But economic equality was never far from the centre of the social justice agenda. Perhaps, inevitably, the emergence of new radicalised civil society produced a reaction. It took two forms. In Eastern Europe it inspired the Velvet Revolutions. But it also provoked a reaction on the political Right in the West that seized the opportunity to reform welfare, while turning the issue of identity politics into a culture war. The Arab Spring amply demonstrates the idea of a burgeoning global associational revolution, albeit with an unexpected outcome in terms of Western expectations. While there are shared norms of civic engagement across the planet, there are also divergent cultural norms that shape the outcomes of popular revolts, proving that civil society takes many forms: radical, liberal and conservative. The Occupy movement demonstrates that radical civil society is very much alive and part of our contemporary political experience – linking popular protest to 'a revolution of the mind' in the Spinozian tradition of radical humanism.

SEVEN

American exceptionalism, multicultural civil society and Plato's noble lie

> When a conservative looks upon a democratic movement from below, this (and the exercise of agency) is what he sees: a terrible disturbance in the life of power.
>
> Corey Robin, *The Reactionary Mind* (2011, p 13)

> It is chiefly the formative role of apocalyptic religion in America that prevented it from establishing a variant of European civilization in the new world.
>
> John Gray, *Black Mass* (2007, pp 109–10)

The American essayist Gore Vidal (1925–2012), while parodying the United States as a quintessential reactionary society, dismissed external critics, 'these people, these foreigners. They wander in, read one issue of *Rolling Stone* and they think they know everything about it [America]' (*Observer*, 9 August 2012). It is a powerful rebuke to the would-be foreign writer to be respectful of American exceptionalism. The 9/11 terrorist attacks on the US reminded the world that we live in an era where we are witnessing what Tariq Ali (2002) has called *The Clash of Fundementalisms*. Fanatical Islamic anger towards the West was mirrored in aggression towards the Middle East. Whatever the rights and wrongs of the 2003 Iraq War and the war in Afghanistan, these wars have unleashed powerful political passions that express themselves as a 'jihad' on the Arab side and a 'crusade' on the Western side, evocative of the Middle Ages. Religious virtue is not simply a preserve of Islamic fanatics. It has become a defining influence in the Anglo-Saxon world. The consequences for civil society are profound. America is the quintessential modern multicultural civil society. It is the 'melting pot', to where the poor and hungry of the world have been drawn in the hope of building a new and better life. America is the embodiment of modernity, with which it has an enchanted relationship (Drury, 1997, p 14). That is the American dream. Of course, not all Americans came voluntarily. Afro-Americans largely came to America as slaves and struggled for emancipation over many generations. The election of an Afro-American President, Barack Obama, in 2008, was a defining moment in America's multicultural journey. Yet the forces of diversity and progress in America are challenged by a vibrant conservative civil society, most recently symbolised by the rise of the Tea Party. America has its culture wars. This chapter is about multiculturalism and civil society in America. It is also about the neo-Tocquevillian spirit that defines liberal American civil society. In America civil society has a historic importance because of the high consensus nature of party politics. Gore Vidal (cited in his Obituary, *Guardian*, 2 August 2012), the ultimate acerbic critique of American culture, observed:

> there is only one party in the United States, the Property Party ... and it has two right wings: Republican and Democrat. Republicans are a bit stupider, more rigid, more doctrinaire in their laissez-faire capitalism than Democrats, who are cuter, prettier, a bit more corrupt – until recently ... and more willing than the Republicans to make small adjustments when the poor, the black and the imperialists get out of hand. But essentially, there is no difference between the two parties.

Vidal had an impressive political pedigree, and twice failed to be elected to national office. His harsh judgement on US politics needs to be set in that context. Vidal also favoured the aphorism over the argument. Nonetheless, his savage caricature of the US party system bears an uncanny likeness to a political system where oligarchical interests have subordinated the democratic will of the people – through their capacity to dominate the communicative power of media advertising. That is Vidal's point! But Vidal is wrong to suggest that a manufactured consensus has undermined democracy in America. It is very much alive in civil society, an enduring Tocquevillian legacy.

Multiculturalism, social movements and recognition

Multiculturalism is a hermeneutic that encompasses politics, society and welfare states. It represents a wide range of ideas that are not easy to define. Perhaps it is more helpful to describe what it means. Quite simply, in terms of social policy, multiculturalism means a double focus on equality and distinctiveness (Blum, 1998, pp 73–9). Nancy Fraser has played a central role in theorising multiculturalism. Her ideas have been widely debated because they have profound implications for established concepts of equality. Fraser (1997, p 11) records the political and ideological tensions between 'the eclipse of a socialist imaginary centered on terms such as "interest", "exploitation", and "redistribution"' and 'the rise of a new political imaginary, centered on notions of "identity", "difference", "cultural domination" and "recognition"'. She sets herself the task 'of developing a critical theory of recognition, one which identifies and defends only those versions of the cultural politics of difference that can be coherently combined with the social politics of equality' (Fraser, 1997, p 12). Fraser (1997, p 26) makes the case for a transformative politics of recognition (that deconstructs group power identities) combined with transformative politics of redistribution (based on the principles of socialist solidarity). This means going far beyond the 'surface' reallocations of resources of the welfare state and the 'surface' reallocations of respect of mainstream multiculturalism, in search of a truly equal society. Fraser's analysis is clearly a very challenging one and underlines the radical implications of the multicultural debate for citizenship.

Multiculturalism is ultimately about the politics of recognition. Taylor (1994, p 75) has commented in this regard:

> The thesis is that our identity is partly shaped by recognition or its absence, often by the misrecognition of others and so a person or group of people can suffer real damage, real distortion, if the people or society around them mirror back to them a confining or demeaning or contemptible picture of themselves. Non-recognition or misrecognition can inflict harm, can be a form of oppression, imprisoning someone in a false, distorted and reduced mode of being.

Frantz Fanon (1925–61) was among the first to raise this issue of multiculturalism in post-war society, through the publication of his *Black Skin, White Masks* in 1952 (Fanon, 1967a). His vision of emancipation for the ethnically oppressed built on a long tradition of protest by Afro-Americans, from Frederic Douglas and Booker T. Washington to Martin Luther King and Barack Obama. It also built on the anti-colonial struggles against Western imperialism.

Recognition is mediated through forms of signification, that is, through modes of intelligibility and ideological frames of sense-making that organise individuals and groups into socioeconomic hierarchies of power and privilege (McLaren, 1994, pp 55–6). New social movements have sought to develop this system of power through cultural politics that is redefining the meanings of civil society. The transformative impact of new social movements on social policy is opening up new vistas. Over the past 40 years new social movements have emerged, championing multicultural causes as diverse as feminism, anti-racism, gay rights, disability awareness and grey power. They pose a fundamental challenge to conventional politics organised around political parties (Byrne, 1997). New social movements have created political and cultural spaces where civil society can flourish. As such, the social politics that dominated most of the 20th century, embodied in the welfare state, is rivalled by a new political agenda based on identity politics. Progressive politics, so long concerned with class inequalities and redistributive justice, has become more complex, embracing a diverse set of agendas, including the politics of recognition. In this changed political, social and cultural landscape, civil society, as noted above, is challenged to reinvent itself into new forms suited to the climate of the times.

The new social movements are making a vital contribution to this process of renewal and redefinition. Feminist social policy has fundamentally reshaped women's relationship with the welfare state. Disability awareness has brought the impact of a social movement that is simultaneously a service-user movement into the centre of what constitutes the definition of inclusive citizenship. Similarly, grey power is transforming cultural attitudes towards older citizens and the need for generative welfare strategies that support dignity and independence in an ageing population. Anti-racism challenges institutionalised discrimination in our society and demands new practices. Gay rights have heightened our awareness of the relationship between sexuality, culture and power. Poor people have also found a voice in this world of moral protest. America has been the principal theatre of cultural politics in the modern world. It is this enchanted relationship with modernity and its values (liberty, equality and solidarity) that provokes conservatives into thinking that America is on the road to nihilism – a journey that is taking it away from the purported values of the Founding Fathers (nation, family and religion).

Poor people's movements and civil rights

The term 'poor people's movements' was coined by Francis Fox Piven and Richard Cloward in their monumental study, *Poor People's Movements* (Piven and Cloward, 1979), which is 'about several protest movements that erupted among the lower-class groups of the United States during the middle years of the twentieth century' (p xix). These groups included: the Unemployed Workers' movement; the Industrial Workers' movement; the Civil Rights movement and the Welfare Rights movement. Piven and Cloward (1979, pp 3–4) assert, in reference to the political import of these poor people's movements:

> The emergence of a protest movement entails a transformation of consciousness and of behaviour. The change in consciousness has at least three distinct aspects. First, 'the system' – or those aspects of the system that people experience and perceive – loses legitimacy. Large numbers of men and women who ordinarily accept the authority of their rulers and the legitimacy of institutional arrangements come to believe in some measure that these rulers and these arrangements are unjust and wrong. Second, people who are ordinarily fatalistic, who believe that existing arrangements are inevitable, begin to assert 'rights' that imply 'demands for change'. Third, there is a new sense of efficacy; people who ordinarily consider themselves helpless come to believe that they have some capacity to alter their lot.

These marginalised groups that compose poor people's movements have existed in a world that has remained largely untouched by the social emancipation secured by forces of modernity. This social emancipation had brought the industrial worker into the political arena as a fully fledged actor. But Marx had dismissed what he called the *lumpenproletariat*, or underclass, as having no historical potential for emancipation.

Marx was wrong. The Civil Rights movement in the United States was to demonstrate that class was not the only element in the struggle for equality. Afro-Americans in the Southern states of America challenged a caste system through the Civil Rights movement. It demonstrated the link between economic and cultural oppression, epitomised by the system of racial segregation that was the hallmark of Southern politics in the US. The US Supreme Court decision in *Plessy v Ferguson* (1896) gave Southern whites *carte blanche* to enact discriminatory legislation (Carter, 1995, p 40).

White supremacy was ensured for more than half a century. Another US Supreme Court decision, *Brown v Board of Education* (1954), called for an end to segregation in public schools. Governor George Wallace of Alabama vowed to uphold 'segregation now ..., segregation tomorrow ... segregation forever' (cited in Carter, 1995, p 11). His 1963 theatrical gesture of blocking the admission of two black students to the University of Alabama in an unsuccessful but televised attempted to 'stand in the schoolhouse door' was to galvanise conservative America.

Carter (1995, p 12) has described George Wallace as the 'alchemist of the social conservatism'. He contested the US presidential elections in 1964, laying the foundations for subsequent Republican political domination of the electoral process.

Between 1957 and 1965 four civil rights bills were enacted, with the express intention of desegregating America. They were the product of the Civil Rights movement led by a black American clergyman and Nobel Prize winner, Dr Martin Luther King (1929–68). In 1957 King played an instrumental role in the foundation of the Southern Christian Leadership Conference (SCLC), a black church organisation opposed to racial segregation. As in South Africa under apartheid, the churches were the only place where black people had the right to associate. Religion and political aspiration gave birth to a powerful social movement. King and other civil rights leaders organised a March on Washington in 1963 to demand jobs and civil rights. On 28 August 1963, King delivered his most famous speech:

> I have a dream that one day this nation will rise up and live out the true meaning of its creed: 'We hold these truths to be self-evident, that all men are created equal' … I have a dream that my four little children will one day live in a nation where they will not be judged by the colour of their skin but by the content of their character.

Martin Luther King personified the Civil Rights movement, but it was a broadly based democratic social movement that demonstrated extraordinary courage in the context of violent repression. The assassination of Dr King in 1968 was the culminating act of violence in a sustained campaign of murder, church burnings and intimidation by the white population (often assisted by the state agencies, notably J. Edgar Hoover's FBI) against the Civil Rights movement that is recorded in Taylor Branch's masterly trilogy: *Parting the Waters* (1988), *Pillar of Fire* (1998) and *At Canaan's Edge* (2006). King and the Civil Rights movement represented a triumph of heroism over hatred. As King famously put it, 'I refuse to hate'. His espousal of non-violence, which was unwavering, bestowed upon the Civil Rights movement in the face of exceptional adversity a reputation for towering virtue that became unchallengeable (Wills, 2006, p 20).

The high point of the Civil Rights movement in America coincided with a variety of other social movements that challenged hierarchy and authority. The 'Sixties', as noted above, also witnessed the women's movement, the student's movement, the anti-Vietnam war protest movement. There was an exultant sense of liberation. It seemed that the world was becoming more socially just in a climate of change driven by hope. Even claimants felt empowered to organise the Welfare Rights movement. It seemed that there was not just one civil society in the United States but a vast diversity of civil societies challenging for equal recognition.

Piven and Cloward (1979, p 320) have put the Welfare Rights movement in political context:

> To say that the welfare rights struggle enjoyed some legitimacy is not to say that it enjoyed much. Welfare rights never became ennobled by the honour of its cause. With a few exceptions, powerful and prestigious figures, whether black or white, did not flock to its demonstrations (as they had to those of the civil rights movement in the South), nor did they contribute money to finance organising. This was to remain a movement of paupers, of a pariah class.

They contrasted the Welfare Rights movement with the Civil Rights movement, concluding that 'the civil rights movement was widely extolled as a force strengthening the American character and American values by furthering democratic ideals: the welfare rights movement was widely denounced as a force wrecking the American character by undermining the most cherished value of self-reliance' (Piven and Cloward, 1979, pp 320–1). Both the Civil Rights movement and the Welfare Rights movement did, however, impact on political consciousness, dividing America into socially progressive liberal and social conservative viewpoints that were to shape politics into the new millennium. Their legacy was to be bitterly contested and, in the case of welfare rights, reversed. The most recent manifestation of a poor people's movement in the US is the Latino *Movimiento*. Like its predecessors, *Movimiento* is a struggle for both recognition and redistribution.

The legacy of the Civil Rights movement casts a long shadow. Appiah and Gates (2005, p 105) comment: 'the enactment of the Civil Rights Act of 1964 and the Voting Rights Act of 1965 reinforced the guarantees of full citizenship ... The desegregation of public facilities was quickly implemented, and the rapid increase in black voting had far-reaching consequences for politics in the South, as well as the nation as a whole.' However, they also added a cautionary note: 'even so, patterns of discrimination, such issues as high rates of incarceration of black men, are still widely evident and point to areas in which racist assumptions continue to influence social policy'. Bruce Western, in his book *Punishment and Inequality* (2006), supports concerns regarding incarceration, which increased seven-fold over a 30-year period and in which a vastly disproportionate number of poor people from ethnic minorities are located. The shift towards punishment of the poor and away from welfare marks a major setback for ethnic rights in US public policy. There are also growing concerns about the disenfranchisement of many citizens from ethnic minorities – notably, those with criminal convictions.

The Great Society and the war on poverty

The Great Society was the project of President Lyndon Johnson in the 1960s. It sought to eliminate poverty and racial injustice by declaring a war on poverty. The emergence of welfare rights and community development as an anti-poverty strategy during the 1960s led to what Hughes and Mooney (1998, p 59) have called 'a prolonged assault on a number of deviant communities'. However, it would be inaccurate to view the poverty programmes and community development in terms of state regulation. They had a remarkable empowering dimension that defined them as radical social action. According to Knight (1993, p 50), 'community development is a method that involves the formation of organisations of ordinary people in geographical areas so that their collective identity gives them a greater say in the forces that affect their lives'. The Great Society, echoing Roosevelt's New Deal, was a genuine initiative to bring American innovative genius to the resolution of the problem of poverty and racial inequality. The boldness of the vision cannot be overstated. It sought to create an inclusive American civil society. This was the core ambition of the Great Society project.

The poverty programmes represent a rejection of charity-based models of social intervention in favour of social inclusion. These programmes, which were established in the 1960s in response to the 'rediscovery of poverty', rejected the individualisation of poverty in terms of family pathology. Their liberal and social democratic sponsors predicated them on the assumption that poverty was largely a localised problem confined to decaying inner-city areas and remote rural communities, where racial violence and social isolation had become endemic. Optimistically, it was believed that these problems could be overcome by targeted social intervention. The history of poverty programmes is one of progression from a consensus to a radical model of social change in the United States, and consequent disillusion on the part of the state. In the United States the Community Action Programmes (CAPs) were part of the 'War on Poverty' established as a result of the Economic Opportunities Act 1964, the cornerstone of President Johnson's 'Great Society' policy to eradicate poverty. The 'War on Poverty' had originated from the action-research-oriented Ford Foundation's Grey Area Projects, and similarly conceived President's Committee on Juvenile Delinquency.

In practice, the War on Poverty was based upon a welfare rights strategy that was intended to empower the poor of inner-city communities, particularly the black poor. It was very much a locally based initiative, with up to 1,000 projects. Piven and Cloward (1971, p 288) state that the type of welfare rights service that became most prevalent in the 1960s was 'the storefront center, staffed by social workers, lawyers, churchmen, students and slum-dwellers themselves'. These agencies were highly effective in empowering poor people to apply for welfare, in some cases increasing local welfare rolls by more than a third in one year. Such success was likely to produce a powerful reaction from neoconservatives deeply opposed to welfare. Wadden (1997, p 71) concludes:

> Despite these tales of success, however, by the mid-1980s it had become not only the political chant of the New Right but almost the conventional wisdom to reflect on the failure of the War on Poverty. Most immediately it might be supposed that this was because the poverty rate had not been reduced in the aftermath of the 1960s. Yet perhaps the starkest evidence in justification of the specific attempt to tackle poverty came with an examination of the official poverty rate. In 1960, 39.9 million citizens, constituting 22.2 per cent of the population, lived below the official poverty line. By 1979 these numbers had fallen to 26.1 million and 11.7 per cent, respectively.

In retrospect, the War on Poverty was the product of Great Society optimism. It was in many respects the apogee of American liberalism. From the start it attracted vitriolic criticism from the New Right. Piven and Cloward (1971, p 256) note that local programmes 'were charged with fiscal mismanagement and embezzlement and with encouraging demonstrations, protest and even riots'. Charles Murray (1984, p 145), in his book *Losing Ground*, which became the touchstone of New Right social policy, declared apocalyptically: 'the War on Poverty had become a domestic Vietnam'. In the face of this conservative critique there was a loss of liberal nerve, which ultimately paved the way for welfare reform. The redistribution of wealth achieved in the 1960s and

1970s in the United States was to be reversed during the 1980s and 1990s by both Republican and Democrat administrations – a trend that has continued into the 21st century, despite the election of an Afro-American President, Barack Obama, in 2008.

The War on Poverty represents reformist social policy at its zenith in a Western context. Social policy and New Deal liberalism had forged a powerful consensus around the promotion of welfare rights and the empowerment of the poor. The connection with the Civil Rights movement of the 1960s, committed to desegregation, was a close one. But as Martin Luther King was assassinated in 1968 and replaced by the Black Panthers and Malcolm X, a hardening of attitudes towards equality began. Class, gender and race issues coalesced in a resurgent New Right determined to destroy the Great Society, which it regarded as anathema.

American exceptionalism, neoconservatism and Plato's Noble Lie

Michael Ignatieff (2012, p 6) has commented: 'affirming belief that America is an exceptional nation has become a test of patriotism in American politics'. Corey Robin (2011, p 3) also presents American exceptionalism in a critical light, arguing that, historically speaking, American conservatives usually get their way:

> Since the modern era began, men and women in subordinate positions have marched against their superiors in the state, church, workplace, and other hierarchal institutions. They have gathered under different banners – the labor movement, feminism, abolition, socialism – and shouted different slogans: freedom, equality, rights, democracy, revolution. In virtually every instance, their superiors have resisted them, violently and non-violently, legally and illegally, overtly and covertly. That march and demarche of democracy is the story of modern politics or at least one of its stories.

Robin (2011, p 7) concludes:

> Conservatism is the theoretical voice of this animus against the agency of the subordinate classes. It provides the most consistent and profound argument as to why the lower orders should not be allowed to exercise their independent

will, why they should not be allowed to govern themselves or the polity. Submission is their first duty, agency, the prerogative of the elite.

Neoconservatism emerged during the 1960s as the voice of 'middle-America' – conservative and God-fearing. It fundamentally questioned the modernist project of American liberalism, which it viewed as a form of nihilism (Drury, 1997). At a philosophical level, neoconservatives denied the Enlightenment distinction between reason and revelation. If the Enlightenment represents the triumph of Athens over Jerusalem in the modernist narrative, neoconservatives are seeking to put Jerusalem back at the centre of modern American life, in an alternative fundamentalist Christian narrative inspired by America's pilgrim past. The link between religious fundamentalism and neoconservatism was an essential part of the emergence (during the 1970s and 1980s) of the New Right as a political synthesis between neoliberalism (privatisation, deregulation and public expenditure cuts) and conservative values (religion, family and nation). The presidency of Ronald Reagan, from 1981 to 1989, marked its high point. It was to generate a new apocalyptic vision of America's future, coupled with a hubristic belief that the year 1989 represented a global conservative restoration.

John Gray (2007), in his book *Black Mass: Apocalyptic Religion and the Death of Utopia*, argues that religion has returned in a perverted form: a 'black mass' of political myths. He focuses on 'the Americanization of Apocalypse'. Leo Strauss (1899–1973), a German Jewish émigré, emerges as the intellectual architect of neo-conservatism in the United States. The liberalism of the 1960s had unsettled American conservatives because of its perceived radical cultural agenda. It seemed the project of American exceptionalism, as the custodian of Western political values, was under fundamental attack from within. Leo Strauss emerges as the philosopher of the American Right – anti-liberal, anti-modern and quintessentially elitist (Drury, 1997).

According to Leo Strauss, American liberalism is a reflection of the country's love affair with modernity. As Shadia Drury (1997, p 14) puts it, in the Straussian worldview America is spellbound by modernity, with potentially fatal consequences: 'for America poses the greatest obstacles to her own salvation: she is enchanted with modernity'. The Straussian crusade against modernity, in Shadia Drury's analysis, has a messianic quality and amounts to an effective counter-revolution in the making. Drury (1997, p 15) asserts:

The role of Strauss's American disciples is to arrest America's development in the direction of more advanced modernity, and to enhance the small remnants of ancient wisdom that America's early stage of modernity still contains. America is to be divested of her modernity – gently, almost imperceptibly, without trauma and without violence. And since this is a supremely un-American activity, it is a very dangerous proposition and must therefore be undertaken with utmost care, not to mention secrecy. It requires great tact and a multiplicity of resourceful strategies, for it is nothing short of a counterrevolution. The Straussian revolution must be a quiet one.

In prosecuting their political task Straussians are clearly sensitive to the political implications of their rejection of popular democracy. They view their mission to bring about a conservative restoration in America as historically ordained by the Founding Fathers in the Declaration of Independence, the Constitution of the Federalist Papers (Drury, 1997). This gives their project a purported legitimacy in the goal of the Salvation of America. But the ideal of Plato's *Republic* – a society ruled by philosopher kings – has had a controversial intellectual history. Noble lies notwithstanding, the people have an affinity with democracy. Civil society is the antithesis of the virtuous ruling class. That is its virtue!

Leo Strauss's worldview was located in classical civilisation, as described by the ideas of Plato and Aristotle but also shaped by Nietzsche (Drury, 1997, p 17). He was an elitist, who subscribed to Plato's Noble Lie that religion (and, arguably, the idea of the nation) is a necessary myth. Liberalism, in Strauss's view, represents the triumph of freedom over order. Consequently, Strauss (like his intellectual mentor Carl Schmitt) was an anti-liberal elitist. Strauss in turn became the intellectual mentor of a neoconservative network that, it is suggested, had a deep influence on George W. Bush and his regime (Gray, 2007, pp 134–45). The apocalypse that emerged in the form of the 2008 financial crash is in many respects the consequence of the triumph of neoconservatism, which unleashed the market from the control of the state. But it was also a political disaster for neoconservatism. It has challenged what John Gray (2007, p 111) calls 'the abiding American belief in the country's exceptional role in the world'. China increasingly challenges American global dominance and belief in its exceptionalism. The Tea Party represents a reaction to this change.

The Tea Party and insurgent populism

The rise of the Tea Party in the United States has been one of the most striking political phenomena in recent history. Who is it and what does it think? First, it is not a conventional political party. It is composed of approximately 1,000 organisations across America. There are about 200,000 grassroots activists, of whom very few are 'strong' supporters. Typically, local Tea Parties are small, with meetings often composed of 'no more than a few dozen people' (Tanenhaus, 2012, p 8).

The Tea Party is, arguably, a movement of insurgent populism located in the undercurrents of US political culture. A survey by Harvard academics Theda Skocpol and Vanessa Williamson found that the Tea Party was primarily driven by a reaction to cultural change:

> Tea Party members rarely stressed economic concerns to us – and they never blamed business or the superrich for America's troubles. The nightmare of societal decline is usually painted in cultural hues and the villains in the picture are free social groups, liberal politicians, bossy professionals, big government, and mainstream media. (Cited in *New York Review of Books*, 8 March 2012, pp 8–9)

Paradoxically, Skopol and Williamson reported that 'fully 83% of South Dakota Tea Party supporters said they would prefer to "leave alone" or "increase" social security benefits, while 78% opposed cuts in Medicare prescription drug coverage, and 79% opposed cuts in Medicare payments to physicians and hospitals ... 56% of the Tea Party supporters surveyed did express support for "raising income taxes" by 5% for everyone whose income is over a million dollars a year' (cited in *New York Review of Books*, 8 March 2012, pp 8–9). Some commentators argue that Tea Party conservatism is not rooted in a coherent political programme but a 'mood' (Tanenhaus, 2012, p 8). Anheier et al (2012, p 14) assert:

> The Tea Party has often been described as an 'astroturf' movement as opposed to a grassroots one, since funding and organisers have been provided by wealthy supporters ... Yet given the extent of its mobilisation, it has evidently touched some populist chord – in a weird combination of ideas including nostalgia for a 'pure' white America, conservative 'family values', a distorted conception of freedom that involves cutbacks in the role of the federal

government (except for the military) and in taxation, as well as opposition to the wars in Iraq, Afghanistan and Libya and support for greater decentralisation.

There are signs that the apocalyptic passions that drove the Tea Party political movement are beginning to subside (Tanenhaus, 2012, p 8). While it is possible to suggest that the conservative philosophy of Leo Strauss is becoming popularised, it is perhaps more accurate to attribute the Tea Party to populist culture and media influences in US political culture. The influence of Ayan Rand (1905–82) in popularising conservative values in her influential novels, such as *Atlas Shrugged* (1957), is seminal. Rand depicted heroic individualism as America's salvation. She shaped an anti-statist anarcho-capitalist narrative as the American way. It resonates with a strand in public opinion that is drawn towards a form of insurgent populism that has historically been part of American political culture. The Tea Party is probably ephemeral, but it has a pedigree in American conservatism. It is the authentic voice of conservative civil society in 21st-century America – anti-statist and anti-secular.

Neoconservatism: the end of welfare in America

The United States, the homeland of the Anglo-Saxon liberal model of welfare based on neoliberal economics and neoconservative political values, presents a very different picture to that of the European Union. A conservative restoration is reshaping America. The neoconservative movement, as already noted, has been in gestation in the United States since the 1960s and is inspired by Leo Strauss and his disciples. Hutton (2002, p 95) has observed in relation to the singular influence wielded by Strauss over the American political elite that he provided it with a philosophy for a conservative restoration:

> The good society, [Strauss] insisted was constructed upon virtuous morally centred citizens of good character, and the case against state-led attempts to socially engineer more equality was that they undermined such virtue by relieving individuals of the necessity of facing the consequences of individual actions. He thought that religion and nationalism helped to entrench such virtue, and that liberalism and secularism undermined it – and that unless the US was watchful it faced the same fate as the Weimar Republic.

More than two decades after Strauss's death in 1973, it is a widely held view that the inspiration for the 1994 Republican manifesto, *Contract with America*, to Strauss. The decision by the Republican Party to embrace the conservative evangelical movement and support faith-based charity and pro-life positions is undoubtedly attributable to Strauss. Shadia Drury (1997, p 9) puts the Straussian vision of America's future into stark relief:

> So why do Strauss and his followers continue to paint liberalism as nihilistic and sceptical? The answer lies in the fact that liberalism has a sceptical temper where politics is concerned. For the sake of truth, liberals reject the imposition of those in power of a single and indisputable reality. The liberal stance conflicts with the Straussian conviction that society requires unwavering faith and unflinching devotion. And even though the result is zealotry and fanaticism, Strauss does not flinch from it; for zealotry and fanaticism are preferable to nihilism and scepticism, because the latter weaken society, while the former strengthen it.

The respected American critic Harold Bloom (2005, p 4) has rhetorically posed the question 'What defines America?' adding: 'Democracy is a ruined word, because of its misuse in American political rhetoric of our moment.' Bloom asserts that 'even as [President] George W. Bush extolled his Iraq adventure, his regime daily fuses more tightly together elements of oligarchy, plutocracy and theocracy' (Bloom, 2005, p 4). He argues that a new religion is emerging in the United States, quite distinct from its European origins, which celebrates wealth, neglects poverty and seeks to place intelligent design (creationism) on an intellectual par with Darwin's theory of evolution. Some 45% of Americans believe that the Earth was created precisely as described in the Book of Genesis and is not more than 9,000 years old. To them, Darwin is 'the Satan of America'. In a society where opinion polls reveal that 93% of the population believe in God and 89% are certain that God loves them in a personal way, the importance of religion as a cultural force cannot be overestimated (Bloom, 2005).

Leo Strauss has upheld Plato's Noble Lie that the political masses need religious belief – even if it is 'bunk' because he viewed it as the antidote to liberal nihilism. As Holmes (1993, p 65) puts it, in the Straussian view of the world, 'religion is socially useful because it infantilises most human beings and anesthetises them to the anguish an unscreened <u>view of nature would provoke in weak minds</u>'. The parody of European Christianity that has emerged in the form of American Christian fundamentalism provides the consoling myths that insulate the mass of the American population from a more critical reality. While 'telly evangelism' may appear to the European post-Christian mind as risible, Bloom (2005, p 4) concludes that 'contemporary America is too dangerous to be laughed away'. Strauss has redesigned American democracy. Corey Robin (2011, p 173) asserts in relation to the enigmatic nature of Leo Strauss's influence that his 'quiet odes to classic virtue and ordered harmony veiled his Nietzschean vision of torturous conflict and violent struggle'. Regardless, Strauss laid the intellectual foundations for the resurgence of America's conservative civil society.

Rapture: the credo of cultural conservatism

In his satirical novel, *Candide* (1759) (Voltaire, 1993), the French Enlightenment philosopher Voltaire (1694–1778) called into question faith in the idea of an ultimate purpose. In his masterpiece Voltaire tells the story of a young man, Candide, and his innately optimistic mentor, Pangloss, on their travels, where they experience every conceivable misfortune. The occurrence of the Lisbon earthquake in November 1755, which almost totally destroyed the city, was a severe check to the climate of optimism that shaped the 18th century. Voltaire, in common with his fellow 18th-century *philosophes*, recognised the precariousness of progress, devoting his life to excoriating fanaticism and superstition, which were epitomised, in his view, by religion and the rule of divine right.

The modern world was built on the idea of progress in its various manifestations: liberal, Marxist, feminist and so on. These secular grand narratives suggested the possibility of a better, more equal future. The belief in political and social progress was mirrored by material and scientific advances. It suggested that humankind was making real progress. But the 20th century shattered that optimism, our belief in progress in the moral sense was undermined by devastating technological war and the Holocaust. Hywel Williams concludes:

> But there is a further reason for scepticism. The history of the 20th century dissolved the connection between the material or scientific progress and a better moral order. Technological advance was twice turned to the business of mass slaughter in global war, as well as to genocide and ethnic cleansing. Material progress was seen to mingle with

moral regress. The model T Ford and the gas chamber were the inventions that defined the century. (Williams, 2005)

In the wake of this shattered dream emerged an old force from a previously rejected past – cultural conservatism in the form of the rebirth of religious fundamentalism. Evangelists such as Jerry Falwell and Pat Robertson emerged, preaching a gospel that denounced simultaneously moral permissiveness and state welfare. Doing good was God's preserve, virtue the preserve of the religious. Secularism, socialism and modernism were in their eyes the credo of the damned. In their stead, American evangelists offer the Rapture credo, 'the world cannot be saved'. Bob Moyers, in the *New York Review of Books*, explained the Rapture credo and its cultural roots in the Middle East, the cradle of Christianity, Judaism and Islam:

> The plot of the Rapture – the word never appears in the Bible although some fantasists insist it is the hidden code to the Book of Revelation – is rather simple, if bizarre. Once Israel has occupied the rest of its 'biblical lands', legions of the Antichrist will attack it, triggering a final showdown in the valley of Armageddon. As the Jews who have not been converted are burned the Messiah will return for the Rapture. True believers will be transported to heaven where, seated at the right hand of God, they will watch their political and religious opponents writhe in the misery of plagues – boils, sores, locusts, and frogs – during the several years of tribulation that follow. (Moyers, 2005, p 8)

The emergence of a call for faith-based charities in the US, following the abolition of welfare in 1996, is the most visible sign of evangelical influence over social policy. The election of a US president in 2000 who was a born-again Christian put an evangelical in the White House. The 2012 Republican primary campaign was driven by a militant brand of social conservatism that seeks to define American civil society within fundamentalist Christian tenets, evoking the presidency of George W. Bush. However, the Straussian project of reinventing America as a conservative society ruled by a Platonic elite no longer seems a potent lineat to American democracy and civil society. That doesn't mean that cultural conservatives have given up on resacralising America.

Faith-based charity in America: resacralising society

On 29 January 2001, President George W. Bush signed an Executive Order establishing a White House Office of Faith-Based and Community Initiative (OFBCI). The website www.georgebush.com had promised, during the 2000 presidential election campaign, the expansion of charitable choice to all federal laws, unleashing 'armies of compassion' in a new wave of welfare reform:

> Governor Bush envisions a different role for government – a role based on the belief that government should turn first to faith-based organizations, charities, and community groups to help people in need. Resources should be devolved, not just to the states, but to the charities and neighbourhood healers who need them most, and should be available on a competitive basis to all organizations – including religious groups – that produce results. As President, Governor George W. Bush will commit himself and the nation to mobilizing the armies of compassion – charities and churches, communities and corporations, ministers and mentors – to save and change lives as he has done in Texas. This is the next bold step of welfare reform. (Bush–Cheney, 2000)

However, the problems of religious fundamentalism and cultural essentialism in the US soon put the future of President George W. Bush's faith-based charity project in doubt. Conservative Christian bodies expressed alarm at the prospect of fringe religious (as they saw them), such as the Church of Scientology, the Hare Krishnas and followers of the Reverend Sun Myung Moon (the 'Moonies'), benefiting from state assistance. Louis Farrakhan's Nation of Islam organisation was attacked by a leading Jewish group, the Anti-Defamation League, as unworthy of government support (*New York Times*, 20 February 2001). Manifestly, social movements and community groups committed to change were excluded.

Liberals expressed concern that President Bush's partnership between church and state violated the First Amendment to the United States Constitution. It enshrines separation between church and state, and it is difficult to see how Bush's faith-based charity project would not have violated the Constitution of the United States. There were suggestions that churches would eschew their evangelical mission. But this is hardly realistic, given that evangelicalism constitutes the *raison d'être* of every religion. Americans United for Separation of Church and State declared in February 2001: 'In a nation where the government must remain neutral on religious matters and funding for ministries is supposed to be derived voluntarily from believers instead of being mandated by the state, many Americans get more than a little nervous when the President starts offering clergy ways to "get around" the First Amendment' (cited in the *Guardian*, 13 March 2001). Religious belief is at the core of conservative civil society in the United States.

There was a deep sense of unease among liberals that the faith-based charity project was part of a conservative restoration bent on globally rolling back the welfare state. The *Observer* (4 February 2001) reported: 'The reformed structures, it is argued, will roll back the follies and errors of the liberal 1960s and Lyndon Johnson's Great Society, injecting new moral vitality into the fight against poverty – establishing a model for conservatives in Europe to follow…. Opponents say that this means a government abrogating its responsibilities to the poor.'

These reservations put the future of the faith-based charity initiative in doubt. The Bush administration had originally envisaged a bill to approve federal funds for religious groups and to preserve tax deductibility of donations to such groups. But this was put 'on hold'. Even the religious Right was having second thoughts about the proposed partnership between church and state. Robert Boston of Americans United for Separation of Church and State commented on the atavistic suspicion that the religious Right feels towards government: 'There is an innate mistrust of government among the religious right: with government funding comes government regulation. Suddenly a lot of the groups are having second thoughts' (*Guardian*, 13 March 2001). The 2010 mid-term election results confirmed this political trend. Led by the Tea Party, America moved sharply to the Right in a profoundly anti-statist political mood. During the 2012 presidential election campaign Republicans have continued to pursue an anti-statist agenda but failed to win over a majority of voters. Multiculturalism was the victor.

Despite these second thoughts, Michelle Goldberg (2006) argues in a study titled *Kingdom Coming: The Rise of Christian Nationalism* that the faith-based regime is beginning to supplant the New Deal that defined the *zeitgeist* of America's minimalist welfare state. Goldberg (2006, p 107) concludes:

> The diversion of billions of taxpayer dollars from secular social service organizations to such sectarian religious outfits has been one of the most underreported stories

of the Bush Presidency. Bush's faith-based initiatives have become a spoils system for evangelical ministries, which are now involved in everything from prison programs and job training to teenage pregnancy prevention, supplanting the safety net that was supposed to catch all Americans. As a result of faith-based grants, a growing number of government-funded social service jobs explicitly refuse to hire Jews, gay people, and other undesirables; such discrimination is defended by the administration and its surrogates in the name of religious freedom.

It would appear, if Goldberg is correct, that government finance during the presidency of George W. Bush was being diverted away from secular social services and towards faith-based charities. Exclusionary employment practices are resulting from their religious ethos, with implications for discrimination against minority groups.

George W. Bush, elected to his second term as President of the United States in 2004, was determined to maintain the allegiance of the evangelical conservative movement. His espousal of the Terri Schiavo case in 2005 bore eloquent testament to his dedication to the evangelical conservative cause. Terri Schiavo, a brain-damaged woman who had been in a persistent vegetative state for 15 years, had her feeding tube removed on the authority of a Florida state judge at the request of her husband. The Schiavo case had been heard by 19 judges in seven courts and unsuccessfully appealed to the Supreme Court three times. President Bush and the Republican congressional leadership saw it as a test case of conservative evangelical power. Tom DeLay, the then Republican congressional majority leader, declared:

> One thing God has brought to us is Terri Schiavo. This is exactly the issue that's going on in America, the attacks on the conservative movement against me and many others.... This is a huge nationwide concerted effort to destroy everything we believe in ... and we have to fight back. She talks and she laughs and she expresses likes and discomforts. (*Guardian*, 24 March 2005)

The Democrat political commentator Sidney Blumenthal responded:

> For the first time public policy in the US is being made on the basis of pitting invisible signs versus science. As in tribal cultures, a confederacy of shamans – Bush, Frist and

DeLay – have appeared to conduct rights of necrophiliac spiritualism. Only the shamans can interpret for the dying and control their spirits hovering between heaven and earth. The public opinion polls show overwhelming disapproval of the Republican position. But these polls are just so much social science. In this operation, for the tribe, there is no way of proving failure. (*Guardian*, 24 March 2005)

In this 'Rapturous' climate of evangelical fervour, the removal of social services from the secular sphere would appear to be highly possible. A religious future, evocative of the medieval religious world, would seem to constitute a possible future for American civil society. The only problem is that America remains a liberal democracy. The diversity of civil society in the United States means that there is a permanent tension between its liberal, conservative and radical components. But there is a sense that we are witnessing in conservative civil society in the United States a new theology of power. Its reach may be global.

A new theology of power?

In a world where religion and politics once again seem to be converging as the centre of power and influence, this is why it is possible to speak of a new theology of power. Its influence is likely to impact on civil society. Teeple (1995, pp 150–1) has characterised the much-vaunted triumph of neoliberalism and the global market as a coming tyranny, observing that:

> Capitalism must increasingly confront the world that it has made, the results of its own expansion: seriously degraded nature, an increasingly impoverished working class, growing political autocracy and declining legitimacy, and new forms of resistance.... Here, largely unfettered by political considerations, is a tyranny unfolding – an economic regime of unaccountable rules, a totalitarianism not of the political but of the economic.

Mason's (1997, p 7) comment in relation to 1930s Germany comes to mind, in which he argues that fighting communities 'need to engage in self-deception'. Other commentators have taken a more optimistic view, detecting a new complexity in which a more radical democratic imaginary can emerge. Walzer (1983) has suggested a break with the old normative idealism embodied in collectivist and universal notions of 'the social' and advocated new thinking around pluralist frameworks of complex equality that involves taking democratic rights beyond traditional conceptions of citizenship.

Behind Walzer's vision is the assumption that culture and society shape the nature of government. This is true to a degree. It is essential to the neo-Tocquevillian vision of the pivotal role of intermediate institutions as the generative force in society. However, an older tradition of thought, stretching from Aristotle to Montesquieu, suggests that fundamentally the state shapes society, not the other way round. If we accept this view, we are thinking not about civil society in the all-embracing sense envisaged by De Tocqueville, but about the Roman virtue of *civitas*, that is, public-spiritedness, sacrifice for the community and, of course, social obligation. However, Walzer's conception of a radical democratic imaginary indicates the critical role played by civil society in political change.

Tocquevillians versus Gramscians

Alberto Luzárraga (2010) presents American civil society as a battle between the followers of Alexis de Tocqueville and of Antonio Gramsci. He cites the *Wall Street Journal* of 19 December 2000 in support of his thesis:

> [The *Wall Street Journal*] defines the ideological split in America as a contest between present-day Tocquevillians and disciples of the 20th-century Italian philosopher Antonio Gramsci, who drew on the ideas of Friedrich Hegel and Karl Marx. The Tocquevillians incline towards individualism, religious belief and patriotism. The Gramscians see any society, including America, as an arena where the 'marginalised' are necessarily at war with the privileged classes. Good old fashioned class warfare, in other words.

Luzárraga's novel analysis captures the dichotomy between traditionalists and progressives in American civil society and political culture. Robert Putnam (2000), in his iconic study of civil society in the United States, *Bowling Alone*, has cast doubt on the Tocquevillian legacy. Putnam's core argument is that postmodern America is characterised by social disengagement. The visual media has created a society that is increasingly atomised with shrinking social capital. Traditional forms of participation in social networks are in decline. However, it may be that they are changing. Face-to-face interaction in the age of social networks is being replaced by virtual encounters and digital activism, for example, Facebook, texting, blogging and so on. Technology is not susceptible to either secular or religious control, but it has transformed social relations.

Lester Salamon and Kassey Spence (2009) take a more optimistic view of social engagement in the United States than that suggested by Robert Putnam. On the basis of a 2009 survey of 1,400 non-profit sector organisations engaged in the fields of activity (including children's and family services, elderly housing and services, education, community and economic development), they examined the impact of public expenditure. Salamon and Spence discovered a neo-Tocquevillian paradox. The recession had impacted severely on non-profit organisations, but volunteerism enabled them to enhance their effectiveness. Communitarianism is, apparently, very much alive in American culture. Salamon and Spence (2009, pp 1–2) conclude that 80–90% of these non-profit organisations transferred their service delivery systems from professionalised to volunteers. The volunteers were prepared to take on more activity and their recruitment increased. However, Salamon and Spence (2009) acknowledge, 'it will be important to avoid thinking of volunteers as substitutes for paid staff'. What this development tells us is that the Tocquevillian spirit of social engagement is still very much alive and well in America. In the context of the economic crisis, active citizens are willing to help their neighbours. That is very hopeful. But active citizenship cannot be a substitute for social citizenship based on entitlement. It is simply charity, with all its limitations in human rights terms.

Conclusion

The United States of America is an exceptional society. Its historical narrative differs from that of Europe. But its institutions have proved to be more durable. Apart from the American Civil War (1861–65), Americans have managed to resolve their political differences peacefully. This may be explicable in terms of the powerful cultural influence of civil society, first noted by Alexis de Tocqueville in the 1830s. While religion plays an apocalyptic role in framing the national psyche, there is at the heart of American culture an enthusiasm for modernity that ultimately transcends the vagaries of history. The social in American political culture remains remarkably communitarian – the neo-Tocquevillian paradox. However, there is also a radical civil society in America that is part of a broadly based progressive coalition. This is the Gramscian tendency in American politics. The world that Alexis de Tocqueville described has been replaced by a multicultural civil society. It has resulted in a sharp ideological divide within American civil society. De Tocqueville's liberal version of civil society is challenged by radical civil society, made up of a coalition of progressive political causes (feminist, ethnic rights, gay rights and so on) seeking 'the right to have rights', in Arendt's famous phrase. It is also challenged by conservative civil society, most flamboyantly represented by the Tea Party.

EIGHT

Global civil society: myth or reality?

> From the beginning we conceived global civil society as a 'fuzzy and contested concept'.
>
> H. Anheier, M. Kaldor and M. Glasius,
> 'The global civil society year book' (2012, p 2)

> Hunger, disease, and waste of lives that is extreme poverty are an affront to all of us.... History will be our judge, but what's written is up to us.
>
> Bono, Foreword to Jeffrey Sachs,
> *The End of Poverty* (2004, p xv)

The eclipse of the socialist imaginary has undermined the principal modernist narrative of change. Its passing has left a political and moral vacuum at the heart of society. Decades of virtuous achievement in terms of struggles for social justice have been swept away in a society that has exchanged state-centred social politics for individualised consumer choice. But, arguably, the individual choices of consumer society would not have been possible without the social struggles of the past. Globalisation brought a change in the direction of civil society, altering the focus from past preoccupations. Campfens (1997, p 4) notes: 'Relations have since changed between the state and civil society, because of the struggles with global restructuring and changing ideologies; as a result new actors have appeared on the scene.' What Campfens is clearly referring to is the growing influence of globalisation in terms of shaping a neoliberal project that has served to downsize the welfare state. The eclipse of the socialist imaginary has given a new lease of life to civil society internationally in terms of the role of NGOs. Humanitarian NGOs are the world's conscience. Humanitarianism expressed through a concern with tackling world poverty through philanthropic activity has become a dominant political norm in the age of global capitalism. Deakin (2001, p 172) has likened this development to the emergence of a new entity, 'global civil society'. While he acknowledges that international organisations such as the International Committee of the Red Cross, Save the Children Fund and Oxfam have been around for a very long time, there has been a 'new policy agenda' since the collapse of communism that has laid down the parameters for the emergence of a global civil society. Its influence is evident in approaches to development policy and international aid. This chapter explores the nature of global civil society and its changing role within nation-states that are being recast by globalisation, prompting new conceptions of state and society relations. Karl Polanyi (1886–1964), in his monumental study, *The Great Transformation*, originally published in 1944 (Polanyi 2001), argued that the 19th century was the age of capital, which was reversed during the 20th century by socialism. Will the 21st century produce a third project, and what will be the role of civil society in shaping it? We must now turn our attention to seeking answers to these questions.

Civil society, globalisation and the state: the NGOisation of the public sphere

Barber (1984, p 14) has observed that 'from the perspective of this political zoology, civil society is an alternative to the jungle – to the war of all against all that defines the state of nature'. This statement invests a lot of credibility in the social and moral potential of civil society. It envisages the civic domain as essentially democratic, providing 'free spaces' where citizens can take control of democracy, learning the competencies of social responsibility and participation. Kaldor (2005, p 43) notes the political influence of civil society discourse over time, observing that 'the changing content reflects changing historical circumstances, but, in my view, it is possible to identify a shared meaning that has to do with the process of agreeing on rules and common procedures for dealing with conflict, an ethical space where public and private, individual and universal values are reconciled'. This analysis places a very positive construction on the concept of civil society and its potential for good. Similarly, Keane (1998, p 69) notes that civil society has become 'a positive synonym for voluntary association, diversity and liberty, among its supporters on the political Left'. He further asserts: 'So we see the waxing moon of civil society and the beginnings of a world-wide search for new equilibriums between state and non-state institutions' (Keane, 1998, p 34). For Keane (1998, p 32), civil society is forging a new language: 'So striking is the popularisation of the term that it could even be said that the language of civil society is currently undergoing vertical and horizontal globalisation.' He concludes: 'This development was wholly unexpected and it has consequently filled some with the millenarian hope that the Age of Civil Society is nigh' (Keane, 1998, p 65). The Union of International Associations has recorded nearly 17,000 international NGOs (*International Herald Tribune*, 15 August 2002). But Frantz Fanon's critique of Western development attitudes in his seminal book *The Wretched of the Earth* (Fanon, 1967b) continues to haunt the authenticity of our intentions towards the developing world.

Kirby (2006, pp 203–11), in a study of the impact of globalisation titled *Vulnerability and Violence*, observes that 'there is extensive evidence that global civil society, in engaging with key economic and political powers in this globalised world order, has become a significant social actor'. He cites examples: 'Campaigns against Nestlé for its infant milk formula, against Nike for its labour conditions, against toy makers in China and other developing countries for their labour conditions, against pharmaceutical corporations for their control of HIV/AIDS drugs and their refusal to allow developing countries like South Africa and Brazil to manufacture cheaper generic drugs, against Monsanto for genetic engineering, and against Shell for its activities in Nigeria, have all gained a high level of international media coverage and elicited changes in the practices of corporations involved (though critics claim such changes are often more cosmetic than substantial)' (Kirby, 2006, p 205). The Fair Trade Network, which seeks to support poor producers in developing economies, offers another illustration of the positive influence of civil society on global ethics (Kirby, 2006, p 205). But Kirby (2006, p 206) sombrely concludes:

> Yet for all its activism, global civil society's achievements have been modest at best. It may have helped modify some of the harder edges of neoliberal globalisation, slightly lessening the extent of vulnerability faced by some groups (for example, some workers in sectors of global manufacturing targeted by campaigners) and strengthening in a modest way some coping mechanisms (such as environmental regulations). Overall, however, it has done little to curb the extension of market values into almost every domain of our social lives. This may not be due to any failure on the part of global civil society but rather due to the fact that large sectors of it may either uphold and promote neoliberal globalisation (for example, business lobbies, professional associations and philanthropic foundations) or else co-operate with states and inter-governmental organisations in projects and programmes that are in no way inconsistent with neoliberal

globalisation (after all many civil society organisations are
subcontracted by states to provide services).

A fundamental weakness in civil society as an organising principle is that
it can 'mean all things to all people'. Kaldor (2003, p 2) notes that the
term 'civil society' can be enthusiastically embraced by interest groups
as diverse as neoliberals, post-Marxists and Islamicists. In fact, Kaldor
suggests that there is a mimetic quality to civil society, with new social
movements emerging in the 1970s and 1980s, international NGOs
dominating the global scene during the 1980s and 1990s, nationalist
and fundamentalist movements mushrooming during the 1990s and,
finally, the anti-capitalist/anti-globalisation, Occupy and *los indignados*
movements dominating the new century. Kirby (2006, p 207) responds
to Kaldor's observation that a more accurate representation might be 'to
see them as competing against one another and therefore to see global
civil society as a terrain of struggle. What unites the different forms
of actors competing on this terrain is that they are non-hierarchical,
decentralised and often local groups that network with one another
across state boundaries.' In this sense, global civil society constitutes
a movement for social change and transformation. Democracy is at
its core. However strong the pressures of corporate funders and state
bureaucracies to conform to the 'top-down' managerialism of the
neoliberal elite that sets the international agenda, there are demonstrable
signs that civil society is value driven. Hilary Wainwright (2005, p 97)
views civil society's embeddedness in the democratic process as the
hallmark of its transformative influence and potential 'as a force for
achieving and deepening democracy or rebuilding it in a radically
new context'. That new context is shaped by the civic republican
tradition of democracy informed by the right to associate. On the
face of it, civil society offers the prospect of a political future that
is shaped by a deepening democracy. As Kaldor (2003, p 12) puts it,
'global civil society for the activists, therefore, is about "civilizing" or
democratizing globalization, a global rule of law, global justice and
global empowerment'.

But this optimism is challenged by sceptical commentators. Rieff
(1999, p 11) declares:

> When we put our faith in civil society, we are grasping at
> straws. Apart from a few principled nationalists, libertarians
> and Marxists, most well intentioned people now view
> the rise of civil society as the most promising political
> development of the post-cold war era. By itself, that fact

only points to how desperate we are, on the cusp of the millennium, to identify any political paradigm offering some realistic prospect for a more humane future.

Rieff (1999, p 12) goes on to provide a searing critique of civil society, arguing that any idea that simultaneously enjoys the support of the US government and the European Union poses no threat to powerful vested interests: 'Far from being oppositional, it is perfectly in tune with the Zeitgeist of an age that has seen the growth of what proponents like Bill Clinton and Tony Blair are pleased to call the "Third Way" and what might be called Thatcherism with a human face.' He accuses the advocates of civil society of being 'the useful idiots of globalisation', assisting the privatisation of democracy building: 'Further by undermining the state, they undermine the only remaining power that has at least the potential to stand in opposition to the privatisation of the world, commonly known as globalisation' (Rieff, 1999, p 12). Rieff asserts that in a world consisting of etiolated nation-states, putting society's faith in local concerns and single-issue campaigns represents a return to pre-democratic forms. He concludes that civil society 'is, indeed, the new medievalism, with the leaders of the NGOs as feudal lords.... Yet as things stand it is this unaccountable, undemocratic congeries of single-interest groups that is being proposed as the only viable alternative to the nation-state.'

Clough (1999, p 16) shares Rieff's scepticism about the limitations of civil society, warning that 'attempting to create twenty-first century versions of twentieth-century institutions founded on seventeenth-century assumptions is a recipe for failure'. He argues that we exist in a world where the nation-state paradigm is being eroded and replaced exponentially by the market and civil society, but insists that much progress needs to be made before the emergence of a clear alternative form of governance will be achieved. Clough (1999, p 18) makes several important suggestions:

1. That government at local, national and international levels needs to become more inclusive, collaborative and adaptive in its dealings with civil society.
2. Civil society, for its part, must recognise that partnership with government brings new obligations to be democratically accountable in forging an ethic of global governance.
3. Civil society can do much to promote with government the elimination of poverty, oppression and war.

The relationship between civil society, globalisation and the state raises profound normative questions that ought to inform any discussion of the meaning of citizenship and association in postmodern society. Debates among contemporary social theorists about the transformative potential of civil society have devolved on this complexity. Gramsci's ideas have proved to be seminal in unpacking the issues. Mayo (2005, p 46) concludes:

> Civil society according to this more complex view is potentially a key site of struggle, particularly key when it comes to the battle of ideas about capitalism and the extent to which it may even be feasible to consider alternatives for transformation. Far from seeing capitalist globalisation as necessarily linked to the strengthening of civil society, whether as cause or effect – or both, such approaches see civil society then as an increasingly important arena for these struggles, globally as well as locally.

But a sceptical public has yet to be convinced about the value of civil society. The World Summit on Sustainable Development, known as the 'Earth Summit', in Johannesburg in 2002, became a forum for voicing concerns about globalisation. The close linkage between sustainable development and poverty eradication was the core of the debate. The compromise reached did not satisfy representatives of civil society and developing countries. Voters were not impressed either. An opinion poll published in the *Observer* (8 September 2002) revealed that 7 out of 10 British citizens thought that the Earth Summit had made 'no difference to the future of the planet' and 'a significant majority of voters say government and businesses should do more to protect the environment'. The failure of the Rio + 20 Earth Summit in 2012 confirmed this public scepticism. Public cynicism has been further fuelled by reports that the G8 countries are failing to meet their targets for alleviating poverty in Africa. *The Times* (30 June 2006) reported that nearly a year after the global Live8 concerts, which were part of the Make Poverty History campaign, a study had found that progress on commitments made had been 'painfully slow, proceeding at best at half-pace'. This raises fundamental questions about the effectiveness of global civil society in tackling world poverty. Kaldor (2003, p 9) asserts: 'Humanitarian NGOs provide the safety net to deal with the casualties of liberalisation and privatization strategies in the economic field…. Thus critics have charged that the term is reactionary, a way of evading the responsibilities of states for welfare and security.' Her critique raises fundamental questions about development.

Poverty, global civil society and international aid

The *Independent* (10 September 2003) proclaimed: 'There are terrible inequities that need to be addressed if the 2.7bn people in the world [out of 6bn] who live on less than $2 a day are to be enabled to stand on their own feet.' It went on to expose a contradiction at the core of international aid: 'Through the complex web of taxes, tariffs and quotas that governs trade we take far more from the poor than we give them. For every $1 we give in aid, we take $2 through unfair trade. Unfair trade costs the world's poor $100bn a year.' The *Independent* further noted a deep imbalance in world trade, with 40% of the world's population receiving only 3% of the world's income from trade, compared with 14% of the population living in the richest countries making 75% of the profit from world trade. Rich governments spend $1 billion per day on subsidising farmers, notably in the US and the EU. The currently stalled round of World Trade Organization talks that commenced at Doha in 2001 promised to put developing countries at the centre of multilateral trade negotiations. Progress has been painfully slow, with the EU deferring reform of the Common Agricultural Policy (CAP) until 2013. Currently, the average European family pays more than $1,000 per year in agricultural support, with 5% of farms (usually agribusinesses) receiving half the total CAP subsidies. Similarly, in the US the poorest 50% of farmers receive 5% of government agricultural subsidies. If EU trade barriers were lifted on Mozambique's imports, its export earnings would be boosted by $100 million per year – almost as much as it receives in European aid. The moral calculus of aid is undermined by the financial calculus of trade, which allows the West to continue exploiting the developing world.

In 2000, the United Nations set out, as one of its Millennium Development Goals, to reduce the number of people in the world living in subsistence poverty. At the 2000 Millennium Summit in New York the international community agreed on eight goals for health, education, women's rights and the environment and to halve extreme poverty by 2015, based on 1990 levels. But there is very little evidence that the political will exists within the international community to achieve the UN's Millennium Development Goals. The rhetoric of the rich countries is not being matched by financial support and the removal of discriminatory trade barriers.

The Global Conference on Scaling Up Poverty Reduction, co-sponsored by the World Bank and the Chinese government, convened at Shanghai in 2004. It set out to re-energise efforts to achieve the UN Millennium Development Goals. The main aims of the conference were to identify the economic, social and governance components that have enabled countries to reduce poverty, to share lessons about successful development across regions and countries and to disseminate those lessons to policy makers, practitioners and researchers. While more than half of the populations of developing countries continue to live in poverty, the conference noted that 50 years of development have enabled millions to shake off poverty. The conference was committed to the principle of poor people's being enabled to be the central force in changing their circumstances, rather than being the objects of Western charity. *China Daily* (26 May 2004) concluded that 'the world's poor certainly have the right to benefit from the fruits of civilization and economic development. Without their participation, a sustained development of mankind will be tantamount to building castles in the air. Poverty reduction should be fought like the war against terror. The war against poverty should be a worldwide effort joined by countries rich and poor.'

Undoubtedly, this assertion of the need for determined and coordinated international action is correct. Extreme poverty is a regional issue, with 93% of the world's poor living in Asia or Africa. The remainder are concentrated in Latin America and Eastern Europe. Significant progress has been made in poverty eradication in Asia, where poverty has fallen dramatically, from 58% in 1981 to 15% in 2001. On the other hand, about 10% of the populations of Latin America are still living in extreme poverty. In post-Soviet Eastern Europe, extreme poverty has risen from negligible levels to about 4% (*Irish Times*, 17 July 2006). Development is widely viewed as the panacea for world poverty. But demonstrably, development has been very uneven, with a deep structural inequality between Northern and Southern hemispheres. This has led some commentators to conclude that post-war development has failed, despite the fact that development has occurred in terms of absolute growth; the disparities between countries and between people within them have widened (Kothari and Minogue, 2002, p 2). They point out that the Development Dictionary opens with the sombre assertion 'the idea of development stands like a ruin in the intellectual landscape' (Kothari and Minogue, 2002, p 2). Kothari and Minogue (2002, p 13) conclude: 'The concept of development agency is most valuable in revealing the "open secret" of development, that its character and results are determined by relations of power, not by the rhetoric of fashionable populist labels such as participation, civil society or poverty reduction.' Nonetheless, there is clear evidence of a global civil society led by elite NGOs that are also vibrantly active in local communities.

Global civil society and NGOs

The emergence of a global civil society has been reflected in the changing nature of civil society (Salamon, 1994; Keane, 2003; Kaldor, 2003). The first generation of civil society emphasised traditional charity and welfare activities. A second generation of civil society became more development orientated, with an emphasis on aid programmes in the developing world: NGOs such as Médecins Sans Frontières, Trócaire, Oxfam and many others. Some of these NGOs evolved into a third generation of civil society that has sought to adopt a more 'catalytic role' based on 'people-centred and sustainable development at local level'. Finally, a fourth generation has sought to align global civil society with new social movements, for example, environmentalist, human rights and women's movements (Korten, cited in Campfens, 1997, p 4).

The fourth-generation vision was very much in evidence at the Earth Summit in Johannesburg in 2002. Civil society promoted an agenda of progress towards sustainable development and poverty eradication. The links with new social movements in terms of environmentalism, human rights and women's issues were clearly evident. The final communiqué, with its absence of targets, proved to be a severe disappointment to representatives of civil society. Equally disappointing was the method of implementation. George Monbiot (*Guardian*, 3 September 2002) reported that 'the world's biggest corporations, with the UN's blessing, have negotiated a series of "partnership agreements" – voluntary commitments obliging those companies to respect the environment and defend human rights'. Monbiot concluded that these partnership agreements were worthless and the concept of 'corporate social responsibility', which underpins them, meaningless without the force of law. The Rio + 20 Earth Summit in 2012 was a fitting end note.

The connection between local development and international development is fundamental, since there is a shared focus: *development*. However, development practice may be 'state led', 'market led', or 'community led'. Modernisation theory assumed that development would be state led. Neoliberalism wants the market to dominate but aspires to keep the state in a partnership. Community-led development is more problematic. Kothari and Minogue (2002, p 14) observe:

What of the third element of the triad: 'community' or 'civil society'? Despite the considerable attention paid to this element in the development literature and the substantial recognition afforded to it by official development agencies, it is difficult to think through what would be a positive and collaborative relationship the community would have with the market, given the ample evidence across all types of political economy of the deeply damaging effects on communities of market failures and imperfections. It was precisely to remedy such damage that the state was given a leading role in development in the past, but with the new formulation of state–market partnership, who will protect the community?

The role of NGOs has become increasingly important in international development. The renaissance of civil society in the developed world has been mirrored by the growing importance of NGOs in the developing world. Paul Francis (2002, p 72) observes: 'Non-governmental organisations were seen as more effective deliverers of development goods and services, especially to populations that were socially, politically and spatially marginal.' NGOs have also acted as a counterweight to tyrannical regimes, bringing Western democratic values of elections, the rule of law and good governance to bear on societies that were viewed as being in need of fundamental reform. But, as Francis (2002, p 73) notes, there have been difficulties. First, there is the problem of framing a coherent development strategy within the context of a field as heterogeneous as civil society that by no means has a shared sense of purpose. Second, civil society is a Western concept. Its imposition on developing countries raises questions about its legitimacy. Is it a form of cultural imperialism? Third, there is the argument that the impact of external funding provided by NGOs 'far from contributing to the health of civil society, may create dependency among local partners and undermine institutional sustainability' (Francis, 2002, p 74). It could be argued that, far from promoting local democracy, NGOs may be imposing Western values that are currently shaped by neoliberalism. Some critics of NGOs have argued from this viewpoint. We have already noted that Mary Kaldor is a stringent critic of the role of NGOs in international development.

Kaldor (2003, p 88) views NGOs as an instrument of neoliberal world governance: 'Markets plus elections became the ideological formula of the 1990s. NGOs came to be seen as an important mechanism for implementing this agenda. They can provide a social safety net without extending the role of the government.' She further suggests that social movements are being de-radicalised through 'NGOisation'. Hardcore neoliberal organisations, such as the International Monetary Fund (IMF), have, according to Kaldor, begun dialogue with NGOs. A distinction has opened up between Northern and Southern NGOs, reflecting the structural imbalance of wealth between the Northern and Southern hemispheres. Kaldor (2003, p 92) asserts that 'effectively what this means is that those NGOs who are Northern and therefore close to the centres of power and funding, whose emphasis is service provision, who are solidaristic rather than mutual benefit and whose organization tends to be more formal and hierarchical, have come to dominate the NGO scene'. She adds that governments 'may be nervous about advocacy, they are biased toward NGOs from their own countries, and also prefer to deal with formally organised professional NGOs' (Kaldor, 2003, p 92). Kaldor damningly concludes: 'In extreme cases, it is argued that NGOs are merely the handmaidens of capitalist change, with little serious concern for effective poverty alleviation strategies.... They are seen as the modernizers and destroyers of local economies, introducing Western values and bringing about "*economicide*"' (Kaldor, 2003, p 93). This is very harsh criticism, which ignores the humanitarian subjectivity of aid workers and NGOs. Radicals have looked to a more critical response that addresses the root causes (as they see them) of world poverty, which they locate in the capitalist system. This represents the fourth generation of civil society.

Anti-globalisation and world development

A new social movement, called the anti-capitalist/anti-globalisation movement, has arisen in response to neoliberal domination of the world development agenda. It campaigns on issues as diverse as: sweatshops in developing countries that provide cheap goods (notably clothing), often through the exploitation of child labour; the cancellation of 'Third World' debt; the dangers of biotechnology; inequities in world trade; and constraints on trade unions organising at a global level (Cockburn and St. Clair, 2000, p 2). In reality, it is constituted by a diversity of social movements opposed to globalisation, often operating at a local level in a semi-autonomous fashion and linked loosely to a wider network. The anti-globalisation movement differentiated itself from earlier anti-capitalist movements by the specificity of its agenda. It is refreshingly engaged with real issues, rather than abstract political theory, albeit the anti-capitalist/anti-globalisation movement is not without its theorists. The anti-capitalist/anti-globalisation movement has found a voice in a series of publications that question the current world status quo. The anti-globalisation activist Naomi Klein produced a searing critique of globalisation and the corporate world in her widely acclaimed book, *No Logo*. She argues: 'Economic trends that have so accelerated in the past decade have all been about massive redistribution and stratification of world resources: of jobs, goods and money. Everyone except those in the very highest tier of the corporate elite is getting less' (Klein, 2000, p 122).

Klein (2000, p 442) concludes that 'political solutions – accountable to people and enforceable by their elected representatives – deserve another shot before we throw in the towel and settle for corporate codes, independent monitors and the privatization of our collective rights as citizens'. This is an important statement, since it challenges Margaret Thatcher's famous aphorism that 'there is no alternative' to neoliberalism. Manifestly there is, as several commentators have argued.

Noreena Hertz, in her book *The Silent Takeover* (2001), takes up the issue of growing oligarchical power. She demonstrates the influence of corporations over governments across the globe, taking over state responsibility for key social services, including technology for schools and healthcare in the community. She argues that 'participation in the market has been substituted for participation in politics', concluding that 'the political state has become the corporate state' (Hertz, 2001, pp 10–11). In this reconfigured world, the active citizen is replaced by the passive consumer. Hertz (2001, p 60) warns against 'abstaining from a discussion of the limits of Anglo-American style capitalism, a system that favours the rich so blatantly, and puts the profit motive above all else is not a conscionable option'.

Not all commentators concerned with promoting social equality globally share this pessimistic analysis. Michael Hardt and Antonio Negri, in their influential book, *Empire*, published in 2000, argue that globalisation is an entirely new phenomenon that involves a rupture with the past. Hardt and Negri assert: 'Our basic hypothesis is that sovereignty has taken a new form, composed of a series of national and supranational organisms united under a single logic of rule. The new global form of sovereignty is what we call Empire' (2000, p xii). *Empire* has been widely acclaimed as a new political testament that reframes the socialist imaginary to fit the times we live in. The Slovenian sociologist Slavoj Žižek has dubbed *Empire* 'nothing less than a rewriting of the *Communist Manifesto*' (Žižek, 2001).

Hardt and Negri (2000, p 40) view the emergence of *Empire* as a positive development; because of its lack of rulers and national boundaries, 'the source of imperial normativity is born of a new machine, a new economic-industrial-communicative machine – in short, a globalised bio-political machine'. Other commentators have blamed the anti-capitalist/anti-globalisation movement for getting the issues wrong. The Nobel laureate Amartya Sen (2001) has concluded that the critics of globalisation have chosen 'the wrong battleground', adding: 'Even though many sections of the poor in the world economy have done really badly for a variety of reasons, involving domestic as well as international agreements, it is hard to establish an overall and clear cut trend.' Clearly, the development of China has been prodigious, while Africa remains locked into underdevelopment.

There are considerable tensions between the anti-capitalist/anti-globalisation movement and the elite corps of international NGOs. Batliwala (2002, p 400) notes that 'transnational grassroots movements are struggling with several ironies: the resistance to resourcing them from funders who have pigeonholed them as "local" and cannot see a role for them in the global arena; and the struggle to enter global advocacy spaces dominated by more elite representatives who have been speaking for them'. It is clear that while international NGOs reflect the traditional structures of the voluntary sector, transnational social movements opposed to globalisation cross-nationally more closely resemble the community sector in its most democratic form. The vital ingredients of a vibrant social movement approach are emphasis on a mass base and direct stakeholder involvement in decision making as collective actors engaged in shaping policy at local, national and global levels. The anti-capitalist/anti-globalisation movement possesses these characteristics. It is the essence of 'globalisation from below' that, in classic Gramscian terms, challenges the hegemony of 'globalisation from above'. In that sense, it offers an alternative metanarrative of progress based on equality and democracy. E-activism enables anti-capitalist/anti-globalisation campaigners to cooperate globally.

The new *Movimiento* among the Hispanic immigrants in America is a good illustration of the connection between the anti-globalisation movement and more traditional protest movements. Lovato (2006, p 13) asserts that 'the US Movimiento is as much the northernmost expression of a resurgent Latin America left as it is a new, more globalised, human rights centred continuation of the Chicano, civil rights and other struggles that facilitated immigrant rights work here'. This 'local–global sensibility' has also expressed itself in immigrant support groups such as Voces de la Frontera, which seeks to support mainly Mexican and Central American immigrant workers at local level, who are working in agriculture, catering, construction and manufacturing. Lovato (2006, p 11) believes that 'the leaders of the new Movimiento merge traditional labor and civil rights strategies and tactics with more global, networked – and personalised – organising to meet the challenges of the quintessentially global issue of immigration'.

The emergence of information technology has led to the proliferation of websites linking up the world of civil society in its struggle for sustainable development, human rights and the eradication of world poverty in the age of globalisation. According to the Worldwatch Institute, the environmental and social research organisation, 'it is clear that the Earth Summit ushered in a new era of global transnational citizen activism that is radically transforming the landscape of international diplomacy' (*International Herald Tribune*, 15 August 2002). While NGOs are committed to dialogue and diplomatic approaches to the promotion of social and political change, more radical groups have contested the legitimacy of globalisation itself through direct action.

The alternative global civil society favoured by radical activists is epitomised by the World Social Forum (WSF), which originated at the southern Brazilian city of Porto Alegre. It has been likened to a people's United Nations. The *Guardian* (25 January 2003) commented:

> For four days the city, whose participatory method of administration has made it the United Nations' model of good government, will be host to more than 100,000 activists for peace and social justice. The first WSF in 2000 was the brainchild of organisations involved in the anti-capitalist protests of the late 90s; they wanted to develop alternative ways of living. The event is held at the same time as the business-led World Economic Forum in Davos, Switzerland, in order to draw attention to the idea that, in the words of the WSF logo, another world is possible. The choice of Porto Alegre was symbolic too. For 15 years the city's governing Workers' Party – which now rules Brazil through the leftwing President Luis Inacio Lula da Silva – has been deciding the budget through a process of popular participation, redistributing wealth, reducing poverty and eliminating corruption as a result. The diversity of the WSF, a hallmark of each of the last three years' events, illustrates that the left may at last have retained the tension of a good debate without the fractious infighting of old. One of the most central of these debates is the relationship between civil society and political power.

However, the WSF has been criticised for being elitist and institutionalised (Pleyers, 2012, pp 166–81). But there are signs that it has addressed this problem. What appears to be emerging from the WSF is a very positive paradox. In the age of globalisation, participation at local level provides a democratic alternative possibility. Citizen involvement brings local government and civil society together in partnership. It draws on the traditions of civic republicanism dating from antiquity and of grassroots democracy rooted in modern democratic practice. While much of the recent focus has been on developments at Porto Alegre, participation in governance is not a new idea. In fact, it is a very old one. But can civil society protect social citizenship rights in a globalised world dominated by neoliberalism that speaks with a new, ideological edge, shaped by an 'ideas industry' called think-tanks? Are we witnessing the privatisation of policy making?

World poverty, social policy and Poor Law politics

Jeffrey Sachs (2006), the director of the Earth Institute at Columbia University in New York, in an influential book entitled *The End of Poverty*, has endorsed the popular humanitarian sentiment 'to make poverty history'. He does not say when it will happen, but argues that it could happen. Sachs is an economist whose focus is on development. But, arguably, in itself development is no panacea for poverty. Only the redistribution of wealth eliminates poverty. Throughout most of human history poverty has been viewed as an unavoidable reality. The Christian view was fatalistic: 'Ye have the poor with you always' (Mark 14: 7). Modernity challenged that view. As Stein Ringen (2005, p 3) puts it: 'A counter theory emerged 200 years ago when the idea of societies without poverty was invented.' Modernist thinkers, such as Tom Paine in his influential book *The Rights of Man* (1791–92) (Paine, 1969)and Karl Marx and Friedrich Engels in *The Communist Manifesto* (Marx and Engels, 1967), redefined poverty as an issue of social justice. These were, arguably, the most important modernist contributions to changing human subjectivity in relation to the distribution of wealth. They undermined charity and turned redistribution into a right to social justice. Pope Benedict XVI's endeavour in his encyclical *Deus Caritas Est* to reassert the positivity of charity represents an attempt to resurrect pre-modern ideation (Pope Benedict XVI, 2006).

International development is based on a modest redistributionist goal of transferring 0.7% of national income from the rich countries to the poor developing nations of the world. That is what the rich countries have promised, but they give only 0.2% of their wealth to the poor.

The United States spends $450 billion per year on arming its military but only $15 billion on alleviating world poverty (Ringen, 2005, p 4). The welfare state represented the first attempt in history to abolish poverty, not through development but through the pursuit of social justice. In developed countries like the United States, where welfare state institutions are weak, poverty is endemic. Developing countries are often referred to as 'the Third World'. We are less apt to speak of 'the fourth world' of poverty in the rich countries of the West. The Scandinavian countries, where the welfare state ethos is strongest, have been most effective in eliminating poverty. As Stein Ringen (2005, p 4) puts it, 'if there is a small corner of the world in which poverty has been eradicated, it is Scandinavia'. Without the redistribution of the world's wealth, it is hard to see how world poverty can be eliminated. Humanitarian initiatives must be underpinned by social justice.

Sadly, it would seem that international aid, despite the adoption of the ambitious UN Millennium Development Goals in 2000, is shaped by a Poor Law mentality. Sachs (2006, p 223) observes that the former UN Secretary General Kofi Annan 'invited us to think big – and we did – by creating a global-scale effort that could begin to get its collective reach around problems of enormous scope and complexity'. But the rich countries, most notably the United States, failed to respond. Sachs (2006, p 285) laconically concludes: 'The effort required of the rich is indeed so slight that to do less is to announce brazenly to a large part of the world *you count for nothing*. We should not be surprised, then, if in later years the rich reap the whirlwind of that heartless response.' Stein Ringen (2005, p 4) explains this 'heartless response' in terms of an inadequate global social policy vision: 'There is still no more of a global mind-set than in the age of poor laws and poor relief. The IMF is the world's committee of poor-law custodians. It orders those who depend on it to live by its decrees.' This failure of development policy to alleviate world poverty has given rise to the post-development school that regards the whole process as an elaborate 'hoax' (Thomas, 2000, p 22). This is a doomsayer's view of the world. Development theory is inherently problematic because it is overly reliant on economic policy that is largely shaped by neoliberal ideas. Hence the Poor Law ethos. Social policy offers an alternative vision that reflects the principles of redistribution, social justice and equality. That is the only strategy that will end world poverty because it offers a return to a structural view of development. However, as Deacon (1997, p 201) has argued, there are still serious risks of tokenism: 'Regardless of detail, a broader political and moral question is whether it is helpful to see some of those in these epistemic communities who are concerned to fashion either a global safety net or a global citizen's income as being on the side of the angels, as the humanizers of capitalism globally. Are they, alternatively, like national social reformists of old, to be accused of creating a fig-leaf to cover naked global imperialism?' This observation raises big questions to which there are no easy answers. Clearly, if the agenda of the developed world is global imperialism, there is little point in international development. However, the United Nations' Millennium Development Goals do offer the hope of global social justice. The United Nations provides a democratic and ethical alternative to the global imperialism of Western powers, led by a rampant United States. Like global civil society, the United Nations enjoys significant levels of symbolic power.

Conclusion

We must now ask ourselves whether global civil society is a myth or a reality. There is a very strong volume of evidence that supports the post-development theorists' conclusion that we are dealing with a 'hoax'. This raises the alarming possibility that it would be better to do nothing. The consciousness-raising efforts of popular cultural icons such as Bono and Bob Geldof are, in terms of this pessimistic analysis, in vain. Philanthropic foundations lack the means to make a real difference. We are, it would seem, dealing with a vast charade. Advocacy think-tanks are distorting the message. The West exploits the developing world and offers tokenistic aid in response. This view suggests that global civil society is a myth, and a cruelly deceptive one at that. But to accept this doomsayer's analysis, however logically and persuasively it is argued, is to give in to the impossibility of world development. It is to write off the humanitarian efforts of NGOs. The UN Millennium Development Goals suggest that it is realistically possible to eliminate extreme poverty in the world by 2015 at a cost of 0.7% of the gross domestic product of the world's richest countries. This has yet to happen and there are real concerns about a lack of political will. NGOs are at the forefront of the campaign to ensure that it happens. Popular humanitarian consciousness-raising events such as Live8 help to alter minds and, ultimately, to create the political climate where the UN Millennium Development Goals may be achieved. Humanitarianism does have value. But there are deeper issues at stake. Global civil society will not become a reality until there is agreement about the need for social justice based on an equitable redistribution of the world's wealth. That is not simply an economic policy objective; it involves a need to reframe the issue within the context of social policy.

Global civil society can be the agent of that change. The significance of the idea of global civil society comes down to its symbolic power to influence the way we think about the developing world. Its capacity to transform world poverty is primarily constituted in its capacity to be a communicative social change actor that promotes a cause that only international governance has the resources to tackle.

References

Ainger, K. (2012) 'Make Change Contagious', *Guardian*, 9 May.

Ali, T. (2002) *The clash of fundamentalisms: Crusades, jihads and modernity*, London and New York: Verso.

Alighieri, Dante (c.1309–1320) *La Divina Commedia*, Firenze: Le Monnier.

Allen, W.S. (1966) *The Nazi seizure of power: The experience of a single German town*, London: Eyre and Spottiswoode.

Aly, G. (2006) *Hitler's beneficiaries: Plunder, racial war and the Nazi welfare state*, New York: Metropolitan Books.

Anderson, B. (2011) 'Cameron's "little platoons" get lost in the woods', *Financial Times*, 9 February.

Anderson, P. (1998) *The origins of postmodernity*, London: Verso.

Andrle, V. (1994) *A social history of twentieth Century Russia*, London: Edward Arnold.

Anheier, H. (2010) 'Civility' in *International Encyclopedia of Civil Society, Volume 1* (eds H. Anheier, S. Toepler and R. List), Springer, New York, pp 475-8.

Anheier, H. and Seibel, W. (2001) *The non-profit sector in Germany*, Manchester and New York: Manchester University Press.

Anheier, H., Kaldor, M. and Glasius, M. (2012) 'The global civil society year book: lessons and insights 2001–2011', in M. Kaldor, H. Moore, S. Selchon (eds) *Global civil society 2012*, London: Palgrave Macmillan.

Appiah, K. and Gates, H. (eds) (2005) *Africana: The encyclopaedia of African and African American experience, Volume 2* (2nd edn), Oxford: Oxford University Press.

Archambault, E. (1997) *The non-profit sector in France*, Manchester and New York: Manchester University Press.

Arendt, H. (1958) *Origins of totalitarianism* (2nd edn), New York: Meridian Books.

Asen, R. and Brouwer, D.C. (2001) *Counterpublics and the state*, Albany: State University of New York Press.

Ashford, E.E. (1986) *The emergence of the welfare state*, Oxford: Blackwell.

Atherton, C. (2002) 'Welfare states: A response to John Veit-Wilson', *Social Policy and Administration*, vol 36, no 3, pp 306–11.

Ayçoberry, P. (1999) *The social history of the Third Reich*, New York: The New Press.

Badiou, A. (2010) *The communist hypothesis*, London: Verso.

Badiou, A. (2012) 'Interview', *Guardian*, 19 May.

Bailey, R. (1973) *The squatters*, Harmondsworth: Penguin.

Barber, B. (1984) *Strong democracy: Participatory politics for a new age*, Berkeley, CA: University of California Press.

Barnes, P. (2006) *Capitalism 3.0: A guide to reclaiming the commons*, San Francisco: Berret-Koehler.

Batliwala, S. (2002) 'Grassroots movements', *Voluntas*, vol 13, no 4, pp 393–409.

Bauman, Z. (1998) *In search of politics*, Cambridge: Polity Press.

Bauman, Z. (2000) *Liquid modernity*, Cambridge: Polity Press.

Baxter, C. (2011) 'Behind Murakami's mirror', *New York Review of Books*, 8 December, pp 23–5.

Beck, U. (1993) *Risk society*, London and New Delhi: Sage.

Beck, U. (1997) *The reinvention of politics*, Cambridge: Polity Press.

Bell, D. (1962) *The end of ideology*, New York: Free Press.

Bentham, J. (1843) *Works* (edited by J. Bowering), Edinburgh.

Blaagaard, B. (2012) 'Passionate publics in mediated society', in M. Kaldor, H. Moore and S. Selchon (eds) *Global civil society 2012*, London: Palgrave Macmillan.

Blond, P. (2008) 'The true Tory progressives', *Guardian*, 30 May.

Blond, P. (2010) *Red Tory*, London: Faber and Faber.

Bloom, H. (2005) 'Reflection in the evening land', *Guardian Review*, 17 December, pp 4–5.

Blum, L. (1998) 'Recognition, value and equality', in C. Willet (ed) *Theorising multiculturalism*, Oxford: Blackwell.

Bobbio, N. (1987) *The future of democracy*, Cambridge: Polity Press.

Bobbio, N. (1996) *Left and Right*, Cambridge: Polity Press.

Bono (2004) Foreword in J. Sachs, *The end of poverty*, London: Penguin.

Bourdieu, P. (1998) *Acts of resistance*, Cambridge: Polity Press.

Bourdieu, P. (2000) 'Pierre Bourdieu in conversation with Gunter Grass', *The Nation*, 3 July.

Boychuk, T. (2007) 'Big society, small government', *Macalester International*, 18, pp 201–13.

Branch, T. (1988) *Parting the waters*, New York: Simon and Schuster.

Branch, T. (1998) *Pillar of fire*, New York: Simon and Schuster.

Branch, T. (2006) *At Canaan's edge*, New York: Simon and Schuster.

Brodsgaard, K.E. (2009) *Hainan: State, society, and business in a Chinese province*, London: Routledge.

Brogan, H. (2006) *Alexis de Tocqueville: A life*, New Haven: Yale University Press.

Browning, C.R. (2001) *Ordinary men*, Harmondsworth: Penguin.

Bruntland, G. (1987) *Our common future*, Oxford: Oxford University Press.

Burke, E. (1790) [2004] *Reflections on the French Revolution*, London: Penguin.

Burleigh, M. (2000) *The Third Reich: A new history*, London: Pan Macmillan.

Buruma, I. (2012) 'Tony Judt: The right questions', *New York Review of Books*, 5–25 April, pp 28–31.

Bush–Cheney (2000) *Presidential Election Manifesto*.

Byrne, P. (1997) *Social movements in Britain*, London: Routledge.

Campfens, H. (ed) (1997) *Community development around the world*, Toronto: University of Toronto Press.

Camus, A. (1960) *The plague*, Harmondsworth: Penguin.

Camus, A. (1962) *The rebel*, London: Penguin.

Carter, D.T. (1995) *The politics of rage*, New York: Simon and Schuster.

China Daily 26 May 2004.

Clough, M. (1999) 'Reflections on civil society', *The Nation*, 22 February, pp 16–18.

Cockburn, A. and St. Clair, J. (2000) *5 days that shook the world*, London and New York: Verso.

Cohen, J.L. and Arato, A. (1994) *Civil society and political theory*, Cambridge, MA: MIT Press.

Cohn, N. (1961) *The Pursuit of the Millennium*, Harper and Row, New York.

Colas, D. (1997) *Civil society and fanaticism: Conjoined histories*, Stanford, CA: Stanford University Press.

Connolly, L. and Hourigan, N. (2006) *Social movements and Ireland*, Manchester: Manchester University Press.

Conservative Party (2008) *A stronger society: Voluntary action in the 21st century*, Green Paper No 5, London: Conservative Party.

Costoriadis, C. (1987) *The imaginary institution of society*, Polity Press, Cambridge.

Dahrendorf, R. (1994) 'The changing quality of citizenship', in B. Van Steenbergen (ed) *The condition of citizenship*, London: Sage Publications.

Davies, N. (1997) *Europe: A history*, London: Random House.

Davis, D.B. (2006) *Human bondage*, Oxford: Oxford University Press.

Davis, M. (2006) *Planet of slums*, London: Verso.

De Sousa Santos, B. (2006) *Democratizing democracy*, London: Verso.

De Swann, A. (1988) *In care of the state: Health, education and welfare in Europe*, Cambridge: Polity Press.

De Tocqueville, A. (1956) *Democracy in America* (edited by R.D. Heffner), New York: Mentor.

Deacon, B. (1997) *Global social policy*, London: Sage Publications.

Deakin, N. (2001) *In search of civil society*, New York: Palgrave Macmillan.

Dean, J. (2009) *Democracy and other neoliberal fantasies*, Duke University Press, Durham and London.

Dean, M. (1991) *The constitution of poverty*, London: Routledge.

Delanty, G. (2005) 'Modernity and postmodernity' in A. Harrington (ed) *Modern social theory*, Oxford: Oxford University Press.

Della Porta, D. (2012) 'The road to Europe: movements and democracy', in M. Kaldor, H. Moore and S. Selchon (eds) *Global civil society 2012*, London: Palgrave Macmillan.

Dickens, C. (1971) *Bleak house*, Harmondsworth: Penguin.

Dickens, C. (1984) *Oliver Twist*, London: Folio Society.

Dickens, C. (2003) *Hard times*, London: Penguin Classics.

Doerner, K. (1981) *Madmen and the bourgeoisie*, Oxford: Blackwell Publishing.

Domarus, M. (1992) *Hitler: Speeches and proclamations 1932–1945* (3 vols), London: I.B. Tauris.

Donzelot, J. (1980) *The policing of families*, London: Hutchinson.

Dreano, B. (2012) 'The Arab awakening', in M. Kaldor, H. Moore and S. Selchon (eds) *Global civil society 2012*, London: Palgrave Macmillan.

Drury, S. (1997) *Leo Strauss and the American Right*, New York: St. Martin's Press.

Drury, S. (2005) *The political ideas of Leo Strauss*, London: Palgrave Macmillan.

Ehrenberg, J. (1999) *Civil society: The critical history of an idea*, New York: New York University Press.

Elias, N. (1994) *The civilizing process* (first published 1939), Oxford: Blackwell Publishing.

Engels, F. (1999) [1844] *The condition of the working class in England*, Oxford: Oxford University Press.

Esping-Andersen, G. (1990) *The three worlds of welfare capitalism*, Cambridge: Polity Press.

Esping-Andersen, G. (1999) *The social foundations of post-industrial society*, Oxford: Oxford University Press.

Etzioni, A. (1993) *The spirit of community*, New York: Touchstone.

Evans, R. J. (2005) *The Third Reich in power*, London: Allen Lane.

Fallada, H. (2009) *Alone in Berlin*, London: Penguin.

Fanon, F. (1967a) *Black skin, white masks*, New York: Grove Press.

Fanon, F. (1967b) *The wretched of the earth*, London: MacGibbon and Kee.

Ferguson, A. (2001) *An essay on the history of civil society* (originally published 1782), Cambridge: Cambridge University Press.

Finkel, A., Conrad, M. and Strong-Boag, V. (1993) *History of Canadian peoples, Vol 2*, Toronto: Copp Clark Pitman Ltd.

Foucault, M. (1967) *Madness and civilization*, London: Tavistock.

Francis, P. (2002) 'Social capital, civil society and social exclusion', in K. Kothari and M. Minogue (eds) *Development theory and practice*, Basingstoke: Palgrave Macmillan.

Fraser, I. and Wilde, L. (2011) *The Marx dictionary*, London and New York: Continuum.

Fraser, N. (1997) *Justice interruptus*, London: Routledge.

Fraser, N. and Honneth, A. (2003) *Redistribution or recognition?* London: Verso.

Fredrickson, G.M. (2005) 'The long trek to freedom', *New York Review of Books*, 14 July, pp 40–2.

Friedman, T. (2005) *The world is flat*, London: Allen Lane.

Fukuyama, F. (1992) *The end of history and the last man*, New York: Free Press.

Fukuyama, F. (1995) *Trust: The social virtues and the creation of prosperity*, London: Hamish Hamilton.

Gellner, E. (1994) *Conditions of liberty: Civil society and its rivals*, London: Hamish Hamilton.

Geoghegan, M. and Powell, F. (2009) 'The contested politics of the late modern agora', in *Community Development Journal*, vol 44, no 4, pp 430–47.

Giddens, A. (1994) *Beyond Left and Right*, Cambridge: Polity.

Giddens, A. (1998) *The third way: The renewal of social democracy*, Cambridge: Polity Press.

Goldberg, M. (2006) *Kingdom coming: The rise of Christian nationalism*, New York: W.W. Norton.

Goldhagen, D.J. (1997) *Hitler's willing executioners*, London: Abacus.

Gorz, A. (1982) *Farewell to the working class*, London: Pluto.

Gramsci, A. (1971) *Prison notebooks*, Lawrence and Wishart, London.

Gramsci, A. (1973) *Selections from Prison Notebooks* (edited by G. Howell Smith and Q. Hoare) London: Lawrence and Wishart.

Gray, J. (2007) *Black mass*, London: Allen Lane.

Greenberg, M. (2011) 'In Zuccotti Park', *New York Review of Books*, 10 November.

Guardian 13 March 2001.

Guardian 3 September 2002.

Guardian 25 January 2003.

Guardian 11 March 2005.

Guardian 9 April 2005.

Guardian 1 September 2005.

Guardian 20 February 2006.

Halasz, N. (1963) 'The impassioned affair', in L. Defler (ed) *The Dreyfus affair: Tragedy of errors*, Boston: Heath and Company.

Hall, P. (1998) *Cities in civilisation*, New York: Pantheon.

Hann, C. and Dunn, E. (eds) (1996) *Civil society*, London Routledge.

Hardt, M. and Negri, A. (2000) *Empire*, Cambridge, MA: Harvard University Press.

Hardt, M. and Negri, A. (2004) *Multitude*, London: Hamish Hamilton.

Harriss, J. (2002) *Depoliticizing development*, London: Anthem Press.

Harvey, D. (2005) *A brief history of neoliberalism*, Oxford: Oxford University Press.

Hegel, G. (1821) *The philosophy of right* (translated by T. Knox, 1952) Oxford: Oxford University Press.

Held, D. (1996) *Models of democracy*, Cambridge: Polity Press.

Hertz, N. (2001) *The silent takeover: Global capitalism and the death of democracy*, London: Heinemann.

Hessel, S. (2011) *Time of outrage: Indignez vous*, New York: Twelve.

Heywood, A. (2003) *Political ideologies* (3rd edn), Basingstoke and New York: Palgrave Macmillan.

Higgins, M. (2011) *Renewing the republic*, Dublin: Liberties Press.

Hinsley, F.H. (1962) (ed) *Material progress and world wide problems 1870–98*, The New Cambridge Modern History XI, Cambridge: Cambridge University Press.

Hitler, A. (1938) *Mein Kampf* (English translation by James Murphy), London: Hurst and Blackett.

Hobbes, T. (1968) *Leviathan* (Original 1651), Harmondsworth: Penguin.

Holloway, M. (1966) 'Introduction', in C. Nordhoff (ed) *Dover edition of the communistic societies of the United States*, New York: Dover Publications.

Holmes, S. (1993) *The anatomy of antiliberalism*, Cambridge, MA: Harvard University Press.

Holroyd, M. (1988) *Bernard Shaw: The search for love*, New York: Random House.

Home Office (1998) *Compact between the voluntary and community sector and the state*, London: HMSO.

Huntington, S. (2002) *The clash of civilizations*, London: Simon & Schuster.

Hutchings, G. (2000) *Modern China*, Cambridge, MA: Harvard University Press.

Hutton, W. (2002) *The world we're in*, London: Little, Brown.

Ignatieff, M. (1999) 'Human rights: The midlife crisis', *New York Review of Books*, 20 May.

Ignatieff, M. (2012) 'We're so exceptional', *New York Review of Books*, 5 April, pp 6–8.

Independent 15 January 1997.

Independent 10 September 2003.

International Herald Tribune 15 August 2002.

Irish Times 17 July 2006.

Israel, J. (2001) *Radical enlightenment*, Oxford: Oxford University Press.

Israel, J. (2006) *Enlightenment contested*, Oxford: Oxford University Press.

Israel, J. (2010) *A revolution of the mind*, Princeton, NJ and Oxford: Princeton University Press.

Jackson, J. (2001) *France: The dark years 1940–1944*, Oxford: Oxford University Press.

Jacques, M. (2005) 'It is national sovereignty that has given China and India their edge', *Guardian*, 17 September.

James, C.L.R. (1989) *The Black Jacobins*, London: Allison and Busby.

Joll, J. (1976) *Europe since 1870: An international history*, Harmondsworth: Penguin.

Joll, J. (1977) *Gramsci*, London: Fontana/Collins.

Jonasen, V. (2003) 'The third sector in Denmark', in *EuroSET Report*, Rome: Centro Italiano di Solidarietà di Roma.

Jones, O. (2012) *Chavs: The demonization of the working class*, London: Verso.

Jordan, B. (2010) *Why the third way failed: Economics, morality and the origins of big society*, Bristol: Policy Press.

Judt, T. (2005) *Postwar*, London: Heinemann.

Judt, T. (2010) *Ill fares the land*, New York: Penguin.

Judt, T. (2012) *Thinking the twentieth century*, New York: Penguin.

Kaldor, M. (2003) *Global civil society: An answer to war*, Cambridge: Polity Press.

Kaldor, M. (2005) 'Commentary on Keane: "Eleven theses on markets and civil society"', *Journal of Civil Society*, vol 1, no 1, pp 43–4.

Kaldor, M., Moore, H. and Selchon, S. (eds) (2012) *Global civil society 2012*, London: Palgrave Macmillan.

Keane, J. (1995) *Tom Paine: A political life*, London: Bloomsbury.

Keane, J. (1998) *Civil society*, Cambridge: Polity Press.

Keane, J. (2003) *Global civil society?* Cambridge: Cambridge University Press.

Keane, J. (2009) *The life and death of democracy*, London: Simon and Schuster.

Kedward, R. (2005) *La vie en bleu*, London: Penguin.

Kendall, J. and Knapp M. (1996) *The voluntary sector in the UK*, Manchester: Manchester University Press.

Kendall, J. and Knapp M. (1997) 'The United Kingdom', in L. Salamon and H. Anheier (eds) *Defining the non-profit sector*, Manchester: Manchester University Press.

Kershaw, I. (2008) *Hitler: 1889–1936*, Harmondsworth: Penguin.

Khalaf, R. and Saleh, H. (2011) 'A religious revival', *Financial Times*, 30 December.

Kingsnorth, P. (2012) 'The Old Greens are dead: beware the new ones', *Guardian*, 2 August.

Kirby, P. (2003) *Introduction to Latin America*, London: Sage Publications.

Kirby, P. (2006) *Vulnerability and violence: The impact of globalisation*, London: Pluto Press.

Kirino, N. (2008) *Grotesque*, London: Vintage.

Kirp, D.L. (1999) 'So, it is back to bowling alone?' *The Nation*, 8 March.

Klein, N. (2000) *No logo*, London: Flamingo.

Klein, N. (2006) *The shock doctrine: The rise of disaster capitalism*, London: Penguin.

Klein, A. (2010) 'Civil society theory: Marx', in H. Anheier, S. Toepler and R. List (eds) *International Encyclopaedia of Civil Society, Volume 1*, New York: Springer, pp 430–5.

Knight, B. (1993) *Voluntary action*, London: Home Office.

Kothari, U. and Minogue, M. (2002) *Development theory and practice*, London: Palgrave.

Kramer, R. (1981) *Voluntary agencies in the welfare state*, Berkeley, CA: University of California Press.

Krausnick, H. and Brozat, M. (1968) *Anatomy of the SS state*, St Albans: Paladin.

Laclau, E. and Mouffe, C. (1985) *Hegemony and socialist strategy: Towards a radical democratic politics*, London: Verso.

Landim, L. (1997) 'Brazil', in L.M. Salamon and H.K. Anheier (eds) *Defining the non-profit sector: A cross-national analysis*, Manchester and New York: Manchester University Press.

Lee, P. and Raban, C. (1988) *Welfare theory and social policy*, London: Sage Publications.

Leibniz, G.W. (2006) *Theodicy* (original 1710), West Stockbridge, MA: Hard Press.

Lictheim, G. (1974) *A short history of socialism*, Fontana, London.

Leo, R. (2008) 'Caute: Jonathan Israel's secular modernity' in *Journal for Cultural and Religious Theory*, vol 9. no 2, pp 76–83.

Lis, C. and Soly, H. (1979) *Poverty and capitalism in pre-industrial Europe* (translated from the Dutch by J. Coonan), Hassocks, Sussex: Harvester Press.

Lister, R. (1997) *Citizenship: A feminist perspective*, London: Macmillan.

Lovato, R. (2006) 'Voices of a new movimiento', *The Nation*, 19 June, pp 11–14.

Luzárraga, A. (2010) 'Gramsci and the US body politic', available online: www.futurodecuba.org/Gramsci.

Machiavelli, N. (1961) *The Prince* (originally published in 1532), Harmondsworth: Penguin.

Machiavelli, N. (1970) *The discourses*, Harmondsworth: Penguin.

Malik, N. (2011) 'Egypt's progress from dictatorship to democracy offers hope to the Arab world', *Guardian*, 27 December (G2 section).

Malthus, T.R. (1798) *Essay on the Principles of Population*, London: J. Johnson.

Marshall, T.H. (1973) *Class, citizenship and social development*, Westport, CT: Greenwood Press.

Marsland, D. (1996) *Welfare or welfare state?* London: Macmillan.

Marx, K. (1843a) *Critique of Hegels philosophy of right, collected works (1975–2000)*, London: Lawrence and Wishart.

Marx, K. (1843b) *The Jewish question, collected works (1975–2000)*, London: Lawrence and Wishart.

Marx, K. (1844) *The economic and philosophical manuscripts, collected works (1975–2000)*, London: Lawrence and Wishart.

Marx, K. (1859) Preface to *Contributions to the critique of political economy, collected works (1975–2000)*, London: Lawrence and Wishart.

Marx, K. (1962) *Das Kapital* (first published in 3 vols 1867, 1885, 1893), Moscow: Progress Publishers.

Marx, K. and Engels, F. (1967) *The communist manifesto* (first published in 1848), Harmondsworth: Penguin.

Mason, T. (1997) *Social policy in the Third Reich*, Oxford: Berg.

Massiah, G. (2012) 'Five lessons from the revolutionary uprisings in the Maghreb–Mashreq region', in M. Kaldor, H. Moore and S. Selchon (eds) *Global civil society 2012*, London: Palgrave Macmillan.

Mayo, M. (2005) *Global citizens: Social movements and the challenges of globalisation*, London: Zed Books.

McLaren, P. (1994) 'White Terror and oppositional agency', in D.T. Goldberg (ed) *Multiculturalism: A critical reader*, Oxford: Blackwell Publishing.

McLintock, A. (1995) *Imperial leather*, London: Routledge.

Meier, H. (1995) *Carl Schmitt and Leo Strauss*, Chicago, IL: University of Chicago Press.

Milton, J. (1868) *Aeropagitica* (originally published in 1644), London: A. Murray.

Mishra, R. (1977) *Society and social policy*, London: Macmillan.

Miszlivetz, F. (2012) 'Lost in transformation', in M. Kaldor, H. Moore and S. Selchon (eds) *Global civil society 2012*, London: Palgrave Macmillan.

Molnár, G. (2010) 'Civil society in history: Antiquity', in H. Anheier, S. Toepler and R. List (eds) *International Encyclopaedia of Civil Society, Volume 1*, New York: Springer, pp 341–5.

Monbiot, G. (2012) 'Our economic ruin means freedom for the super-rich', *Guardian*, 31 July.

Montesquieu, C. (1949) *The Spirit of the Laws* (first published in 1748), New York: Hafner.

Mooney, G. (1998) '"Remoralising" the poor', in G. Lewis (ed) *Forming nation, framing welfare*, London: Routledge.

Mouffe, C. (2000) *The democratic paradox*, London and New York: Verso.

Mouffe, C. (2005), *The return of the political*, London: Verso.

Moyers, B. (2005) 'Welcome to Doomsday', *New York Review of Books*, 24 March, pp 8–10.

Munkonen, M. (2010) 'Ancient philanthropy', in H. Anheier, S. Toepler and R. List (eds) *International Encyclopaedia of Civil Society, Volume 3*, New York: Springer, pp 1230–5.

Murakami, H. (2011) *IQ84*, London: Harvill Secker.

Murray, C. (1984) *Losing ground: American social policy 1950–1980*, New York: Basic Books.

Murray, R. (2012) 'Co-operatives and global growth', in M. Kaldor, H. Moore and S. Selchon (eds) *Global civil society 2012*, London: Palgrave Macmillan.

Nash, G. (2005) *The unknown American Revolution*, New York: Viking.

New York Review of Books, 8 March 2012.

New York Times 20 February 2001.

Niemöller, M. (1937) *From U-boat to pulpit*, Chicago, IL: Willet Clark.

Nietzsche, F. (1961) *Thus spoke Zarathustra*, Harmondsworth: Penguin.

Nietzsche, F. (1968) *Twilight of the idols*, Harmondsworth: Penguin.

Nietzsche, F. (1969) *The will to power* (edited by W. Kaufmann), London: Weidenfeld and Nicolson.

Nietzsche, F. (1994) *The genealogy of morality*, Cambridge: Cambridge University Press.

Nordhoff, C. (1966) *The communistic societies of the United States*, New York: Dover Publication.

Norman, J. (2010) *The big society*, Buckingham: University of Buckingham Press.

Novak, T. (1988) *Poverty and the state*, Milton Keynes: Open University Press.

Observer 9 February 1997.

Observer 4 February 2001.

Observer 8 September 2002.

Offe, C. (1984) *Contradictions of the welfare state*, London: Hutchinson.

Orwell, G. (1949) *Nineteen eighty-four*, London: Secker and Warburg.

Orwell, G. (1989) *1984*, London: Penguin.

Paine, T. (1969) [1776] *Common sense*, edited by S. Hook, *The essential Thomas Paine*, New York: Mentor.

Paine, T. (1969) [1791] *The rights of man*, edited by S. Hook, *The essential Thomas Paine*, New York: Mentor.

Paine, T. (1969) *The rights of man*, edited by H. Collins, London: Penguin.

Paine, T. (2005) *The age of reason*, New York: Citadel Press.

Palier, B. (ed) (2010) *A long goodbye to Bismarck?* Amsterdam: Amsterdam University Press.

Parker, S. and Heapy, J. (2006) *The journey to the interface*, London: Demos.

Phillipson, N. (2010) *Adam Smith: An Enlightenment life*, London: Allen Lane.

Pierson, C. (2001) *Hard choices: Social democracy in the 21st century*, Cambridge: Polity Press.

Pinter, H. (2005) 'Pinter in the US', *Guardian*, 8 December, G2, pp 9–13.

Piven, F.F. and Cloward, R. (1971) *Regulating the poor*, New York: Vintage.

Piven, F.F. and Cloward, R. (1979) *Poor people's movements*, New York: Vintage.

Pleyers, G. (2012) 'A decade of world social forums', in M. Kaldor, H. Moore and S. Selchon (eds) *Global civil society 2012*, London: Palgrave Macmillan.

Pocock, J.G.A. (1975) *The Machiavellian moment, Florentine political thought and the Atlantic republican traditions*, Princeton, NJ: Princeton University Press.

Polanyi, K. (2001) *The great transformation* (first published in 1944), Boston, MA: Beacon Press.

Pope Benedict XVI (2006) *Deus caritas est*, Rome: Vatican.

Powell, F. (1992) *The politics of Irish social policy 1600–1992*, New York: Edwin Mellen Press.

Powell, F. (2001) *The politics of social work*, London and New Delhi: Sage Publications.

Powell, F. (2010a) 'Civil society history II: Medieval period', in H. Anheier, S. Toepler and R. List (eds) *International Encyclopaedia of Civil Society, Volume 1*, New York: Springer, pp 345–9.

Powell, F. (2010b) 'Civil society history IV: Enlightenment', in H. Anheier, S. Toepler and R. List (eds) *International Encyclopaedia of Civil Society, Volume 1*, New York: Springer, pp 353–8.

Powell, F. (2010c) 'Civil Society Theory: Paine', in H. Anheier, S. Toepler and R. List (eds) *International Encyclopaedia of Civil Society, Volume 1*, New York: Springer, pp 438–42.

Powell, F. and Geoghegan, M. (2004) *The politics of community development: Reclaiming civil society or reinventing governance*, Dublin: A.A. Farmar.

Prugh, T., Constanza, R. and Daly, H. (2000) *The Local politics of global sustainability*, Washington, DC: Island Press.

Putnam, R. (1993) *Making democracy work: Civic traditions in modern Italy*, Princeton, NJ: Princeton University Press.

Putnam, R. (2000) *Bowling alone: The collapse and revival of American community*, New York: Simon and Schuster.

Ramirez, M. (2007) 'The politics of recognition and citizenship' in B. de Sousa Santos (ed) *Democratising democracy*, London: Verso.

Richardson, R. (1988) *Death, dissection and the destitute*, Harmondsworth: Penguin.

Rieff, D. (1999) 'The false dawn of civil society', *The Nation*, 22 February, pp 11–16.

Ringen, S. (2005) 'Band of hope', *Times Literary Supplement*, 24 June, pp 3–4.

Robin, C. (2011) *The reactionary mind*, Oxford: Oxford University Press.

Römmele, A. and Schober, H. (2012) 'Wurzburger in Wonderland' in M. Karlelor, H. Moore and S. Selchav (eds) *Global Civil Society*, London: Palgrave Macmillan.

Royal Commission on the Poor Law (1909) *Reports of the Royal Commission on the Poor Laws*, London: HMSO.

Ross, F. (2000) 'Interests and choice in the politics of welfare', in M. Ferrera, A. Hemerijck and M. Rhodes (eds) *Recasting European welfare states*, London: Frank Cass.

Rusche, G. and Kirchheimer, O. (1939) *Punishment and social structure*, New York: Columbia University Press.

Sachs, J. (2006) *The end of poverty*, London: Penguin.

Salamon, L. and Spence, K. (2009) 'Volunteers and the economic downturn', available at: www.nationalservice.gov.

Salamon, L.M. (1994) *The global associational revolution*, London: Demos.

Sandel, M. (2012) *Justice*, London: Penguin.

Sassoon, D. (1996) *One hundred years of socialism*, New York: New Press.

Saul, S. (2010) 'A body on the green', *The Nation*, 29 March.

Schmitt, C. (1988) *The crisis of parliamentary democracy*, Cambridge, MA: MIT Press.

Schmitt, C. (1996) *The concept of the political*, Chicago, IL: University of Chicago Press.

Scull, A. (1979) *Museums of madness*, London: Palgrave Macmillan.

Seligman, A.B. (1992) *The idea of civil society*, Princeton, NJ: Princeton University Press.

Sen, A. (2001) Article on globalisation, *Guardian*, 29 July.

Shirer, W. (1960) *The rise and fall of the Third Reich*, London: Pan Books.

Skidelsky, R. (1999) 'Doing good and being good', *Times Literary Supplement*, 26 March.

Smiles, S. (1859) *Self-help*, London: Murray.

Smith, A. (1759) *Theory of moral sentiments*, London: A. Millar.

Smith, A.M. (1998) *Laclau and Mouffe: The radical democratic imaginary*, London and New York: Routledge.

Sternhell, Z. (2010) *The anti-enlightenment tradition*, New Haven, CT and London: Yale University Press.

Streeck, W. (2011) 'The crisis of democratic capitalism', *New Left Review*, 71, September–October, pp 1–15.

Strong, T.B. (1996) 'Dimensions of the new debate around Carl Schmitt', Foreword in C. Schmitt, *The concept of the political*, Chicago, IL: Chicago University Press.

Tanenhaus, S. (2012) 'Will the tea get cold?' *New York Review of Books*, 8 March, pp 7–9.

Tarrow, S. (1998) *Power in movement*, New York: Cambridge University Press.

Taylor, C. (1994) 'The politics of recognition', in D.T. Goldberg (ed) *Multiculturalism: A reader*, Oxford: Blackwell.

Teeple, G. (1995) *Globalization and the decline of social reform*, Toronto: Garamond Press.

Thane, P. (1982) *The foundations of the welfare state*, London: Longmans.

Thomas, A. (2000) 'Poverty and the end of development', in T. Allen and A. Thomas (eds) *Poverty and development into the 21st century*, Oxford: Oxford University Press.

Thompson, E.P. (1975) *Whigs and hunters*, London: Penguin.

Thomson, D. (1966) *Europe since Napoleon*, Harmondsworth: Pelican.

Times, The 30 June 2006.

Titmuss, R. (1970) *The gift relationship*, London: Allen and Unwin.

Touraine, A. (1981) *The voice and the eye*, Cambridge: Cambridge University Press.

Touraine, A. (2001) *Beyond neo-liberalism*, Cambridge: Polity Press.

Toynbee, P. (2006) 'Compassionate conservatism sounds uncannily familiar', *Guardian*, 13 June.

Van Gelder, S. (ed) (2011) *This changes everything*, San Francisco: Barret-Koehler.

Veit-Wilson, J. (2000) 'States of welfare: a conceptual challenge', *Social Policy and Administration*, vol 34, no 1, pp 1–25.

Voltaire (1993) *Candide* (first published in 1759), Hertfordshire: Wordsworth Classics.

Wainwright, H. (2005) 'Civil society, democracy and power: global connections', in H. Anheier, M. Glasius and M. Kaldor (eds) *Global civil society 2004–2005*, London: Sage Publications.

Walzer, M. (1983) *Spheres of justice: A defence of pluralism*, Oxford: Martin Robertson.

Weber, M. (1919) *Max Weber's complete writings on academic and political vocations*, New York: Algora Publishing.

Webster, P. (1991) *Petain's crime*, Chicago, IL: Ivan R. Dee.

West, C. (2004) *Democracy matters*, Penguin, New York.

Western, B. (2006) *Punishment and inequality in America*, New York: Russell Sage Foundation.

Wheen, F. (1999) *Karl Marx*, London: Fourth Estate.

White, M. (2004) *Machiavelli: A man misunderstood*, London: Little, Brown.

Wiig, P., Fránsehn, M. and Silow, E. (2003) 'The third sector in Sweden', in *EuroSET Report*, Rome: European Social Enterprises Training, Centro Italiano di Solidarietà di Roma.

Williams, H. (2005) Report on holocaust, *Guardian*, 9 April.

Williams, Z. (2011) 'Kicking charities while Serco profits isn't a plan with legs', *Guardian*, 4 August.

Wills, G. (2006) 'An American Iliad', *New York Review of Books*, 6 April, pp 20–6.

Wilson, R. (2011) *After the Celtic tiger: a Nordic vision for a new Ireland?* Dublin: Tasc.

Young, I.M. (2000) *Inclusion and democracy*, Oxford: Oxford University Press.

Younge, G. (2012) 'The itinerant UC Left has found its home in Occupy', *Guardian*, 27 February.

Zinn, H. (1999) *A people's history of the United States*, New York: Harper Collins.

Žižek, S. (2001) 'Review of Empire', *New York Times*, 7 July.

Žižek, S. (2011) 'Don't fall in love with yourselves', in A. Taylor, K. Lessen and editors from N + I (eds), *Occupy! Scenes from occupied America*, London: Verso.

Žižek, S. (2011) *Living in the end of times*, London: Verso.

Zola, E. (1898) *J'accuse*, Paris.

Zola, E. (1986) *Germinal* (first published in 1885), Paris: Sedes.

Index

www.ingramcontent.com/pod-product-compliance
Lightning Source LLC
Chambersburg PA
CBHW060034030426
42334CB00019B/2324